Middle Eastern Lives
in America

Perspectives on a Multiracial America Series
Joe R. Feagin, Texas A & M University, series editor

Breaking the Code of Good Intentions
    by Melanie Bush

Middle Eastern Lives in America
    by Amir Mavasti and Karyn McKinney

Middle Eastern Lives in America

Amir Marvasti
and
Karyn D. McKinney

ROWMAN & LITTLEFIELD PUBLISHERS, INC.
Lanham • Boulder • New York • Toronto • Oxford

ROWMAN & LITTLEFIELD PUBLISHERS, INC.

Published in the United States of America
by Rowman & Littlefield Publishers, Inc.
A wholly owned subsidiary of The Rowman & Littlefield Publishing Group, Inc.
4501 Forbes Boulevard, Suite 200, Lanham, Maryland 20706
www.rowmanlittlefield.com

PO Box 317
Oxford
OX2 9RU, UK

British Library Cataloguing in Publication Information Available

Library of Congress Cataloging-in-Publication Data

Marvasti, Amir B., 1966–
    Middle Eastern lives in America / Amir Marvasti and Karyn D. McKinney.
        p.   cm. — (The Joe Feagin series)
    Includes bibliographical references.
    ISBN 0-7425-1957-0 (hardcover : alk. paper) — ISBN 0-7425-1958-9 (pbk. : alk.
paper)
        1. Arab Americans—Social conditions.   2. Iranian Americans—Social conditions
    E184.A65M37   2004
    305.892′7073—dc22   2004017874

Printed in the United States of America

∞ ™ The paper used in this publication meets the minimum requirements of American
National Standard for Information Sciences—Permanence of Paper for Printed Library
Materials, ANSI/NISO Z39.48-1992.

Contents

Acknowledgments

This work would not have been possible without the generous support of numerous scholars, respondents, and editors. We are especially grateful to Joe Feagin who inspired this work and mentored us throughout the data collection and writing process. We also owe much gratitude to Lori Bechtel, Akbar Marvasti, Nabil Matar, and Hernán Vera. Our special thanks goes to our editors, Dean Birkenkamp and Alan McClare, and their editorial staff at Rowman & Littlefield. As we worked on the book, we benefited from the diligence of three of our students, Eric Liddick, Tracy Reilly, and Vanessa Gonthier, and from the encouragement of our families. Finally, we are indebted to our respondents whose participation and insights moved us to write this book.

Foreword

Much of what is known as "Western civilization" was invented by peoples in the Middle East, and then flowed from there north and west to Europe. In the geographical areas now called Europe and the Middle East, the first developed agricultural societies, the early breakthroughs in domesticating plants and animals, the first great cities, the first large-scale governments and educational institutions, the first major developments in writing and libraries, and many great scientific developments came out of Middle Eastern areas. Three of the world's major religions—Judaism, Christianity, and Islam—all developed first in the Middle East. Scholars and others in the advanced Arab societies of the tenth, eleventh, and twelfth centuries c.e. made major developments in such areas as mathematics, optics, sea-going navigation, and medicine well before the Europeans. Later, Europeans borrowed substantially from this Middle Eastern knowledge and science, as the Greeks and Romans had done in earlier centuries.

Many descendants of these early Middle Eastern peoples are now citizens of the United States, yet their ancestors' great contributions to the development of Western civilization are rarely recognized by most Americans. Nor are their own great contributions to the development of the United States recognized. This book by Amir Marvasti and Karyn D. McKinney is the first lengthy sociological examination of these Middle Eastern Americans and their everyday experiences in U.S. workplaces, schools, and other major institutions. The authors go well beyond the usual discussions of Middle Eastern Americans that focus on immigration patterns and countries of origin. Little previous analysis looks at everyday experiences of Middle Eastern Americans, particularly experiences with hostility and discrimination. Here we get a rich description and analysis of these life experiences. In explicating these matters, Marvasti and McKinney use original data gathered from in-depth interviews, as well as from many informal conversations and participant observation in various institutional settings.

People from Middle Eastern countries have immigrated to the United States now for more than a century. The largest group is Arab immigrants from more than twenty countries, and many of them have been Christian in religion. Those who read this book carefully will learn not only much about these Middle Eastern Americans, both Muslim and Christian, but also much about how U.S. society oppresses, exploits, and discriminates against many of its own hardworking citizens.

Since September 11, 2001, all Middle Eastern Americans have become the object of greatly enhanced and unwanted attention, particularly from Americans with power and influence. Honest, hardworking Americans with Middle Eastern ancestry are more likely than before September 11 to be viewed with suspicion and racialized hostility, and they are more likely to face racial profiling and other types of discrimination. Significantly, most Americans are quite ignorant about Middle Eastern issues, including even about who the September 11 terrorists were. Indeed, most Americans do not realize that not one of the September 11 terrorists was from Iraq or Iran, and that most were from staunch U.S. allies such as Saudi Arabia.

After an opening chapter on history and immigration of Middle Eastern Americans, Marvasti and McKinney systematically examine the multifaceted lives and often difficult experiences of these Americans. First, they assess an oppressive array of "Orientalist" stereotypes that are imposed on Middle Eastern Americans—such as their allegedly terroristic impulses and their allegedly hyperconservative religious views. We come away from these chapters with a clear view of how outrageously inaccurate conventional stereotypes of Middle Eastern Americans are, as well as where they often come from and why they persist.

For example, terrorism is seen by most Americans as an *outside* phenomenon brought suddenly into the United States on September 11 by Middle Easterners, rather than as something that U.S. citizens, sometimes with assistance from the U.S. government, have created in the United States and elsewhere. When domestic terrorists kill many people, as in the Oklahoma City bombing by Timothy McVeigh and his white supremacist associates, their terroristic killings are rationalized as something coming from personality disorders and as unconnected to their social and political socialization and views. Indeed, the oldest, still existing terrorist group anywhere on the globe today operates in every state in the United States, and its members are responsible for hundreds, perhaps thousands, of deaths over its long lifetime: the Ku Klux Klan. Yet the many branches of the Klan operating now across the United States rarely get media attention, even when they are involved in violence against other Americans. When they do, they tend to be viewed just as sick individuals. In contrast, Middle Eastern terrorists—who are virtually never Middle Eastern *Americans*—are always seen as coming out of extremist social, political, and religious settings. They are never seen as just misguided individuals, but rather as representatives of their countries and cultures. In their probing analysis, Marvasti and McKinney force us to take a careful look at these stereotypes, and in the process we learn much about this country's unwillingness to face its own generation of violence and terrorism.

The authors also dissect the many stereotyped images of Islam in the United States, as well as the failure of most U.S. analysts to pay serious attention to the many divisions within Islam. They have an insightful analysis of gendered oppression in the West and the Middle East. They suggest, for example, that the pressure on Muslim women to wear the burka covering is no more limiting and oppressive for women than is the pressure on Western women to be super slim, to engage in extreme dieting (with millions thus developing major eating disorders), and to strive to look good in string bikinis. Both societal pressures are forms of sexism that focus on women's bodies as something to be changed under the ultimate control of men.

This book destroys many negative images of Middle Eastern Americans. For example, Arab Americans, the largest group among Middle Eastern Americans, are well educated as a group—with a higher average level of education than white Americans. The median family income of Middle Eastern Americans is substantially higher than the U.S. median income, and Middle Eastern Americans are better than average community citizens. They are much more likely to vote than citizens in most other American groups, and they are more active than most other groups in keeping up with political debates and candidates.

We might note that the interview data on prejudice and stereotypes presented by Marvasti and McKinney are corroborated in yet other studies. For example, one 1980s opinion survey found that 44 percent of respondents considered Arabs to be barbaric or cruel, while half thought they were treacherous or cunning. More than half thought they were warlike and mistreat women. Such negative images have been circulating for decades, at all levels of the society. Indeed, Terrel Bell, President Ronald Reagan's secretary of education in the 1980s, has written about how White House aides made comments about Arab peoples as "sand niggers."

In the second part of the book, Marvasti and McKinney examine the reality and impact of discrimination targeting Middle Eastern Americans today. They draw here on many rich interviews in order to thoroughly demonstrate how Middle Eastern Americans regularly confront problems of racialized mistreatment from others, and how they learn to combat that discrimination with an array of strategies, including withdrawal, joking, and confrontation. We observe too how discrimination typically operates within institutional settings such as public accommodations, workplaces, and schools, as well as the economic and psychological impact of this discrimination.

In recent years, non-Muslim Americans have verbally and physically attacked Muslim Americans, often blaming them for terrorism around the globe. Thus, journalist Souheila al-Jadda recently reported riding on a bus and being subjected to taunts like "Are you a terrorist?" And "Do you have a bomb in your bag?" Veiled Muslim women are especially likely targets for such stereotyping and open hostility. Indeed, in the last few years numerous Arab American women have been dismissed from jobs because they refused to remove their head coverings, and some Muslim men have been fired just because they look like they are from the Middle East. In addition, violent attacks are often directed against Middle Eastern Americans. In a nine-week period after the September 11 attacks, there were more than 520 violent attacks on people the attackers thought were Middle Eastern. Since then, many more such hate crimes have targeted not only Middle Eastern Americans but also religious and other community facilities. Such attacks have included assaults, arson, and murder, targeting that is often spread by hate-centered Internet sites.

Historically, the U.S. government has vacillated in its definition of Middle Eastern Americans as "white," "not white," or "other." In recent decades, the government, including the Census Bureau, has treated Middle Eastern Americans as white for official purposes. Yet as Marvasti and McKinney show, few other Americans, in every practice, view or treat them this way. For the most part, Middle Eastern Americans are defined by others as not white—which commonplace discrimination constantly demonstrates.

Marvasti and McKinney conclude with a probing analysis of the ongoing reality of racial and ethnic discrimination for many different Americans and how these are real everyday problems that must be dealt with if the United States is ever to become the democracy it proclaims itself to be. The character of a country can be judged by how its majority reacts under crisis, and by that standard the United States gets very mixed marks. Courageously, Americans of many different backgrounds pitched in to help those families, also a diverse group, that suffered great losses from the terroristic acts of September 11, 2001. However, expedient conservative politicians also took advantage of these events to reduce the freedom of all U.S. citizens, such as by governmental actions legitimated under the so-called PATRIOT Act. This act, passed immediately after the 2001 attacks with little thought, has reduced the civil liberties of Americans—and especially those not yet citizens. Many Middle Eastern Americans have been detained or put into prison for long periods without proper charges and without access to attorneys because, to non–Middle Eastern American officials, they somehow look threatening and dangerous. Marvasti and McKinney show that this is not the first time that the U.S. government has targeted Middle Eastern Americans for such official discrimination. In earlier decades the federal government conducted similarly secret surveillance operations targeting Middle Eastern Americans because of their identities or political views on numerous occasions.

Recently, United Nations Secretary General Kofi Annan condemned the spread of "Islamaphobia" across many Western countries. Especially troubling, he noted, was the fact that most Westerners see the Muslim world, and the Middle East, as undifferentiated. He condemned the growing stereotyping and discrimination that is targeting Muslims in the West. These attacks have implications for all peoples, not just those attacked. The late Edward Said, a Palestinian American scholar of great distinction, once pointed out that "Orientalist" attacks on Middle Eastern peoples have serious implications for U.S. policies overseas: "The Middle East experts who advise policy-makers are imbued with Orientalism almost to a person. . . . If in the meantime the Arabs, the Muslims, or the Third and Fourth Worlds go unexpected ways after all, we will not be surprised to have an Orientalist tell us that this testifies to the incorrigibility of Orientals and therefore proves that they are not to be trusted."[1] Making policy judgments on the basis of such distorted perceptions and stereotyping often leads to disastrous political escapades by ill-motivated U.S. politicians, as we have seen in recent military adventures by the U.S. government in the Middle East. No nation, and especially no democratic nation, can long survive such stereotype-based, grand political miscalculations.

Joe Feagin

NOTE

1. Edward Said, *Orientalism* (New York: Vintage Books, 1979), p. 321.

Introduction

During the August 2001 annual meeting of the American Sociological Association in Anaheim, the first author of this book, Amir Marvasti, attended a session on race and ethnicity in which white, Asian, Hispanic, and African American scholars passionately debated how racism and discrimination could best be combated. As a Middle Eastern American, who had his share of experiences with prejudice, Amir stood in the room wondering which ethnic group he should identify with. Although officially classified as white, Amir's swarthy skin, black hair, and large facial features (i.e., Middle Eastern–looking appearance) meant that he would not be accepted as white for practical everyday purposes. His appearance caused him sometimes to be mistaken for a Puerto Rican, but he could not speak Spanish. Clearly, he could not pass as black or Asian either (although, ironically, some concerned colleagues have suggested he don traditional African clothing for airline travel, to attempt to "pass" as African or African American). So he stood there in this meeting, listening in silence without a footing from which to express his unique experiences as a person of color. There was definitely a story to be told about Middle Eastern Americans and their struggles with inequality, for Amir and others like him, dubiously classified as a white, not being recognized as a distinct ethnic group meant not having a voice.

Later that day, Amir ran into one of his mentors, Joe Feagin, in the hotel lobby of where the conference was held. Joe was having dinner with a publisher, Dean Birkenkamp. They asked Amir to join them for a drink. Joe and his publisher were discussing future book projects. Amir complained to Joe about the lack of sociological research on Middle Eastern Americans. Referring to the session he had attended earlier that day, he griped, "I heard every ethnic group being presented in that room except us. It is as though in the minds of sociologists we don't exist. Every day we are stereotyped and vil-

lainized in Hollywood films and in local and national news, but race and ethnicity scholars just don't seem to notice us."

Joe and Dean seemed to agree. Turning to Amir, Joe commented, "Why
don't you write a book about Middle Eastern Americans?" He then turned to
Dean and asked, "You would be interested in something like that wouldn't
you?" Dean was more than interested. He told Amir to submit a proposal for
the book as soon as possible. In the last days of August 2001, coming back
from the conference on the flight from California to Florida, Amir noticed a
Middle Eastern man across the aisle from where he was seated. The man,
who appeared to be in his mid- to late fifties, was reading an Arabic newspaper without attracting much attention from the other passengers. He was cor-
dially treated by a stewardess as he asked for a drink in a less than perfect
English. Amir thought perhaps Middle Eastern people were beginning to
blend into the fabric of American culture. Maybe the worst days of intolerance were over.

After recruiting the assistance of his friend and colleague Karyn McKinney, the first draft of the book proposal was submitted in the first week of
September 2001, days before the terrorist attacks that shocked the world. We
had proposed to study the lives of Middle Eastern Americans and their experiences with discrimination. The book's working title was "Unwelcome
Immigrants: Middle Eastern Lives in the United States." We knew that just
about every ethnic group in America had been "unwelcome" at one point or
another, but we felt the Middle Eastern Americans had been particularly
shunned in recent decades. While our proposal was still under review, September 11 happened. The following account captures Amir's initial reaction
to the tragic events of that day:

> It's just another morning. You drag yourself out of bed, put on the almost clean
> dress shirt and walk out the door with the indifference and anonymity that you have
> used to make your hybrid existence easier. It helps you blend in, you think. You are
> an Iranian exile desperately trying to pass as just another nine-to-five *shmuck*.
>
> Your neighbor, who has never taken an interest in you before, frantically informs,
> "Can you believe they bombed the towers?" You wonder if he had too much to drink
> the night before. You amuse him with: "Which towers?" "The ones in New York!"
> he yells. Reluctantly, you follow with "Wow, that's terrible," having no idea how
> terrible. Listening to the radio on the way to work, the disaster begins to sink in.
> Your first reaction is to pray, not for the victims, no, for yourself. The foul memories
> of past accusations have made you very selfish. You begin a dialog with a god you
> had abandoned for months, "Please let it be a homegrown nut."
>
> When people at work ask if you had heard about the bombing, you are still in
> denial. Still holding your chin up and showing no guilt, you announce, "These mili-
> tia groups have to be stopped. They are going to destroy this country."
>
> But you can't stop the deluge of news reports. They point to the part of the world

that continues to embrace you, even though you have been trying to be rid of it for years. In some strange way, it has embedded itself in your skin, your walk, your unabashedly large nose, and most importantly, your eyes.

Later that night you watch the horrifying images of the towers collapsing and you see your dreams plummeting to the ground with them. Tears well up in your eyes, as much for the victims as for yourself. Who could believe a person's life can change so much in so little time? You know it will only get worse from here.

"What if one of the hijackers has the same first name as me?" you ask yourself and are comforted with the thought that the famous boxer Mike Tyson named his son Amir, and that you know Israelis named Amir. The name thing you can survive, but what about the way you look?

The news reports are flashing images of the suspected terrorists on the screen. Damn! They look Middle Eastern, not very different from yourself. Shamefully, the pain of the victims and their families still has not dominated your thoughts.

Then they show this video of people jumping out of the burning towers to save their lives. How hopeless and tragic. What a horrible way to die. And at least for a few moments you and your situation seem trivial compared to their suffering. These tears rolling down your cheeks are for them, and only them.

The next day comes the business of living through this. Your small act of courage for the day was walking your dog under the hateful gaze of the neighbors. To ease the situation, you address your dog in the thickest American accent you can muster, but it doesn't help that even your dog has an Iranian name. Realizing this, you quickly shift to simply referring to the poor animal as "good dog."

The toughest business of the day was calling your daughter. She had to be reminded that at least for now her dad is not Iranian, and the Farsi words she so enthusiastically memorized are not to be spoken in public, no matter how impressed her friends might be. You consider yourself fortunate for having a daughter who can pass for a number of other ethnicities besides Middle Eastern. "Everybody at school thinks she's Mexican," her mother consoles you.

You have known the bigotry. You have seen them do it to blacks for years, but you never thought you would be a full-fledged target. Ironically, you relied on the sensibility of the racists to hold you in higher regard. You always pictured a scenario where you would indignantly remind them that you are a Persian and not a common African American. But this hatred, you never imagined, and you cannot escape. Perhaps you will follow your Black students' advice and dye your hair and eyebrows blond and try to pass for a mulatto.[1]

September 11 has been described as "the day that changed everything." Many might find this phrase a melodramatic exaggeration, but for Middle Eastern Americans that tragic day was indeed transformative. The decades of fear regarding terrorism became intensely focused on the supposed treacherous character of Arabs and Iranians. Ethnically biased policies and legislation along with growing public distrust soon followed. That large numbers of Middle Eastern Americans could be detained like the Japanese Americans after Pearl Harbor was a real possibility. So real, in fact, that Amir packed a small bag the night of September 11 in preparation for mass detentions. That night and several nights after that, he went to bed fully dressed fearing that should there be a knock on the door, he would not have enough time to properly dress for the unknown journey. We later learned from our interviews that he was not alone in fearing the worst and preparing for it in this manner. While no extreme drastic measures were taken (or have not been taken yet), at least for the weeks immediately following September 11, the daily routines of Middle Eastern Americans were severely disrupted. Going to a grocery store became an act of bravery. Driving to work required strategic planning to avoid long stops at traffic signals for fear of a mob attack. Numerous American flags had to be acquired and prominently displayed to signal not so much patriotism but conformity and innocuousness. To walk in any public place was to risk being the target of angry shouts of "fucking towel head" and "sand nigger," or possibly being shot by a misguided patriot.

Sympathetic e-mails began rolling in shortly after the attacks. Among them one from our publisher, Dean, who reassured us that he had become even more interested in our book. However, we now faced a new challenge in soliciting interviews.

INTERVIEWING MIDDLE EASTERN AMERICANS IN THE POST–SEPTEMBER 11 CLIMATE

Our Middle Eastern American contacts were justifiably skeptical about our research agenda. How were they to know that we were not covertly helping law enforcement authorities collect information about people of Middle Eastern origin? Asking people how they feel about living in the United States has never been an innocuous question. To ask Middle Eastern Americans this question in the post–September 11 environment could easily be construed as a secret intelligence operation. So we had to go to those who trusted us, the first author's family and friends in most cases, who introduced us to others in turn. On a few occasions, we recruited respondents at national conferences such as the annual meetings of Islamic Society of North America, Council on American Islamic Relations, and Middle Eastern Studies Association. Typically, we would stand in hotel lobbies of conferences and approach random subjects for interviews. Our success rate was less than 20 percent. The majority of the people we approached did not turn us down directly but asked for contact information and indicated they would be in touch with us at a time of their choosing. Without exception, we did not hear from these potential respondents.

In the end, we interviewed twenty respondents (fourteen men and six women). Fifteen were naturalized citizens, and four grew up in the United States. They ranged in age from nineteen to fifty-six. Almost all were college graduates or in college. Nine were from Iran, six from Pakistan, two from Egypt, two from Lebanon, and one from Turkey. Nineteen were Muslims and one was a Christian. The in-depth interviews usually lasted an hour and both authors were involved in asking questions.

FIELD OBSERVATIONS AND
PERSONAL EXPERIENCE

Aside from our formal interviews, in this study we also draw on informal sources of empirical data. This data was gathered by both authors in many settings, over many years; through informal conversations, life experiences, collective memories, and visits to conferences, mosques, and other family and community gatherings. For example, many times before an interview would begin, we would find that an interviewee would ask, "So, what will this interview be about?" or "What kinds of questions will you be asking me?" Of course, to put the respondent at ease, as well as to fulfill informed consent requirements, we would explain the purposes and goals of our research. Respondents, not familiar with the stilted protocol of formal interviewing, would often then begin to tell us, "Oh, yes, I can talk about that, because I've had a lot of experiences with discrimination. For example . . ."[2] Sometimes we found ourselves simply without the means to conduct a formal interview although the exchange was useful for our research.[3] In other cases we had to meet with our respondents informally before collecting data. For example, we visited the home of an Iranian woman and her African American husband before conducting a formal interview with her. In fact, we did not even bring up or ask her for an interview until the end of the evening, after she served us an elaborate Iranian meal and after hours of conversation.[4]

Another type of informal data for this book was provided by non–Middle Eastern American spouses of some of our participants. For example, we met the Iranian woman spoken of earlier through her husband, who read the post–September 11 piece by Amir on the Internet and e-mailed him about it.[5] Similarly, the Muslim wife of one of our Iranian respondents, who herself is not Middle Eastern but is from the Midwest United States, was present and interviewed along with her husband.[6]

Our time in the field itself was a form of data collection. Although it is impossible to isolate individual statements and phrases, or "transcribe" the feel of a room or setting, we gathered data simply by being in certain settings. For example, the second author, Karyn McKinney, visited a mosque while on a trip to Chicago and spent an entire afternoon touring not only the mosque itself but also a youth center across the street and having dinner with the members of the mosque at an Arabic restaurant nearby. Although Karyn conducted no formal interviews, the amount of data she gathered in this setting could fill pages.[7]

Other settings similarly yielded experiential data. At one conference, both authors sat at dinner beside a young Pakistani Muslim, who, although he felt he did not "know enough" to be a participant in our study, informally discussed topics relevant to it with us over our three-course meal. At every conference we attended, we met people who were willing to talk "off the record," but too nervous to have the tape recorder emerge. Data was gathered in such settings simply by sitting quietly and watching people. Of course, this was quite likely easier for Amir than for Karyn, as the conference settings were one place where he blended in more easily than she. In fact, in order to meet up with one respondent at the ISNA conference, Amir told him "I'm sort of tall, with dark skin and black hair." As an aside, he mentioned "Oh, and my colleague is short, with red hair." When we finally found our respondent among a sea of Middle Eastern faces, Amir laughed and said, "I guess giving you my description didn't help much." The respondent replied "Oh, no, I immediately skipped over that and started looking for *her* red hair."[8]

Finally, the lives of the authors themselves are a source of experiential data. As previously mentioned, we sought respondents through connections with Amir's family. Additionally, although we did not interview all the members of Amir's family, obviously he has had innumerable conversations with his family and extended family, in which they have told him about their immigration experiences and lives in the United States. Amir and Karyn also draw on their own experiences throughout the book.

WHO IS A MIDDLE
EASTERN AMERICAN?

For the purpose of this book, our definition of Middle Eastern American is practical and derived from the respondents' everyday experiences with their ethnicity and the reactions of those around them. From this perspective, a Middle Eastern person is someone who identifies him- or herself as being from or having ancestral ties to the predominantly Islamic region of the world in Southwest Asia and North Africa. Given this definition of Middle Eastern, we included in this study Pakistanis, Iranians, Egyptians, Lebanese, and a Turk.[9]

Our definition here also assumes that while Middle Eastern Americans, like Hispanic Americans, come from multiple racial, linguistic, religious, and geographical backgrounds, they constitute a distinct ethnic category in the United States. Our approach is based on the fact that Middle Eastern Americans have been viewed by white, mainstream Americans as "others" (see chapter 1 for a detailed history of how early Middle Eastern immigrants were classified racially). Ironically, as indicated in an official report, the U.S. Census, under Directive No. 15, "instructs persons of Middle Eastern or North African descent to report their race as 'white.'"[10] However, the same report notes that, "it is not known how well this instruction is followed. . . . Over the years there has been confusion about how people of these ancestries should respond—'Asian,' 'White,' or 'Other race.'"[11]

As we note throughout this book, far from being treated as "white," Middle Eastern Americans, particularly those with darker skin tones (i.e., those who are Middle Eastern looking), are considered a despised and dangerous minority group. The goal of our research is to bring to light the history and current experiences of this group with discrimination.

THE OBJECTIVES AND ORGANIZATION OF THIS BOOK

The place of Middle Eastern Americans in the racial hierarchy of the United States remains relatively unexplored in scholarly research. This inattention can be attributed to three factors: (a) For the purpose of data collection and analysis, Middle Easterners are not a homogenous group and thus do not easily fit into a particular racial category; (b) until recently, this population has been relatively small compared to other minority groups; and (c) the political conflict between the United States and Middle Eastern countries has cast immigrants from this region as disloyal guests unworthy of equal attention in the realm of ethnic studies.

Nearly all the work focused on Middle Eastern people has considered their experiences in the Middle East. Perhaps in part due to the prolonged conflict with Israel, much of this research explores issues of national identity and political involvement. Very few studies have attempted to detail the immigrant experience for Middle Easterners in the United States, and those that have tend to use quantitative data analysis to gather demographic information about Middle Eastern Americans. Perhaps part of the reason that very few previous studies have qualitatively studied the day-to-day experiences of Middle Eastern Americans is because, until relatively recently, they were fewer in number than most other groups. However, because Middle Eastern groups are some of the fastest growing in the United States today, the time is ripe for an in-depth analysis of their lives, and particularly of their place in the U.S. racial and ethnic hierarchy.

Economically, Middle Eastern immigrants often have been perceived as a "model minority"; however, our previous research and experiences tell us that they are not accepted as part of the American mainstream. Additionally, the discrimination and exclusion they face cannot simply be understood as the same as that experienced by other minority groups. The political tensions between the United States and various Middle Eastern countries has added an element of hostility and suspicion to daily interactions between Middle Eastern Americans and other Americans that is not faced by any other group today.

There is a growing recognition in the sociological study of race and ethnicity of the so-called browning of America, and yet when one reviews the research literature, there is virtually no mention of Middle Easterners, who are part of that demographic shift. The time is overdue for such a study. This book fills that gap in the race and ethnicity literature and makes visible how members of this ethnic group experience discrimination. We bring this message to our readers in an accessible style that thoroughly covers the main themes of the Middle Eastern experience in America.

This book especially focuses on how Middle Eastern Americans adjust to, or resist, prejudice and discrimination within the existing structure of ethnic and racial inequality in the United States. Our work is organized into two parts. Part I looks at the social forces that have shaped the experiences of Middle Eastern Americans. Specifically, chapter 1 looks at the history of Middle Eastern immigration into the United States. A brief introduction of the pattern of immigration and settlement of various groups (e.g., Arabs, Iranians, and Turks) is offered here.

Chapter 2 examines the most prominent stereotypes of Middle Eastern Americans, which tend to focus on Islam and terrorism. Both topics are explored in this chapter from historical and sociological perspectives to challenge the prevailing misconceptions. For example, we take issue with the notion that Islam is inherently opposed to Christianity. Similarly, we challenge the premise that terrorism has been a uniquely Islamic or Middle Eastern phenomenon. At the same time, chapter 2 offers a review of the recent history of U.S. military conflicts with Arab countries and Iran and their impact on the lives of Middle Eastern Americans.

Using content analysis of media accounts, chapter 3 explores how the opposition between the Middle Eastern self and the Western other is rhetorically constructed and particularly reinforced in the post–September 11 climate. This chapter shows how the media dismisses the threat of domestic terror as isolated acts of mentally unbalanced and misguided Americans while at the same time emphasizing how the potential for terrorism among Middle Eastern and Muslim Americans is a culturally embedded phenomenon that is backed by the "uncivilized" and "barbaric" people of the Middle East and their supporters here in America.

Part II of this book describes everyday experiences with discrimination. This part is organized into three chapters. Chapter 4 looks at how Middle Eastern Americans present themselves to others. Specifically, we show how our respondents account for themselves in everyday encounters by educating their fellow Americans using humor and sometimes by directly confronting stereotypes of themselves.

Chapter 5 reviews the history of other ethnic and racial groups in the United States and highlights similarities with the Middle Eastern American experience. This chapter also empirically explores the meaning of the "American Dream" for our respondents in light of their developing understanding of discrimination. Chapter 6 builds on the theme of experiencing and coping with discrimination by focusing on Middle Eastern lives in the context of social institutions. Specifically, we present our respondents' accounts of the discrimination they have faced at work, in schools, and in their communities. We also highlight the economic and psychological impact of this discrimination on their lives and their coping strategies. Chapter 7 explores the possibilities and potentials for the formation of panethnic Middle Eastern American identity. We look at the social conditions that pave the way for the formation of such an identity and the methods used by some of our respondents to promote it. The chapter ends by considering the challenges that national, political, and religious differences pose against the potential for the creation of a panethnic Middle Eastern identity. Finally, chapter 8 summarizes the overall theme of the book into a single message: To speak against discrimination is to fight an insidious social ill. We reject the argument that the criticism of the status quo amounts to "whining." On the contrary, we argue that ethnic and racial discrimination are *real* problems with *real* adverse consequences for *real* people.

NOTES

1. Amir Marvasti, "You Know It Will Get Worse," www.iranian.com, September 6, 2002.

2. Middle Eastern etiquette, when one is familiar with it, is in some ways even more "formal" than U.S. manners. So, not wanting to interrupt the respondent to ask if we could turn on the tape recorder, we sometimes did not get these thoughts on tape, although they contained interesting information and certainly were "data." Often these musings before

the formal interview began would go on for several minutes or even a half an hour before one of us could find a gracious way to break in.

3. Once, while eating in a favorite Iranian restaurant in Orlando, Florida, we asked the restaurant owner, who Amir had spoken with before in Farsi, if he might participate in our study. However, we did not at that time have our tape recorder with us, or our questionnaire and consent forms. He asked what the study was about; and we gave him an overview. He then went on to describe to us in vivid detail his immigration experiences, discrimination he has faced in the United States, and strategies he's used to deal with it, particularly since September 11, for close to an hour. We left him our business card, and told him that we would be back with our forms and tape recorder. However, we also left knowing that we should have been prepared on the spot to interview him, if we were going to bring it up—not only would it be hard to get him to "retell" his story the same way, it would be awkward to ask him again, particularly by Iranian standards of etiquette.

4. During these hours of conversation, however, this woman spoke of her experiences as an immigrant to the United States, as well as the experiences of many of her relatives, that had become part of the collective memory of her family. Amir and I looked at each other with a mixture of delight and dismay as the conversation progressed. All of this, of course, we were not getting on tape as formalized data. However, we made notes from the conversation, and the wealth of information that she shared with us, not only in the formal interview conducted later with her on the telephone but also in this informal conversation, contributed much to our study.

5. In fact, Amir conducted a phone interview with him prior to our visit to their home. Although we did not include his interview in the sample, given that he is not Middle Eastern but African American, this insightful respondent added a dimension to our research that was quite valuable. Several things that he noted about the Middle Eastern community contributed theoretically to this study.

6. Because she wears the chador, although she is light-skinned and looks "American," she often deals with some of the same prejudices that Middle Eastern Americans experience. For example, in the library where she works, often patrons raise their voices to a near-shout and speak very slowly when addressing her, apparently assuming she is "foreign" simply because she is "veiled." After September 11, a car sped up as if to run her down as she tried to cross a street. Obviously, she also observes the experiences of her husband and family. Again, although she is not included in the formal "sample," this woman certainly is part of the study.

7. At the youth center, she listened to a very young imam discuss the programs he is developing to help Muslim youth become involved in U.S. society while still maintaining their Muslim values. In the mosque, she heard two Muslim women describe their feelings about wearing the hijab. One of them stated that rather than seeing it as oppressive, she finds it liberating to not have to be subject to the oppressive beauty standards that American women are so victimized by. Since, Karyn has found it much easier to explain this topic to her women's studies students, and pictures these women's faces each time. Dinner was equally informative, and one of the young women, whose husband and son Karyn had met, hugged her as she left.

8. Karyn learned much from being in settings where she was the minority, particularly when the conferences were Muslim and women were dressed conservatively. Of course, being familiar with Muslim communities, she had dressed relatively conservatively also,

but still did not have on a hijab and thus stood out in the crowd. Still, people were very friendly in most cases, and again, most American women would be surprised to learn that Muslim women are not silenced under their "veils."

9. In defining this ethnic population (i.e., in deciding who is a Middle Eastern American), we had two other options. First, there was the objective, geographically based definition that refers to a set of countries and their people as Middle Eastern. These include Arabic-speaking countries such as Iraq, Jordan, Saudi Arabia, as well as Iran, where the dominant culture and language is Farsi or Persian. This definition, while useful for a census count, for example, did not seem to fit the qualitative and experiential emphasis of our project. The second choice would be based on the idea that the Middle East is a geopolitical construct that is founded on exaggerated distinctions between "Western self" and the "Arab/Muslim Other." This view adds a different flavor to such terms as "the Near East," "the Middle East," or "the Far East." These labels respectively represent degrees of similarity between the "orient" and the "occident" (see Edward Said's *Orientalism* [New York: Vintage Books, 1979]). The latter, though closer to our topic of interest due to its political overtones, also seems inappropriate for this research because it too is somewhat removed from everyday experience.

10. U.S. Census Bureau, "Recommendation from the Interagency Committee for the Review of the Racial and Ethnic Standards," 2000. www.census.gov.

11. U.S. Census Bureau, "Recommendation from the Interagency Committee."

Part I

THE HISTORY, PRESENT STATUS, AND PUBLIC PORTRAYALS

Chapter 1

How They Came to America and Where They Are Today

As we noted in the introduction, in the case of Middle Eastern Americans, specifying who is Middle Eastern American is more complex than in the case of some other groups. In the United States, the group has generally included Arabs, Iranians, and Turks. Today in the United States, there are an estimated two to three million Arab Americans, though the actual number is not known, largely because the U.S. Census, which ironically classifies Middle Eastern Americans as "white," does not include a category for Arab or Middle Eastern Americans.[1] The Middle Eastern population as a whole may be underrepresented in official U.S. population estimates, and specific subpopulations may be overlooked.

For example, it is difficult to place Iranian Americans, who are from the Middle East but not of Arabic ancestry. Most statistical information, from academic or governmental sources, is about Arab Americans, and thus does not explicitly include Iranian Americans. The same can be said for Turkish and Pakistani Americans, who are not officially labeled as Middle Eastern, and yet many self-identify or are identified as such.

In this chapter, we present the background of Middle Eastern Americans. Specifically, we begin by discussing their early history and economic adaptations. We then review the shifts in their identity in the context of two waves of immigration. We also describe their current socioeconomic and geographical distribution, as well as their political and religious affiliations. Finally, given that the data attributed to Middle Eastern Americans is typically based on surveys of the Arab American community, we end this chapter by offering separate demographic profiles for Iranian, Turkish, and Pakistani Americans.

3

EARLY HISTORY

Although some evidence suggests that individual Muslims may have come to the North American continent with exploring expeditions as far back as the 1100s, the earliest substantial group of Muslims to arrive in America were brought as slaves from West Africa between 1530 and 1851, especially from countries that are now Ghana, the Ivory Coast, Niger, Burkina Faso, and Algeria, all present-day Islamic countries. In fact, today about 62 percent of the African continent is Muslim, and historians estimate that between 14 and 30 percent of all slaves were Muslims.[2] Thus, in many ways it is not surprising that African Americans make up 23.8 percent of the Muslim community in the United States today—as one author writes: "When African-Americans convert to Islam . . . they are actually, possibly, returning to their own roots, in a sense 'reverting' to Islam."[3]

A distinction should be made, however, between waves of *Muslim* immigration and of *Middle Eastern* immigration. Although the first large group of Muslim immigrants were African slaves, the first large groups of Middle Eastern Americans to the United States began to come by boat in the late 1800s and were Syrians and Lebanese.[4] There is some confusion as to the nationality of these earliest Middle Eastern immigrants. This is because all inhabitants of the Ottoman Empire were considered Turkish citizens until after World War I. They all spoke Arabic, and most referred to themselves as "Syrian." However, when they came to the United States, they arrived with Turkish passports. Thus, until 1899, U.S. officials simply referred to all such immigrants as Turkish. After this time, a new category was created for Syrians. It was not until the 1930s that the identification of "Lebanese" began to be used, although it is estimated that about 85 percent of the early immigrants came from the region that is now known as Lebanon. Many Lebanese continued at that time to refer to themselves as "Syrian," and similarly, some people who actually came from the area known as Syria started to call themselves "Lebanese." Others used the term "Syrian-Lebanese."

These first immigrants tended to group themselves based primarily on religion, and there was some divisiveness in the immigrant community because of religious differences between Muslims, Christians, and Jews. However, they had been motivated to immigrate by many of the same factors. Like many other groups, these first Middle Eastern Americans came to the United States to escape difficult lives in their home country. During this period of immigration, which began in 1870 and lasted until about 1914, approximately 100,000 Syrian-Lebanese came to the United States.[5] These first immigrants were fleeing the harsh treatment of the Turkish Ottoman Empire, which had ruled over the region for four hundred years.[6] Economic conditions were poor in Turkey, in part due to overtaxing, so large numbers of people were starving and living in poverty; and along with this poverty came poor health. The Turkish government was generally harsh, but particularly persecuted Christians. The promise of religious freedom in the United States, as well as economic opportunities, were the major motivating forces in Syrian-Lebanese immigration in the early 1900s.[7] These reports were sometimes exaggerated, or at least skewed to include only the positive aspects of living in the United States. For example, in *The Syrian Yankee,* Salom Rizk writes of the report his schoolteacher gives of America:

> "It is a country—but not like Syria. It is really a country like heaven and you cannot know what it is like until you have been there. . . ." He told me many more things about America. . . . So many wonderful, unbelievable things my schoolmaster told me . . . the land of hope . . . the land of peace . . . the land of contentment . . . the land of liberty . . . the land of brotherhood . . . the land of plenty . . . where God has poured out wealth . . . where the dreams of men come true . . . where everything is bigger and grander and more beautiful than it has ever been anywhere else in the world . . . where wheat grows waist high, shoulder high, sky high, and as thick as the hair on your head . . . where men do the deeds of giants and think the thoughts of God . . . where they harness rivers of water to turn great machines and drench the land with light . . . where merely the push of a button does the work of thousands of horses and donkeys and camels and men . . . where everybody has a chance to learn, even the humblest child of the humblest Syrian immigrant . . . where every boy and girl can learn to be what he or she wants to be. . . . Now it grew too big, too miraculous, too heavenly. It sounded like the fairylands my grandmother used to tell about, and I knew there were no more fairylands and no more fairies. But I wanted to believe all this, I had to believe it, and I did.
>
> "When can I go there?" I cried. "As soon as we can get word from your brothers, Salom. As soon as you can get a passport." . . . How wonderful! How beautiful! Like the magic lamp of Alladin. Just a piece of paper, but it will open up the gates of heaven—my passport to paradise. I must write to my brothers at once. They will answer. They will tell me what to do. Then I will go to America—to heaven![8]

Although he expresses skepticism about the glowing report of America given to him by his teacher, Rizk, like other Syrians of the time, is eager to immigrate. Like many other autobiographical accounts written by Syrians, his is primarily a positive account of "this land where this [personal triumph] could happen to anyone."[9] As one researcher states:

> One should not overlook the impact the returning emigrant had, with tales and tangible evidence of their swift economic success, in creating a psychological disposition favorable to emigration. Though the accounts were often exaggerated, they did convince many determined villagers that it was possible in a relatively short time to amass a small fortune and return home. . . . One should not belittle the impact of such "success stories." The tales—often told with dramatic gesture around the

flickering light of an oil lamp on a stormy night in a mountain village with all the
relatives and friends packed into the one room cottage——undoubtedly inspired the
determination and adventurous spirit of countless numbers of villagers to do like-
wise and seek their fortunes in the New World.[10]

Apparently not all of the tales of quick economic success were exaggerated,
as many Syrians were able to be economically successful relatively quickly.

EARLY ECONOMIC ADAPTATIONS

The majority of these early Syrian-Lebanese—one in every three—were peddlers (i.e., traveling salesmen) and many subsequently became shop owners.[11]
Part of the reason for the popularity of this occupation was that trading was
a common venture in their home country. An obvious function of the profes-
sion of peddling, of course, was to make money for the immigrant. For the
rural communities often served by the peddlers, these Syrian immigrants
were invaluable, as they brought products that were essential that might have
been otherwise inaccessible. The Syrian peddlers also provided access to
"exotic" products that the white inhabitants of rural America had never
before encountered. A less obvious function of peddling, for early Middle
Eastern Americans, however, was that it helped them to assimilate to U.S.
society more easily, by preventing ghettoization, spreading them throughout
the country, and by bringing them directly into contact with the native population in their own homes.[12]

Operating moving "stores" also allowed Syrians to transition relatively
easily into occupations as shopkeepers. As of 1914, most of these first Middle
Eastern Americans had become stationary business owners, opening grocery
stores. As such, many were successful enough to compete with European ethnic immigrants who had already settled in urban centers. Specifically, Syrians
who arrived in cities began to replace Irish Americans in neighborhoods as
they became more upwardly mobile. Sometimes hostilities arose between
them, both over tensions that developed in neighborhoods, as well as supposed religious differences. For example, according to historical accounts
from Paterson, New Jersey, in 1920, Irish Catholics were hostile toward Syrian immigrants, who they assumed were, as they called them "Mohammed-
ans" or "Turks," until a group of Syrians met with a religious leader in the
Irish community to explain that they were Christians.[13] Thus all was not
happy for the early Syrian entrepreneurs. For example, consider the following
reflections on the hostility and alienation experienced by the early peddlers:

Why did I have to be born in Syria, anyway, and fall heir to all this contempt, ridi-
cule, and abuse? Why should anybody have to suffer for the accident of being born

in the wrong country? Besides, what was wrong with being a foreigner? Weren't all Americans foreigners if you only went back far enough? I was rebellious—and worried. Suppose the American housewives didn't like my accent or my dark face?[14]

Perhaps in response to such pressures, some Middle Eastern Americans slowly moved away from self-employment and into the industrial labor force, especially in Detroit, where Henry Ford promised a $5 wage for an eight-hour work day in his auto factories.[15] Middle Eastern men were attracted to these low-skill jobs and sent word back home about them to encourage relatives to join them. Syrian men most often arrived alone and after they were established sent for their wives and children to join them. The wives who arrived differed from others of the time in that they were relatively independent, which runs counter to many current stereotypes of oppressed Middle Eastern American women. Although early Middle Eastern American families were relatively poor, as were most immigrants, unlike many others, they were literate and Syrian parents required that their children finish primary school.[16] A look at current statistical data will show that this emphasis on education is still part of the Middle Eastern American ethos. The entire family, including children after they completed school, contributed to the family's economic success.

Although less than one-fourth of the Syrian-Lebanese immigrants were professionals or skilled workers, many were able to become economically secure within the first generation. Some of the reasons for this had to do with characteristics and values of the immigrants themselves; while some were the result of circumstances they were fortunate enough to encounter when they arrived. For example, most Syrian-Lebanese owned homes in their countries, so they immigrated in relatively stable financial circumstances. They also accumulated money quickly, and already had the knowledge of how to invest it wisely, as well as certain cultural values of motivation to succeed, industriousness, and independence. Additionally, as mentioned previously, they had experience in trading, which enabled them to take advantage of a niche that allowed them to gain a unique social and economic position. As a whole, what aided the Syrian-Lebanese immigrants was both being in the right place at the right time and having the skills and knowledge to take advantage of fortunate circumstances. Peddling, which became the first occupation of most Syrian immigrants, allowed them to be spread widely throughout the country, which not only helped them become accustomed to the host population, but also helped the host population become accustomed to them.[17]

Although Syrian-Lebanese maintained some social organizations, and some ethnic newspapers, they did not need to establish their own banks, schools, hospitals, and other institutions. As early as 1911, a Syrians' median income was only slightly lower than that of a U.S.-born male, and they worked in most realms of commerce. This trend in the economic status of Middle Eastern Americans has continued. Syrian-Lebanese had entered most of the major professions, and were assimilated into U.S. economic and social life by the 1950s.[18] About half of the current Arab American population consists of descendants of the original Syrian-Lebanese, first-wave immigrants who arrived before World War II.[19]

CHANGING IDENTITIES OVER
ONE HUNDRED YEARS

In the following section, we discuss the internal and external factors that have shaped Middle Eastern American identity since their early immigration experiences over a hundred years ago. Specifically, we highlight how forces from within and outside the Middle Eastern community have shaped what it means to be a Middle Eastern person living in the United States along the lines of race, nationality, and religion.

First-Wave Immigrants

Early Arab immigrants had strong attachments to family and religious sect. Most thought of themselves as temporary sojourners in North America.[20] According to one historian:

> Judging by autobiographical accounts and other historical sources, many of the early immigrants perceived much of the early movement as a transient phenomenon. Their idea or dream was to amass all the wealth possible, in the shortest time, and then to return home to flaunt the material evidence of their success. Their overall aim no doubt accounts for the fact that youthful and uncommitted males were the primary émigrés in the formative phase of emigration.[21]

Their economic assets were available for quick liquidation, should they decide to return home. Most associated primarily with other Arabs, for instance, marrying endogamously, and formed very few connections with "Americans." These early immigrants did not attempt to assimilate, and the issue of identity was not particularly pressing. Political activities in their new country still focused on events in the countries or even villages from which they immigrated. Thus, although there was some degree of unity among Arabs, there were divisions among communities of origin in the United States.[22] Each community, for example, had its own newspaper to represent its interests.

The period surrounding World War I became a turning point in the identification of Arab Americans. First, World War I itself isolated Arabs in the United States from Arabs in their home countries. Second, right after World War I, restrictive immigration quotas were passed that virtually cut off immigration from many areas of the world, including Arab countries. Both of these factors isolated Arabs in the United States. This isolation strengthened solidarity among communities that had previously been fragmented. It also increased assimilation.[23] Arabs began to realize that what had previously seemed to be a "temporary" residence was to be a permanent home, and some accommodations would need to be made in order to survive in the new environment.[24]

Children of immigrants became more involved in American culture. English began to be used more often, in churches, newspapers, and among the new generation. Arab immigrants began to attend citizenship classes to learn English and to become Americanized.[25] Arab community leaders encouraged assimilation, stating that immigrants should not feel like strangers and should contribute to their new country. A "melting pot" approach was beginning to take hold such that families tried to remove all distinguishing ethnic features, going so far as not teaching their children Arabic. By World War II, Arabs in North America had, for the most part, begun to blend in with the host group, and it was not until the second wave of immigration from the Middle East that Arab American identity was rekindled.

In addition to the internal forces in the era discussed earlier, there were also external influences that shaped the early Middle Eastern American identity, particularly regarding whether they were classified as a race (i.e., biologically distinct from whites) or an ethnic group (i.e., only culturally distinct from whites). Various studies show that even prior to their decision to remain permanently in the United States, Arab immigrants faced prejudice and discrimination. They had been sometimes seen as economically parasitic, since they only engaged in trade and they were thought not to reinvest their profits domestically. Others viewed Arabs as inassimilable and inferior to whites.[26] There was a growing generally intolerant view of any non-Northern European immigrant groups, and nativistic tendencies were high in the United States in the early 1900s.

Several policies had forced Arab Americans in varying racial and ethnic classifications, irrespective of their own attempts at self-definition. The U.S. Census identified them as "Turks" or "Other Asians" until 1920, and Arab immigrants objected to this classification, as it connected them with the Ottoman Empire, which most had immigrated to escape. The designation of "Turk" also implied "Muslim" at the time, and most of the immigrants were

Christian. Muslims were viewed negatively, so a misrepresentation as Muslim carried stigma.[27]

By the end of the nineteenth century, Arab immigrants were classifying themselves as "Syrians." There was a later campaign to change the identification to "Lebanese," but this was for the most part unsuccessful, although some clubs and individuals did begin to identify as "Syrian-Lebanese."[28] Aside from what country of origin Middle Eastern Americans at the time chose to identify with, a larger question loomed ahead for them, however:

> Whatever terms were eventually used by the immigrants, it is important to point out that the question of identity was not so much concerned about resolving the origins of the immigrants, but rather was concerned with how they should situate themselves within the "melting pot" of American society. In other words, could the Arabic-speaking Syrians from Asia fit into a country that favored its European roots and practiced varying degrees of prejudice against those perceived as "non-whites?"[29]

Those referred to as Syrians had been granted citizenship since the 1880s, and seen as white in the United States for the first thirty years of their immigration.[30] However, in the early 1900s, theories of "racial inferiority" began to grow, and U.S. (and Canadian) governments asserted that Arabs had no right to become citizens because they were "nonwhite." Syrian immigrants were sometimes referred to as the "most foreign" of all.[31] At various times, these first-wave immigrants were referred to racially as "Caucasian," "white," "black," and "colored." Thus, the question of racial identification began to become more relevant for Arab immigrants.[32] Syrians began to have their requests for citizenship challenged in court.

Syrian immigrants were ruled ineligible for naturalization in 1909 based on legislation of 1790 (which limited citizenship to "free white persons"). At this time, they were considered nonwhite, even though many of them had blonde hair and blue eyes. A Circuit Court of Appeals reversed the decision. However, this matter was brought before a U.S. District Court again in New York. Although this court upheld the earlier decision stating that Syrians could be naturalized, the continued raising of the issue of citizenship is evidence that acceptance of early Middle Eastern immigrants was certainly not complete.[33]

In 1914, George Dow was denied a petition to become a U.S. citizen because he was declared to be nonwhite in accordance with the 1790 U.S. naturalization law.[34] In order to establish their "whiteness," members of the Syrian community sought to establish their identification as "Arabs." The argument was that Arabs, as the purest of the Semitic race, were even whiter than Europeans. It is interesting to note that even while adopting this Arab identity for the purposes of citizenship, it was not taken on in full. The community still referred to itself, for the most part, as Syrian—perhaps because of the recognition of American antagonism toward Arabs and Islam.[35] Still, the self-imposed Arab label did help overturn the Dow decision in 1915. It was decided that the pertinent legislation should not be that of 1790, but instead legislation from 1873 and 1875—and correspondent to these laws, Syrians were closely related to Europeans, and thus "white."

The initial wave of Middle Eastern immigration that had begun with the entrance of the Syrian-Lebanese abated with the passage of a restrictive immigration act in 1924.[36] This act established a quota system that effectively all but barred immigration from Asian, southern European, and Middle Eastern countries. The act set quotas on immigration for countries that were proportional to that country's percentage of the population in 1920. Obviously, since the United States was primarily Northern European in 1920, the highest immigration quotas went to immigrants from countries in Northern Europe.

Although Syrians had finally been called white by the courts, because their racial status had been challenged, it remained insecure for decades to come. For example, there were two conflicting cases challenging Arab racial identity during World War II. In the first, in 1942, a Muslim from Yemen was denied citizenship because he was considered nonwhite and Muslim. In 1944, under the 1940 Nationality Act, another Muslim was given citizenship because, geographically, Arabs had sometimes lived in Europe and had assimilated culturally with Europeans.[37]

Second-Wave Immigrants

A second wave of Middle Eastern immigration began after World War II, in 1946. The 1924 restrictive immigration act, discussed earlier, was not overturned until the late 1960s, when fixed, equal numbers of immigrants were allowed from each country. It was after this change that the second wave of Middle Eastern immigration peaked. This second wave of immigration has been larger than the first, with half a million Arab immigrants entering the United States just since 1970.[38] These new immigrants have arrived from such countries as Iran, Iraq, Palestine, Egypt, and Lebanon since 1968.[39]

The second wave is made up of Muslims and Christians, whereas the first-wave group was more Christian. The second-wave immigrants have tended to be highly educated professionals. The "push" factors (i.e., what forced them out of their homelands) have been different. Whereas the first wave of Middle Easterners came to America mostly because of religious persecution under the Ottoman Empire, the new arrivals came to benefit from the educational opportunities in the United States and escape political conflicts in their home countries. Some of the crises that have brought the new Middle Easterners to

the United States include the 1968 Palestinian-Israeli conflict over the West
Bank and Gaza Strip; the beginnings of civil war in 1975 in Lebanon; the
Iran-Iraq war; the overthrow of the shah and beginning of Islamic revolution
in Iran in 1978; poverty and civil war in Yemen; and war, conflict, and religious oppression in Iraq.[40] A major implication of this recent pattern of immigration is that most members of the second wave do not see themselves as
temporary residents, as the first group did. Rather, they conceive of themselves as permanent members of their new society, and full participants in
it.[41]

Conflict in the Middle East solidified a sense of Arab American identity in
the United States. For example, some cite the 1967 Arab-Israeli war as a turning point for the second-wave immigrants similar to that of World War I for
first-wave immigrants. Witnessing the Arab-Israeli conflict, and particularly
what many viewed as a one-sided U.S. media response, strengthened the
sense of Arab identity among many Arab Americans. New immigrants, along
with third-generation descendents of the early immigrants, who had begun to
think of themselves as "Arabs" rather than "Syrians," came together to form
an ethnic community. Thus, political conflict in the Middle East revitalized
a sense of Arab pride for the new immigrants, and for the third-generation
immigrants, it began a process of "deassimilation," or pulling away from
mainstream America. For the first time since World War II, an organization
was established to give voice to Arab American interests without country or
religious divisions. This group, established in 1967, was labeled the Association of Arab-American University Graduates (AAUG). During this period,
interest in Arab heritage reemerged, evidenced in growing numbers of conferences that took place, political organizations that formed, and publications
that began to appear in the late 1960s and early 1970s. [42]

Some stereotypes of recent Middle Eastern immigrants are based on fundamentally racist conceptions of them as physically distinct from "white"
Americans.[43] However, Census categorizations continue to label them as
"white." There often exists a fundamental contradiction between the official
racial designation of Middle Eastern Americans and their racial identification
by average Americans, many of whom likely view them as "nonwhite."

Since the 1960s, the notion of Middle Eastern Americans as dangerous
outsiders has been based more on ethnic or religious grounds, which are later
translated into "racial" differences.[44] In light of the political crises in the
Middle East, ethnic and religious differences of Middle Eastern Americans
have received more public attention and scrutiny. Several events—
particularly the 1973 Arab-Israeli war, the Arab oil embargo, and the Iranian
revolution and hostage crisis—influenced the U.S. government and public to
begin to respond to the Middle East, and to Middle Eastern Americans, as a

monolithic religious group.[45] Especially after the Iranian revolution and the hostage crisis, many pundits equated the politics of the Iranian government with Islam.[46] Since large numbers of the new Middle Eastern immigrants were Muslim, they began to be seen in more religious terms than previous immigrants, and often more negatively. Thus from an external view, the Middle Eastern American identity, since the 1960s, to a large extent has been based on religious difference. The convergence of politics and the Muslim identity is best illustrated in the words of an Arab American political activist from Detroit:

> I was actually a delegate to the 1992 convention when the Democrats turned us away and said, "You need to access this party differently." So I am familiar with how bad it can be. It's not necessarily my being an Arab American that would be a problem, but rather my political views. And now in this day and age it's being a Muslim that's a problem. Today Muslims are where I think Arab Americans were two decades ago.[47]

WHERE THEY ARE TODAY

As previously discussed, Middle Eastern Americans have come from many different nations. Arab Americans alone have origins in some twenty-two countries in the Middle East and North Africa.[48] The 1990 Census found that almost half of all Arab Americans are from Lebanon (Syrian-Lebanese).[49] According to 2003 demographics gathered by the Arab American Institute (AAI), 47 percent of all Arab Americans are from Lebanon, and those remaining are from the following countries, in descending order of population: Syria (15 percent), Egypt (9 percent), Palestine (6 percent), Iraq (3 percent), and Jordan (2 percent). The other 18 percent are from a variety of Middle Eastern nations.[50]

Geographical Distribution

Compared to the U.S. population, Arab Americans are more likely to settle in or near urban areas.[51] Ninety-one percent of all Arab Americans live in urban areas, as compared to 75 percent of the overall U.S. population.[52] Recently, some suburbanization has begun to take place, particularly for younger generations.[53] Arab Americans tend to be concentrated in certain areas of the country. Sixty-six percent of Arab Americans live in ten U.S. states; and 33 percent live in only three states: California, Michigan, and New York.[54] Today, the Detroit, Michigan, area is still the one with the largest populations of Middle Eastern Americans. Working-class Arab Americans, particularly, settled in Dearborn, Michigan, a suburb of Detroit, after the 1967 Arab-Israeli war. It is now the largest Muslim community in the United States; and along with other nearby Detroit suburbs, southeastern Michigan has one of the largest populations of Arab people outside the Middle East— approximately 250,000.[55] Of course, as far back as the 1980s, there were particularly hostile attitudes toward Arab Americans in Detroit. Consider, for example, the following excerpt from a 1986 magazine article:

> "An Arab is an Arab is a terrorist" is an assumption shared by many Americans. It is swirling round the streets of Dearborn, a town in Michigan where a fifth of the population is Arab-speaking and where the muezzin booms out the call to prayer five times a day. Most of the residents are old-timers, many of them American citizens. The town is enriched by its Arab coffee houses, shops and restaurants. But the mayor, Mr. Michael Guido, helped to ensure his recent election by promising to deal with the Arab "problem." . . . Arab-Americans in Michigan are afraid that American frustration over Middle Eastern terrorism could erupt into local violence. They are in "a zone of danger," according to Mr. William Webster, the FBI's director. In November the west-coast director of the American-Arab Anti-Discrimination Committee was killed when a bomb exploded at his California office; bombs have also gone off at the committee's Boston and Washington offices.[56]

Geographical concentration makes many other Arab groups equally vulnerable to racially motivated attacks. Forty-eight percent of all U.S. Arabs live in only twenty metro areas.[57] Along with the Detroit Middle Eastern community, other midwestern cities that have large concentrations of Middle Eastern Americans include Milwaukee, Cleveland, Chicago, and Toledo. Still, the Midwest does not have the highest proportion of Arab Americans of any area of the country. Twenty-eight percent of all Arab Americans live in the Midwest, but about 40 percent live in the Northeast, in such cities as Washington, New York, and Boston.[58] A southern city with a large concentration of Arab Americans is Jacksonville, Florida, and about 20 percent of all Arab Americans in the United States live in the South. Approximately 12 percent of the U.S. Arab population lives in the West, particularly in such cities as San Diego, San Francisco, and Los Angeles, which has a neighborhood referred to as "Tehrangeles."[59]

Social Activities and Involvement

Arab Americans who live in the Northeast United States are more likely to have been born in the United States, while those who live in the West are most likely to be immigrants.[60] As a whole, most Arab Americans are not immigrants. As of 2000, various studies report that between 63 and 80 percent of Arab Americans were born in the United States.[61] Nearly 82 percent are citizens.[62] Middle Eastern Americans apparently have found a way to strike a balance between full assimilation and maintenance of tradition and community. Many Middle Eastern communities seem to practice a sort of selective assimilation.

For example, Middle Eastern people tend to be some of the least segregated in their housing patterns. Of all the ethnic groups in a 2000 study (Asian, Hispanic, Jewish, Italian, Arab, and African Americans), Arab Americans, along with Italians, reported living in the most diverse neighborhoods. Correspondingly, of all the groups surveyed they claimed the most friendships with individuals who were of ethnic background different from their own.[63] Previous studies of large Middle Eastern communities have shown that Arab Americans do not seem to take the racial composition of a neighborhood into account as a factor in their choice of whether to live in a particular area. Researchers have speculated that perhaps because they come from a part of the world that is divided along religious, rather than racial lines, Arab Americans tend to not become involved in racial tensions and be relatively inattentive to racial differences.[64]

Even though they are some of the least geographically segregated groups, Middle Eastern Americans do maintain a sense of community. Studies have shown that this sense of community may be *interactional* rather than *territorial*.[65] In other words, even though families or social groups might not live close to one another, through social interactions, they maintain a sense of community. For some, the interactions may center around a mosque or church, or even a coffee house. For some Middle Eastern Americans, it remains very important to pass on cultural traditions and language across generations. For example, the American Federation of Ramallah, which is primarily a lending organization for Palestinians (see later), also offers summer camps and cultural heritage classes for young people.[66] A recent study of Detroit leaders of the Middle Eastern community found that among the issues that concerned them the most were those of cultural and language preservation.[67] While Arab Americans have assimilated linguistically in a significant way, the Arabic language is being maintained in Middle Eastern homes. English is the only language spoken at home for only one-third of all Arab Americans; and nearly half of all Arab Americans older than seventeen speak another language besides English at home.[68] Only about 18 percent speak little to no English.[69] Given their above-average success in business and education (see later), it is reasonable to assume that these are the very young, the very old, and the most recent immigrants.

A particular way in which it seems many Middle Eastern Americans have chosen to remain relatively unassimilated is in their family arrangements. For example, the typical Arab American family is larger than the average American family, with 32.6 percent of households having four or more persons.[70] Many Middle Eastern Americans, it seems, marry within their own ethnic group.[71] Although some suggest that intermarriage is increasing with each new generation, a study drawing on data from early 2000 found that 60 percent of married Arab Americans had selected a spouse from their own ethnic background.[72] Further, 85 percent stated that they would rather that their children remain in their community when grown, a statement that would seem to imply their preference for endogamy.[73] Some Middle Eastern young people born and raised in the United States even return to their country of origin to find a mate. For example, many Palestinian American young people of marriage age each summer visit their homeland to attempt to find a suitable spouse.[74] In some Middle Eastern American families, arranged marriages are practiced, or a slightly modified version, in which the parents initially select a person they consider a suitable candidate for their son or daughter and make introductions, but then it is ultimately the son or daughter's decision whether to follow through with an engagement. Nearly half of the Arab American and other Middle Eastern American populations are under the age of twenty-five. Given this fact, it will be these young Middle Eastern Americans, and their social choices, that will shape the culture of Middle Eastern America for decades to come.[75]

Despite the fact that Middle Eastern Americans maintain their cultural traditions and communities, they are an active part of the larger communities in which they live. Indeed, the contributions of many Middle Eastern Americans have been known to U.S. society for decades, even if the individuals themselves have not been recognized as Middle Eastern.[76] There are many prominent Middle Eastern Americans. In business, some of these are former head of the Federal Aviation Administration and former CEO of Pan-American Airlines Najeed Halaby, whose daughter, Lisa, married King Hussein to become Queen Noor of Jordan; former president and CEO of Ford Jacques Nasser, five-term vice president and then president of International United Auto Workers union the late Stephen Yokich, former president of Mattel Toys Ned Mansour, chairman and CEO of Del Monte Produce Mohammed Abu-Ghazaleh, president and CEO of Polo Ralph Lauren Roger Farah, pollster John Zogby, founder of Kinko's Paul Orfalea, founder of Alamo Flag Company, the largest retailer of flags in the United States today, Tony Ismail.[77] Many other Arab Americans could be listed who are important to U.S. and world business, particularly in banking and investment, but whose companies have less name recognition than these.

Arab Americans who are significant in law, political life, and education in the United States are former dean of the White House press corps Helen Thomas, consumer advocate and sometime presidential candidate Ralph

Nader, founder of MADD Candy Lightner, treasurer of Amnesty International Dr. Rabih Aridi, lawyer of "Erin Brokovich" fame Edward Masry, media critic Dr. Jack Shaheen, and prominent Middle Eastern studies professor the late Edward Said. Middle Eastern Americans have made significant contributions to medicine and the sciences. In this area, Middle Eastern Americans include heart pump inventor Dr. Michael DeBakey, the late Challenger astronaut Christa McAuliffe, director of the National Institutes of Health Elias Zerhouni, geologist George A. Doumani, who helped prove the theory of continental drift, Farouk el-Baz, who helped plan the Apollo moon landings, and two Nobel Prize winners in chemistry.[78]

Middle Eastern Americans have always made contributions to the arts and entertainment culture, since the poet Khalil Gibran. Some who have done so in the twentieth century and are still doing so today are retired heart surgeon and sculptor Dr. Hussam A. Fadhi, industrial designer whose work appears in MOMA Karim Rashid, Pulitzer Prize–winning author Steven Naifeh (*Jackson Pollack: An American Saga*), poet and children's author Naomi Shihab Nye, the Haggar Clothing Company family, super-model Yamila Diaz-Rahi, singer Paul Anka, the late Herbert Khaury (a.k.a. "Tiny Tim"), the late Frank Zappa, singer Paula Abdul, pop star Shakira, entertainer Casey Kasem, actor Jamie Farr of *M.A.S.H.*, actor Tony Shalhoub of *Monk*, actor Yasmine Bleeth, actor Salma Hayek, actor Shannon Elizabeth, actors Danny and Marlo Thomas, Oscar winner F. Murray Abraham, the first woman to head a network—chair of Fox, Lucie Salhany, director Tom Shadyac (*Ace Ventura, Liar Liar, The Nutty Professor, Patch Adams*), screenwriter and novelist William Peter Blatty (*The Exorcist*), Oscar winner for best screenplay Callie Khoury (*Thelma and Louise*). Finally, Middle Eastern Americans have been high-achieving athletes, such as Heisman Trophy winner Doug Flutie; NFL players Jeff George, Bill George, Abe Gibran, and Drew Haddad; NBA center Rony Seikaly; baseball players Joe Lahoud and Sam Khalifa; auto racer Bobby Rahal; world marathon record holder Khalid Khannouchi; and tennis player Andre Agassi.[79]

Educational Attainment

Middle Eastern people have an intellectual tradition that dates back to the time when, between the tenth and twelfth centuries, knowledge developed by Arab cultures was passed to Europe. For example, Arab scholars made a breakthrough in seafaring when they created the compass. They also contributed significantly to mathematics, medicine, and other sciences.[80]

As previously stated, the first Syrian-Lebanese immigrants insisted that their children finish at least their primary education before going to work for the family. The value placed on education, and the tradition of pursuing higher education, continues today in Middle Eastern American families and communities.[81] The educational status of the average Arab American is higher than that of white Americans. Thirty-six percent of Arab Americans have a bachelor's degree, as compared to 27 percent of white Americans.[82] Fifteen percent of Arab Americans have graduate degrees, as compared to 8.9 percent of all Americans, according to 2000 Census figures.[83] Of the school-age population of Arab Americans, 7 percent are in pre-primary school, 53.6 percent are attending elementary or high school, and 39.5 percent are enrolled in college.[84] Although some Arab American parents send their children to Muslim schools, most Arab American children attend public schools, as do the rest of U.S. children.[85]

Despite their exceptional educational achievements, Middle Eastern Americans are nonetheless vulnerable to discrimination in schools. Some researchers and organizations have recently noted that many public schools need to implement programs to better inform their teachers about the diverse cultures of Middle Eastern Americans. Also, teachers should be taught techniques that they can employ to help Middle Eastern students deal with prejudice and discrimination that can arise during times of political problems in the United States and abroad.[86]

Income and Economic Success

The high value that Middle Eastern Americans place on education has been linked in some studies to an understanding of its role in assisting economic progress in the United States. Middle Eastern Americans, compared to other ethnic groups in the United States, are relatively economically successful. Those in the first wave were usually poor; however, they began a tradition of business ownership that has continued. Currently, a larger proportion of Arab Americans are self-employed entrepreneurs than in most other ethnic groups.[87] In fact, at least one study asserts that they have the highest per capita ownership of businesses of *any* ethnic group.[88] According to 1990 Census data, 10.8 percent were self-employed or worked in a family business, compared to 7.3 percent of all Americans.[89] Another recent study of Detroit leaders of various Middle Eastern organizations found that they believed their shared commitment to entrepreneurship as important to founding communities to be a shared cultural trait, along with such things as language, religion, and Middle Eastern history.[90]

Some Middle Eastern American communities have established groups to formally assist new immigrants as they find employment or start their own businesses after immigrating. For example, the American Federation of

Ramallah is a nationwide Palestinian organization that has regional and local chapters. Newly arrived Palestinians are able to receive guaranteed bank loans and financial advice and then gradually pay back the loan. As they repay the loan, they add a percentage to help other immigrants who come after them. Such a system can be invaluable for new arrivals, since it allows them to avoid mainstream banks, in which they may face anti-Arab discrimination or which may simply be difficult to deal with in the early days after arriving in a new country. It also gives new immigrants an opportunity to form bonds with others in their ethnic community, through formal legal channels and because the organizations sponsor social events.[91] Such a borrowing system allows the borrower to retain his or her dignity, since the borrower pays back the loan with interest and thus also receives the satisfaction of knowing that he or she will be helping the next struggling immigrant. This process is explained below by an Arab community leader:

> I don't think I know of anyone that's gone into business that hasn't borrowed large sums of money from their relatives and friends. That money is given to them without any form of collateral, no notes, no interest, and paid back. And the only prerequisite for that is, you know, you work hard. And when they do pay them back, then they're obligated to help others. You know, a lot of nationalities come to me and say "How come the Chaldeans and Arab people are so successful?" . . . It's because of their work ethics. Because of their family relationships. Because they help each other. I can show you where it's not uncommon for ten, twelve people to loan someone five hundred, a thousand, five thousand dollars. You know, and when they have it they pay it back. And then they help someone else. But that progression started right from day one and it just continued and it's still going on.[92]

Many of the second-wave immigrants, especially those who immigrated since the 1960s, have been more highly educated. Thus, in addition to the large proportion of Middle Eastern American entrepreneurs, the group includes higher than average percentages of professional, managerial, technical, and sales workers (approximately 73 percent), and lower percentages of government workers than most other ethnic groups.[93] Seventy-seven percent of Arab Americans work in the private sector, according to 2003 Arab American Institute reports, while 12.4 percent are government employed.[94] It is also important to remember that many left their home countries not due to poverty, as was the case with the first wave (as well as many other U.S. immigrant groups), but because of political upheavals. Consequently, some came with monetary, educational, and entrepreneurial resources that they could begin to use once settled in a community in the United States. This is not to suggest that such a period of settlement is not still quite difficult, but particularly if the family has a Middle Eastern community or other family to help them, coming to the United States with these resources does place one in a different status than arriving impoverished.[95]

Because of their higher education, entrepreneurship, and immigration experiences, according to various reports, Arab Americans have an average household income that is approximately 22 percent higher than that of the U.S. population.[96] According to statistics gathered by the Arab American Institute, the average family income for Arab Americans in 2003 was $53,337, as compared to $43,803 for all Americans.[97] It is important to note, however, that in addition to the family income being higher for Middle Eastern Americans, the proportion of families living below the poverty line (approximately 11 percent) is higher for Arab Americans than for the rest of the population.[98] This is likely due to the fact that the more recent arrivals have not yet had time to establish themselves and are working for lower wages than those who have been in the country longer.[99] In order to account for such outliers, and also the extremely wealthy who might skew the average up, demographers sometimes compare median incomes rather than means, or averages. When one compares the median income of Arab Americans with all other Americans, a disparity still exists. The median income of Arab Americans in 2003 was $39,580, while for all Americans, the median income was $35,225.[100]

For some immigrant groups, a higher family income is based on the fact that there are simply more family members working. This does not seem to be the case for Middle Eastern families. For example, in 1990, for all persons, 13 percent of families had no workers, 28 percent of families had one worker, 45.6 percent had two workers, and 13.4 percent had three or more workers. For Arab Americans, 9.2 percent of families had no workers, 33.7 percent had one worker, 44.5 percent had two workers, and 12.6 percent had three or more workers.[101] Figures were similar for Turkish and Iranian American families.[102] If anything, Middle Eastern families have relatively *fewer* members working than average Americans. Individual income data also show that the higher income of Middle Eastern Americans is not due to having more working family members per household. According to the 1990 Census, per capita income for all persons in the United States was $14,420.[103] This is significantly lower than the individual incomes of Turkish Americans ($20,363), Iranian Americans ($18,040), or Arab Americans ($17,348) in that same year.[104]

Arab Americans indeed have been a relatively financially successful immigrant group. As of early 2000, 30 percent earned more than $75,000 per year—this placed them second only to Jewish Americans. Correspondingly, one of the lowest proportions of any ethnic group studied, only 22 percent, reported earning less than $25,000 a year.[105] According to a 2003 report, only

5.9 percent were unemployed, and 65 percent were in the labor force.[106] In the same study, more than half (56 percent) stated that their financial situation had improved in the last four years; and the largest percentage of any group in the study (87 percent) claimed to have a positive outlook on the future.[107] Generally, Middle Eastern Americans have been a group that has done its best to learn the "rules" of the economic game in the United States, and members have been motivated to work hard not only to play by those rules themselves but also to help each other in doing so. This strategy seems to have served the Middle Eastern American community well and allowed its members to make valuable contributions to the larger communities in which they establish themselves.

Political Involvement

Middle Eastern Americans' participation in U.S. politics has not always been welcomed. At least in theory, most ethnic groups are encouraged to join the democratic process as a way of assimilating; however, this has not always been the case for Middle Eastern Americans. Consider, for example, the words of an Arab American political activist on this topic:

> We have come a long way and we are unique in that most of what we do, even in the most benign stuff, our basic political involvement is considered to be a threat by some people. . . . The reality of our having been a threat by simply working on a campaign, or hosting a fundraiser for a political candidate, or participating in some other benign type of political activity has in some ways affected the taste of our community for American politics. That's something we need to be aware of as we tag along. Our work is like that of any other ethnic constituency, and it doesn't need to be any different. We have interests that relate to our domestic concerns and interests that relate to our foreign policy concerns.[108]

Nonetheless, of all ethnic groups in the United States, Middle Eastern Americans are one of the most politically active. Arab Americans vote in greater percentages (69 percent in early 2000 reports) than average Americans.[109] Political participation in the form of voting has grown in recent years, since in 1996, the percentage of Arab Americans who voted was 62 percent. In a recent study, only Jewish Americans and African Americans were registered to vote in higher numbers than Arab Americans.[110] Aside from voting, Arab American political participation is evidenced in several other ways. For example, Arab Americans are more likely than any other group studied to have visited a presidential candidate's website (13.1 percent).[111] They have also, more than other ethnic group members, watched presidential debates (81.6 percent).[112] Perhaps most significantly, a larger proportion of Arab

Americans than any other group studied have donated money to a presidential campaign, at 16 percent. Others having donated to presidential campaigns include 15.6 percent of Jewish Americans, 14.1 percent of African Americans, 12.8 percent of Hispanic Americans, 11.9 percent of Italian Americans, and 10.2 percent of Asian Americans.[113]

It is apparent that both the major political parties are beginning to see Muslim Americans as an important political constituency. Both because they are growing in numbers, and because Arab Americans are geographically concentrated in some key battleground states, such as Michigan and Ohio, candidates have begun to give them the recognition that they merit as a community.[114] During the national conventions for both parties in the campaigns of 2000, for the first time ever, Muslim clergy led prayers.[115] In the 2000 election, both George W. Bush and Al Gore met with Arab American community leaders, and subsequently publicly made appeals to the Arab American community.[116] George W. Bush specifically stated his concerns that the community was being unfairly "racially profiled," and that this would not be tolerated under his administration, if he were elected. However, as noted earlier, sometimes stereotyping has gotten in the way of Middle Eastern American's attempts to participate fully in the political system. For example, in recent years there have been instances when candidates have publicly returned the political contributions of Arab Americans, out of fear of being associated with a person who has been stigmatized.[117]

A few Syrians held public office by the 1930s; however, national representation did not begin to happen for Middle Eastern Americans until the mid-1900s. Only in 1958 did an Arab American finally get elected to Congress, and it was not until 1980 that the first Arab American senator, James Abourezk from South Dakota, was elected. In recent years, more Middle Eastern and Muslim Americans have been elected to office at the local and state levels, and some organizations seek both to increase these numbers as well as to begin to see more candidates elected at the national level.[118] As of the early 2000s, four Arab Americans have served in the Senate, including former Senate majority leader George Mitchell; and six Arab Americans are now serving in the House of Representatives.[119] About twenty-five others presently serve in some capacity on the congressional or federal level as staff persons.[120] At the state level, Arab Americans have been elected governor of Oregon and New Hampshire.[121] Currently, the governor of Maine is an Arab American, John Elias Baldacci.[122] More than thirty Arab Americans have been mayors of U.S. cities.[123] Altogether, there are currently approximately 120 Arab Americans serving in elected positions at the state and municipal levels, especially as judges and state representatives.[124] In addition to being elected, some Arab Americans have been appointed to positions of influence, such as John Sununu, who served as White House chief of staff in the 1980s; Donna Shalala, President Clinton's health and human services secretary (now the president of the University of Miami); and, most recently, Office of Management and Budget director Mitchell Daniels and Spencer Abraham, energy secretary, both appointed by George W. Bush.[125] Several Middle Eastern Americans have served as ambassadors.[126] Numerous Arab Americans are appointed public servants at the state and local levels of government.[127]

In late July 2003, John Abizaid, an Arab American of Christian Lebanese descent, was appointed head of U.S. Central Command, and is thus the person in charge of U.S. military action in the conflict in the Middle East. Abizaid, who has a thirty-year military career and speaks Arabic, was educated both in the Middle East and in the United States, where he received a master's degree in Middle Eastern Studies from Harvard University.[128] Obviously, Abizaid's identity as an Arab American both subjects him to increased scrutiny and places him in a unique position to positively influence both Middle East policy and the way Middle Eastern people in the United States are treated. As Jean AbiNader of the Arab American Institute stated, "There's concern . . . that the US is discriminating against Arab-Americans because of their ethnicity and religion. . . . To have someone in that kind of position, who is clearly not just there for show, is really important."[129]

Lieutenant General Abizaid's appointment, while extremely significant, is not the first prominent Arab American contribution to the U.S. military. Army officer Major General Fred Safay served with General Patton, and Brigadier General Elias Stevens served on the staff of General Eisenhower. The man some call the world's first jet ace, a Korean War hero, was U.S. Air Force colonel and Arab American James Jabara. A Navy ship, the U.S.S. *Naifeh*, was named in honor of an Arab American, Navy lieutenant Alfred Naifeh, in 1944. An Arab American, General George Joulwan, was the NATO Supreme Allied Commander of Europe more recently.[130] Middle Eastern Americans have served their country with distinction in the armed services.

Despite the strides that Arab and other Middle Eastern Americans have made as a presence in political life, several Middle Eastern American organizations are not only beginning to make increasing voter participation part of their agenda but also putting forth Middle Eastern Americans themselves as candidates.[131]

Political Attitudes

Middle Eastern Americans have not traditionally been easy to place politically, as either "liberal" or "conservative" or "Democrats" or "Republicans."[132] As of the early 2000s, Arab Americans were divided fairly evenly in their party affiliations, between Republicans, Democrats, and Independents.[133] This is both because they are a diverse community and because they tend to be liberal on some issues and conservative on others. The community is split on some social issues. For example, while 52 percent of Arab Americans describe themselves as pro-life, 45 percent are pro-choice. Consensus exists, however, on the matter of parental notification for abortion for young women under the age of eighteen—78.5 percent of Arab Americans surveyed believed parents should be notified in these cases.[134] This is perhaps reflective of the ethic of parental involvement in children's lives that seems evident in many Middle Eastern families we interviewed.

Domestic Issues

As a group, Arab Americans have tended to have more conservative views on education and crime in recent years. In regards to education, in a study conducted in early 2000, Arab Americans tended to agree, for example, with the use of federally funded vouchers to give parents a choice of schools to which they can send their children.[135] A possible reason for this view is that Arab American parents often value private schooling because it may allow their children the opportunity to be taught customs and traditions of their Arab heritage, as well as the Arabic language. For other parents, a choice of private schooling might allow them to send their children to a Muslim school.[136]

In the same 2000 study, Arab Americans were found to have conservative attitudes toward crime and punishment. Most (72 percent) favor the death penalty in the case of capital murder. Eighty-three percent favored prosecuting as adults fourteen- to sixteen-year-olds who have committed crimes using guns. However, 76 percent also favor new gun control laws, which is a traditionally more liberal political position.[137] This is characteristic of the Arab American political stance. That is to say, it is difficult to pigeonhole them as either liberal or conservative.

Arab Americans' attitudes tend to be more traditionally liberal in the area of health care. Ninety-two percent believe that social security and Medicaid should be strengthened. Similarly, 86 percent support using government funds to create a federally sponsored health insurance program. Finally, 89 percent believe that patients should have the right to sue their health insurance companies (HMOs).[138]

Foreign Policy Issues

Obviously, the foreign policy issue of most relevance to Middle Eastern Americans is the ongoing conflict in the Middle East. Most Arab Americans, two-thirds, place it in their top five issues of concern. Seventy-seven percent of those born in the United States and 83 percent of immigrants agree that a political candidate's stance on the conflict is important in deciding their vote (this is 79 percent of Arab Americans overall). The area of Middle Eastern issues is one in which there is a great deal of consensus among Arab Americans, whatever their nationality, religion, or heritage (see the tables 1.1 and 1.2). In fact, interestingly, the only question in 2000 on which there was disagreement among the respondents was on lifting sanctions against Iraq; 54 percent supported lifting the sanctions, while 40 percent did not.[139]

Middle Eastern organizations may be having some influence on the general public's attitudes toward the Palestinian-Israeli conflict. At least one recent opinion poll shows that most U.S. respondents, not just Middle Eastern Americans, support a balanced approach to solving the conflict.[140]

Religious Affiliation

The religious affiliations of Middle Eastern Americans is one of the areas of their lives that is most misunderstood. Although certainly Islam is associated with the Middle East, since Muhammed the Prophet was born and lived there and the three most holy Muslim sites are there, not all Middle Eastern people are Muslims; in fact, the majority of the world's Muslims do not live in the Middle East and are not Arabs.[141] The country with the largest Islamic population in the world is Indonesia, with about 180 million Muslims.[142] Many other non-Arab countries in the world have large populations of Muslims, such as India (120 million), China (18 million), and Malaysia (12 million). Islam is second in the world only to Christianity in its membership, with approximately 1.2 billion Muslims.[143]

This pattern is beginning to be seen in the United States, as well; some predict that by the year 2010, Islam will be the most practiced religion in the

Table 1.1   Arab Americans' Attitudes toward Foreign Policy Issues: U.S. Position on Arab-Israeli Conflict

Statement	Agree	Disagree	Not Sure
Independent Palestinian state	87.2%	6.6%	6.4%
U.S. policy biased toward Israel	74.4%	16.6%	8.9%
U.S. policy is evenhanded	46.9%	36.6%	6.5%
U.S. policy shows respect to Islam	63.1%	26.0%	10.8%

Source: "Arab Americans: Protecting Rights at Home and Promoting a Just Peace Abroad," in Race and Ethnic Relations: Annual Editions, 01/02, 11th ed., ed. J. Kromkowski (Guilford, Conn.: McGraw-Hill, 2001), p. 147. From a study completed for the Arab American Institute by Zogby International, titled Issues, Attitudes and Views.

Table 1.2   Arab Americans' Attitudes toward Foreign Policy Issues: The Middle East

Issue	Important	Neither	Not Important	Not Sure
Securing the rights of Palestinians	74.1%	14.3%	8.6%	3.0%
Sovereignty of Lebanon	80.4%	9.7%	7.0%	2.8%
Normalized U.S. relations with Arab countries	83.2%	8.0%	7.7%	1.1%
Status of Jerusalem	74.0%	13.9%	9.3%	2.7%
Promote human rights in Arab world	87.3%	6.4%	5.3%	1.0%

Source: "Arab Americans: Protecting Rights at Home and Promoting a Just Peace Abroad," in *Race and Ethnic Relations: Annual Editions,* 01/02, 11th ed., ed. J. Kromkowski (Guilford, Conn.: McGraw-Hill, 2001), p. 147. From a study completed for the Arab American Institute by Zogby International, titled *Issues, Attitudes and Views.*

United States, second only to Christianity and displacing Judaism.[144] Already, over 1,400 mosques, most built since 1981, are spread across the United States.[145] Estimates today of the American Muslim population range from three to six million.[146] However, most Middle Eastern Americans are Christians. Forty-two percent of Arab Americans are Catholic, including Roman Catholic, Maronite, and Melkite (Greek Catholic). Twenty-three percent of Arab Americans are Orthodox, which includes Antiochian, Syrian, Greek, and Coptic. The same percentage, 23 percent, are Muslim, including Sunni, Shi'a, and Druze; and the remaining 12 percent are Protestants.[147] The American Muslim Council in 1992 reported the Muslim population of North America to be composed ethnically as shown in table 1.3.[148]

Although even after adding together Arab, Iranian, and Turkish Muslims,

Table 1.3   Muslim Population by Ethnic Group or Country of Origin, 2003

Ethnic Group or Country of Origin	Percentage of Muslim Population
African American	42.0%
South Asian	24.4%
Arab	12.4%
African	5.2%
Iranian	3.6%
Turkic	2.4%
Southeast Asian	2.0%
Caucasian	1.6%
Undetermined	5.6%

Source: Council on Islamic Education, "Teaching about Islam and Muslims in the Public School Classroom," 3rd ed., online. Available www.aaiusa.org (accessed July 30, 2003).

these Middle Eastern Muslims only make up 18.4 percent of the U.S. Muslim population, many Americans believe that most Muslims are Arabs. This is obviously not true, yet Islam has been associated with Middle Eastern Americans, in part because it was immigrants from the Middle East who first brought Islam to the United States. Only about 10 percent of the early Syrian immigrants were Muslim; most were Christian.[149] However, when the Ottoman government began to force Muslims into service in the Turkish army, in order to flee the draft, several thousand came to the United States.[150] Between 1913 and 1914, more than 9,000 Syrians immigrated to avoid the draft, and it was many in this group that were Muslim.[151] The Arabs who established the community in Dearborn in the early 1900s were also Muslim; and the "Little Arabia" there today is still largely Muslim.[152]

As we will discuss in chapter 2, Islam is divided into two major sects, Sunnism and Shi'ism. Most American and world Muslims are Sunni. In the United States, Shi'ites make up about 10 to 16 percent of all Muslims. The world distribution of Sunnis and Shi'ites is proportional to the American distribution.[153] The main difference between Sunnis and Shi'ites is in their beliefs regarding the succession of the leaders of the Islamic faith after Mohammed.[154] Another difference lies in the fact that Sunni Muslims adhere only to the Koran for religious guidance, while Shi'ite Muslims also look to the authority of imams, certain religious leaders, for their writings and verbal teachings.[155] In the Sunni faith, any leader of a mosque is referred to as an imam; while in Shi'ism, only a select few clerics are imams; in fact, to most Shi'ites, there have been only twelve. Despite these differences, the two sects of Islam share the most fundamental Muslim beliefs.

Islam is characterized by five primary tenets, or pillars. These are guiding principles that Muslims live by, or agree to follow in their everyday lives. Many other Americans, particularly Christians, who tend to be less familiar with Islam than are Jewish people, are surprised to learn how similar many of these guidelines are to those that they follow. For example, Muslims make a declaration of their faith in God, called the *shahada*, just as most Christians make a confession of their faith and devotion to God. For Muslims, this declaration includes a statement of a belief in the unity of God, and that Mohammed is the prophet of God who communicated God's message in the Koran. Also similarly to Christians, Muslims are required to give alms to the poor, a pillar of Islam referred to as *zakat*. A third tenet of Islam that is akin to Christianity is *salaat*, the obligation to pray. For Muslims, prayer is to be made toward Mecca at five specific times each day. The final two pillars of Islam are not as closely paralleled in Christianity. All Muslims are required to fast during Ramadan, the ninth month of the Muslim calendar. Although fasting is not mandated in most Christian denominations, it is encouraged and used by many to help them increase their faith, or work through a spiritual crisis. Thus the idea of fasting is not unfamiliar to Christians. The final pillar of Islam is the *hajj*, or the pilgrimage to Mecca, in Saudi Arabia, which is the holiest city of Islam. Any Muslim who is physically and financially able should, at some point in his or her life, journey to Mecca to visit the Ka'aba, which is a stone mosque built by the Prophet Abraham. During the hajj, Muslims, who are all dressed similarly in togalike garments to represent the equality of all people before Allah (God), walk around and touch the Ka'aba and pray.[156] Again, although no similar pilgrimage is required of Christians, it is not a concept unfamiliar to them, since many journey to Jerusalem and the Holy Land to see places where Jesus is historically said to have lived and traveled. Similarly, Jewish people visit the Wailing Wall in Jerusalem, which they consider holy.

The mandates of Islam are well within the ideals of the other major world religions, although in U.S. society, it is sometimes more difficult for Muslims to practice their faith than it is for Christians or Jews. For example, fasting during Ramadan is more difficult in our society, in which the workday is longer than in typical Middle Eastern cultures. Employers are not always understanding about certain requirements Muslims must follow, such as wearing the hijab for women, traveling to Mecca for the hajj, or pausing work to pray during the day.[157] As Islam grows as a faith in the United States, however, more employers are beginning to realize the need to allow their employees the freedom and facilities to practice the tenets of their faith.

Islam can be difficult to practice in the United States also due to the stereotypes that surround it. Because of stereotypical ideas about what Islam means, Muslim Americans sometimes face prejudice and discrimination. Contrary to the perceptions of many, Islam does not require either coercive conversion of those of other faiths or violent "jihad" or holy wars against "infidels." The word "Islam," itself, roughly translated means "submission" or "surrender" to God.[158] Aside from the five pillars, Islam is characterized by a code of conduct for everyday life that includes specific hygienic practices, instructions for maintaining modesty for both men and women, mandates against the consumption of alcohol or pork, and various other guidelines that are considered important for Muslim families and for upholding a Muslim way of life in a country that offers many opportunities for self-indulgence.[159] Just as every other major religious group has a radical faction, which often receives more attention than the more average, mainstream majority, Muslims struggle with the negative impact of the actions of those on the fringes of their faith. As Joe Feagin writes:

> [U]nlike the various denominations of Christianity, Islam is not yet a fully accepted religion in the United States. Its practitioners still suffer widespread prejudice and

stereotyping. . . . The U.S. media sometimes connect mainstream Islam to extremist terrorism. The U.S. media refer to some incidents as involving "Islamic terrorists"—as though the religion of Islam routinely generated this terrorism. Yet the same U.S. reporters and editors would never refer to the terrorists in Northern Ireland as "Christian terrorists," even though Christian sectarianism (Catholics versus Protestants) is centrally linked to bloody terrorism on that island. Clearly, in neither case is the broader religion, Islam or Christianity, responsible for extremist terrorism.[160]

NON-ARAB GROUPS

As stated at the beginning of the chapter, the U.S. Census classifies all Middle Eastern Americans as "white," and thus much of the statistical information available comes from other sources, such as Arab American organizations. Because of this, groups that are considered "Middle Eastern" but not "Arab" are not necessarily included in many reports. Similarly, reports that focus on Muslim Americans are equally problematic. Not all Muslims are Middle Eastern, and not all Middle Eastern Americans are Muslims. Therefore, having Muslim American serve as a proxy category for Middle Eastern American will not do.

Many of our respondents are from non-Arab countries, such as Iran, Turkey, and Pakistan. Thus, we include some demographic profiles about Middle Eastern Americans of non-Arab origin. With the exception of Pakistanis, this information is compiled from the 1990 Census data's "ancestry" survey.

Iranian Americans

As of 1990, the Census Bureau counted 220,714 persons of Iranian ancestry living in the United States, 58 percent of whom were male and 42 percent of whom were female. The median age of Iranian Americans is 30.8, thus they are a relatively young population. Twenty-three percent of the population is less than fifteen years of age. This reflects the fact that most Iranian Americans have immigrated recently, since the Iranian Revolution in the late 1970s. Many young Iranians immigrated in order to escape the revolution, and also to avoid service in the war with Iraq, in which thousands of their contemporaries died. Like other Middle Eastern Americans, Iranian Americans tend to live in households with more members than do average Americans. While 56.3 percent of all Americans were likely to live in households with only one or two people, this was true for only 44.4 percent of Iranian Americans, who were much more evenly distributed among one- (20.1percent), two- (24.3

percent), three- (20.4 percent), and four-person (22.5 percent) households. Nearly 13 percent lived in households with five or more people.[161]

Iranian Americans, like Arab Americans, have been educationally and economically successful in the United States. As of 1990, 69.4 percent were in the labor force, and of those, 78.4 percent worked in managerial, professional, technical, sales, or administrative careers. Seventy-eight percent worked in the private sector, and 12.4 percent more were self-employed or worked for a family business. About 10.6 percent of Iranian American families fell below the poverty line in 1990, similar to the Arab American rate discussed earlier.[162]

Also similar to Arab Americans, Iranian Americans have a higher than average household income. According to the 1990 data, their average household income was $49,533, as compared to that of the national average of $38,453. Iranian American median household income was $36,813, compared to all Americans of $30,056. They also have higher than average educational attainment. Fifty-six percent have a bachelor's degree or higher; and 26 percent had a graduate degree or higher. This is compared to the national average in 1990, which showed 20.3 percent with bachelor's degrees or higher and only 7.2 percent with graduate degrees or higher.[163]

Thus it seems the Iranian American statistical profile is much like that of Arab Americans as a group, suggesting that were their data combined with that of Arab Americans to form a composite of Middle Eastern Americans, it would not dramatically change the overall profile of this panethnic group— except perhaps in the area of education, where Iranian Americans have slightly higher degree achievement than Arab Americans.

Turkish Americans

According to the U.S. Census in 1990, there were 66,492 Turkish Americans. Fifty-five percent were male and 45 percent female. The average age of Turkish Americans was 32.8 in 1990. Turkish Americans are more likely to live in smaller households than some other Middle Eastern families. In 1990, 54 percent lived in households with either one or two members, a figure that is similar to the national average.[164] This is one way in which they differ from Arab and Iranian Americans.

Financially, Turkish Americans have been at least as successful as other Middle Eastern Americans. In 1990, their average family income was $51,712, higher even than Arab and Iranian family income; and their median family income was $37,091. Sixty-seven percent were employed, and of those, 70.6 percent were in managerial, professional, technical, sales, or administrative work. Seventy-seven percent of Turkish Americans work in the private sector. Additionally, 9.9 percent are self-employed or work in a family business. Of Arab, Iranian, and Turkish Americans, Turkish have the lowest poverty rate, 7.4 percent.[165] They are the only Middle Eastern group to have a poverty level that is even lower than that of average Americans, 10 percent in 1990.[166] Like Arab and Iranian Americans, Turkish Americans have placed a high value on education. Forty-one percent have a bachelor's degree or higher, and 22.1 percent have obtained a graduate degree, second only to Iranian Americans and slightly more than Arab Americans.[167]

Turkish Americans, like Arab and Iranian Americans, have had financial and educational success in the United States. Many Turkish Americans arrived earlier than other Middle Eastern immigrant groups, and this may account for their assimilation to U.S. patterns in household size, as well as for their incomes that were even higher than Arab American income in 1990. It also explains the fact that the poverty level for Turkish Americans is lower than that of other Middle Eastern Americans. Fewer Turkish Americans are recent arrivals still seeking work or lingering in low-wage, low-skill jobs while searching for better opportunities or gaining education and training.

Pakistani Americans

It is difficult to locate information about Pakistani Americans, because they tend to be categorized with other groups. Although Pakistanis are from a different national group, in this country information about them is often combined with Asian Indians, and the two are categorized as one ethnic or racial group. Alternatively, Pakistanis are sometimes classified by their religion and placed in the generic Muslim category.[168] The Census does list population numbers for various Asian groups, and according to these figures, there were 153,533 Pakistani Americans in the United States as of 2000, making them 1.5 percent of the total Asian population.[169] Immigration and Naturalization Service Reports from the late 1990s show that immigration from Pakistan has increased in the past two decades, from 61,000 in the 1980s to over 100,000 in the 1990s.[170]

Most Pakistani immigrants settle in urban areas, and 25 percent settle in New York City alone.[171] Although the Census did not provide broken-out data on Pakistani income, some reports suggest that Pakistani Americans have had relative economic success. For example, three out of five are white-collar workers or professionals, and such an occupational distribution places most Pakistanis firmly in the middle to upper class.[172] Indeed, many Pakistani Americans are well educated, some having continued their education in the United States, and provide very well for their families as skilled professionals.

THE CENSUS 2000 REPORT

In December 2003, the U.S. Census Bureau made history by releasing a report on Americans claiming Arab ancestry. An article about the report discusses a family that took part in the Census count:

> Joseph M. Coury IV most often refers to himself as Lebanese-American. . . . His cousins, Mike and Bashir . . . tend to call themselves simply Lebanese. . . . Cousin Rebecca readily extols the wisdom of using the term Arab American because, she said, she believes that it is more politically powerful. . . .
>
> "I could easily conceal it," Mr. Coury, 20, said. "No one would know I was Arab American if I didn't bring it up. But it's a whole identity thing. I have different ethnicities in me, but this is the one that feels tangible. It's important to me, and it's something I want people to know and understand about me. . . ."
>
> "This is an incredible moment in history, where there is a real crystallization of Arab American identity," said Ms. Abou-Chedid. . . . "It's a critical moment to define how we're seen and heard in the world."[173]

The Census report was groundbreaking in that it represented the first such report about Arab Americans.[174] The report also made national news because it showed that the population of those claiming Arab ancestry has grown in recent decades:

> In 2000, 1.2 million people reported an Arab ancestry in the United States, up from 610,000 in 1980 . . . and 860,000 in 1990. The Arab population increased over the last two decades: 41 percent in the 1980s and 38 percent in the 1990s.[175]

Although the report marks an important step in recognizing Arab Americans as a distinct group, some Arab American organizations have disagreed with its population.[176] For example, the Arab American Institute estimates the Arab American population at more than 3.5 million, based on the fact that the first-wave immigrants are now in their fifth generation, and in the past decade, Arab immigration has averaged over 25,000 annually.[177] The Arab American Institute also points out that they offer comprehensive demographic data on Arab Americans and have been an official Census Information Center partnering with the Bureau of the Census for fifteen years. Thus, information taken from their reports has been generally deemed credible. Census reports do have weaknesses, which could give an undercount of the Arab population—one of these is that only one out of every six households is given the "long form" of the Census, which asks the write-in "ancestry" question that would gather the needed data.[178] On the short form, there is only a question asked about race, and there is no racial category for Arab Americans, thus they would remain uncounted.

Still, given the limitations of the sample, the Census report did provide some pertinent information, much of which shows in what ways the Arab American population remained stable since 1990. For example, the Arab American population still remains geographically concentrated in only a few states. About half of all Arabs live in California, Florida, Michigan, New Jersey, and New York. The state with the highest proportion of Arabs is Michigan, and 30 percent of the population of Dearborn is Arab. Although the Arab American population grew in most states since 1990, it grew the most in California, increasing by 48,000.[179]

Lebanese (37 percent), Syrians (12 percent), and Egyptians (12 percent) still make up the largest percentages of national-origin groups. This Census data also shed light on the way in which Middle Eastern Americans are beginning to identify themselves. Panethnic identification has increased since 1990, particularly panethnic identification as "Arab" or "Arabic," which increased by 62 percent. Twenty percent of the Arab American population chose to identify panethnically, as Arab or Arabic (17 percent, or 206,000 people), Middle Eastern (2.4 percent, or 28,000 people), or North African (0.3 percent).[180] As we will discuss in chapter 7, there are many possible explanations for this developing panethnicity.

The Census 2000 report, released in 2003, recognizes the need to enumerate the Arab American population. Although it has shortcomings (such as a failure to account for other non-Arab Middle Eastern groups, and the potential undercount), this may mark an important shift in official demarcation of the Middle Eastern American population. So far, of course, it does not change the fact that, for governmental purposes, Middle Eastern Americans are considered racially white and not a protected minority group.

As we have seen throughout this chapter, people of Middle Eastern origin have been in America for well over a hundred years. They come from various nationalities, speak many languages (e.g., Arabic, Farsi, Turkish, Urdu), and have diverse religious beliefs. Nevertheless, upon entering the United States, they are generally treated as a monolithic group of "brown outsiders."

NOTES

1. Joe R. Feagin and Clairece B. Feagin, *Racial and Ethnic Relations*, 7th ed. (Upper Saddle River, NJ: Prentice Hall, 2003), pp. 324, 328.

2. Asma Gull Hasan, *American Muslims: The New Generation* (New York: Continuum, 2001), p. 17.

3. Hasan, *American Muslims*, p. 21.

4. Asian American Journalists Association, Detroit Chapter, *A Journalist's Guide to Middle Eastern Americans* (Detroit: Detroit Free Press, 1994), p. 4.

5. Vincent N. Parillo, *Strangers to These Shores*, 7th ed. (Boston: Allyn and Bacon, 2003), p. 354.

6. Asian American Journalists Association, *A Journalist's Guide*, p. 4.

7. Parillo, *Strangers to These Shores*, p. 354.

8. Salom Rizk, *Syrian Yankee* (New York: Doubleday, Doran and Company, 1943), pp. 70–73.

9. Rizk, *Syrian Yankee*, p. viii. Here Rizk is quoted in the foreword by DeWitt Wallace.

10. Samir Khalaf, "The Background and Causes of Lebanese/Syrian Immigration to the United States before World War I," in *Crossing the Waters: Arabic-Speaking Immigrants to the United States before 1940*, ed. Eric J. Hooglund (Washington, DC: Smithsonian Institution Press, 1987), pp. 17–35.

11. Asian American Journalists Association, *A Journalist's Guide*, p. 4; Parillo, *Strangers to These Shores*, p. 355.

12. Parillo, *Strangers to These Shores*, p. 355.

13. Parillo, *Strangers to These Shores*, pp. 354–55.

14. Rizk, *Syrian Yankee*, pp. 159–60.

15. Asian American Journalists Association, *A Journalist's Guide*, p. 4.

16. Parillo, *Strangers to These Shores*, p. 355.

17. Parillo, *Strangers to These Shores*, p. 356.

18. Parillo, *Strangers to These Shores*, p. 356.

19. Feagin and Feagin, *Racial and Ethnic Relations*, p. 324; Asian American Journalists Association, *A Journalist's Guide*, p. 4.

20. Michael Suleiman, "The Arab Immigrant Experience," in *Rethinking the Color Line*, ed. Charles Gallagher (Boston: McGraw-Hill, 2004), pp. 473–91.

21. Khalaf, "The Background and Causes of Lebanese/Syrian Immigration," p. 22.

22. Suleiman, "The Arab Immigrant Experience."

23. Suleiman, "The Arab Immigrant Experience."

24. Michael W. Suleiman, "Early Arab-Americans: The Search for Identity," in *Crossing the Waters: Arabic-Speaking Immigrants to the United States before 1940*, ed. Eric J. Hooglund (Washington, DC: Smithsonian Institution Press, 1987), pp. 37–54.

25. Suleiman, "The Arab Immigrant Experience."

26. Suleiman, "The Arab Immigrant Experience."

27. Suleiman, "Early Arab-Americans."

28. Suleiman, "The Arab Immigrant Experience."

29. Eric J. Hooglund, "Introduction," in *Crossing the Waters: Arabic-Speaking Immigrants to the United States before 1940*, ed. Eric J. Hooglund (Washington, DC: Smithsonian Institution Press, 1987), pp. 1–14, p. 7.

30. Suleiman, "Early Arab-Americans"; Suleiman, "The Arab American Experience."

31. Feagin and Feagin, *Racial and Ethnic Relations*, p. 326.

32. Suleiman, "The Arab Immigrant Experience."

33. Parillo, *Strangers to These Shores*, p. 355.

34. Suleiman, "The Arab Immigrant Experience"; Feagin and Feagin, *Racial and Ethnic Relations*, p. 325 (reference to "may be Caucasian").

35. Suleiman, "Early Arab-Americans."

36. Feagin and Feagin, *Racial and Ethnic Relations*, p. 324; Asian American Journalists Association, *A Journalist's Guide*, p. 4.

37. Suleiman, "The Arab Immigrant Experience."

38. Feagin and Feagin, *Racial and Ethnic Relations*, p. 325.

39. Asian American Journalists Association, *A Journalist's Guide*, p. 4.

40. Feagin and Feagin, *Racial and Ethnic Relations*, p. 325; Asian American Journalists Association, *A Journalist's Guide*, p. 4.

41. Suleiman, "The Arab Immigrant Experience."

42. Suleiman, "The Arab Immigrant Experience."

43. Feagin and Feagin, *Racial and Ethnic Relations*, p. 326.

44. "Race" is not a biological distinction, but a social construction. When a group seems "different" in some fundamental way, these differences may set them apart as a distinct race.

45. Fawaz A. Gerges, "Islam and Muslims in the Mind of America: Influences on the Making of U.S. Policy," *Journal of Palestine Studies* 26, no. 2 (1997): 68–80.

46. Gerges, "Islam and Muslims in the Mind of America," pp. 70–71.

47. Sally Howell, "Politics, Pragmatism, and the 'Arab Vote': A Conversation with Maya Berry," in *Arab Detroit: From Margin to Mainstream*, ed. N. Abraham and A. Shryock (Detroit: Wayne State University Press, 2000), p. 366.

48. Parillo, *Strangers to These Shores*, p. 347.

49. Feagin and Feagin, *Racial and Ethnic Relations*, p. 324.

50. Arab American Institute (AAI), "Arab American Demographics." www .aaiusa.org/demographics.htm (accessed July 30, 2003).

51. Feagin and Feagin, *Racial and Ethnic Relations*, p. 325.

52. Parillo, *Strangers to These Shores*, p. 351.

53. Feagin and Feagin, *Racial and Ethnic Relations*, p. 337.

54. Arab American Institute, "Arab American Demographics."

55. Parillo, *Strangers to These Shores*, p. 350.

56. "Middle East in Middle West," *The Economist*, January 11, 1986, U.S. edition, p. 18.

57. Arab American Institute, "Arab American Demographics."

58. Parillo, *Strangers to These Shores*, p. 350.

59. Asian American Journalists Association, *A Journalist's Guide*, p. 4; Parillo, *Strangers to These Shores*, p. 350.

60. Parillo, *Strangers to These Shores*, p. 350.

61. Asian American Journalists Association, *A Journalist's Guide*, p. 5; "Arab Americans: Protecting Rights at Home and Promoting a Just Peace Abroad," in *Race and Ethnic Relations: Annual Editions, 01/02*, ed. J. Kromkowski, 11th ed. (Guilford, Conn.: McGraw-Hill, 2001), p. 145. From a study completed for the Arab American Institute by Zogby International 2000, titled *Issues, Attitudes and Views*; "Quick Facts about Arab Americans," Arab American Institute. www.aaiusa.org (accessed July 30, 2003).

62. Helen Hatab Samhan, "Who Are Arab Americans?" Arab American Institute Foundation. www.aaiusa.org (accessed July 30, 2003).

63. "Arab Americans," p. 145.

64. Parillo, *Strangers to These Shores*, p. 352.

65. Parillo, *Strangers to These Shores*, p. 352.

66. Parillo, *Strangers to These Shores*, p. 360.

67. Reported in Feagin and Feagin, *Racial and Ethnic Relations*, p. 337. Other issues of concern were those of immigration, residency and citizenship, and assimilation and acculturation.

68. Feagin and Feagin, *Racial and Ethnic Relations*, p. 337; "Quick Facts about Arab Americans."

69. "Quick Facts about Arab Americans."

70. "Quick Facts about Arab Americans."

71. Parillo, *Strangers to These Shores*, p. 360.

72. Feagin and Feagin, *Racial and Ethnic Relations*, p. 337; "Arab Americans," p. 145.

73. "Arab Americans," p. 145.

74. Parillo, *Strangers to These Shores*, p. 360.

75. Feagin and Feagin, *Racial and Ethnic Relations*, p. 337.

76. Casey Kasem, "Arab Americans: Making a Difference," Arab American Institute. www.aaiusa.org (accessed July 30, 2003); Feagin and Feagin, *Racial and Ethnic Relations*, p. 333; see also Hasan, *American Muslims,* pp. 3–6, for an enlightening overview of current famous Muslim Americans, including a Nobel Prize–winning chemist, and many CEOs, athletes, and entertainers. She also discusses the Dow Jones Islamic Market Index (DJIM), which she insightfully asserts is an indication of the Muslim presence in the business world.

77. Kasem, "Arab Americans."

78. Kasem, "Arab Americans."

79. Kasem, "Arab Americans"; Asian American Journalists Association, *A Journalist's Guide*, p. 5.

80. Feagin and Feagin, *Racial and Ethnic Relations*, p. 323.

81. Feagin and Feagin, *Racial and Ethnic Relations*, p. 334.

82. Arab American Institute, "Arab American Demographics"; Adalberto Aguirre Jr. and Jonathan H. Turner, *American Ethnicity: The Dynamics and Consequences of Discrimination*, 3d ed. (Boston: McGraw-Hill, 2001), p. 61.

83. Arab American Institute, "Arab American Demographics"; U.S. Census Bureau, "Profile of Selected Social Characteristics: 2000 Data Set: Census 2000 Supplementary Survey Summary Tables Geographic Area: United States." http://factfinder.census.gov/servlet/QTTable?ds_name = ACS_C2SS_EST_ G0 0_&geo_id = 01000US&qr_name = ACS_C2SS_EST_G00_QT02 (accessed July 27, 2003). The figures for all U.S. citizens were calculated for the entire population twenty-five years and older. Further, the statistic the Census Bureau provides is for "Graduate or Professional Degree," and is thus not necessarily an exact match for the figure provided for Arab Americans by the AAI, since their stated statistic is for "Graduate Degrees." "Professional Degrees" may include more than the statistic provided by the AAI. Still, this percentage, 8.9 percent, gives one a rough comparison to the 15 percent provided by the AAI, and the point holds that Arab Americans hold more advanced degrees than the average U.S. population.

84. Arab American Institute, "Arab American Demographics."

85. Feagin and Feagin, *Racial and Ethnic Relations*, p. 334.

86. Feagin and Feagin, *Racial and Ethnic Relations*, p. 334.

87. Feagin and Feagin, *Racial and Ethnic Relations*, pp. 332–34.

88. "Arab Americans," p. 145. It might be more appropriate to say that Middle Eastern Americans as an ethnic group have the highest rates of entrepreneurship, since, at least according to 1990 Census information, Iranian Americans are self-employed at slightly higher rates than Arab Americans (see later, in the section on Iranian Americans). Of course, "self-employed" does not necessarily equate with "entrepreneur," but for all practical purposes, in terms of position in one's community (i.e., running one's own business), the two are very similar.

89. U.S. Bureau of the Census, "Selected Characteristics for Persons of Arab Ancestry: 1990." Internet release date February 18, 1998. www.census.gov/population/socdemo/ancestry/Arab.txt (accessed August 3, 2003); U.S. Bureau of the Census, "Selected Characteristics for All Persons: 1990." Internet release date February 18, 1998. www.census.gov/population/socdemo/ancestry/All_Persons.txt (accessed August 3, 2003).

90. Feagin and Feagin, *Racial and Ethnic Relations*, p. 325.

91. Parillo, *Strangers to These Shores*, pp. 359–60.

92. Gary C. David, "Behind the Bulletproof Glass: Iraqi Chaldean Store Ownership in Metropolitan Detroit," in *Arab Detroit: From Margin to Mainstream,* ed. N. Abraham and A. Shryock (Detroit: Wayne State University Press, 2000), pp. 156–57.

93. Feagin and Feagin, *Racial and Ethnic Relations*, p. 333.

94. Arab American Institute, "Arab American Demographics."

95. As we will hear from respondents later in the book, however, and as other researchers have pointed out (see, for example, Joe R. Feagin and Melvin Sikes, *Living with Racism: The Black Middle-Class Experience* [Boston: Beacon Press, 1994]), one's middle-class status and monetary resources are often not enough to offer protection from discrimination and racism in the United States. In fact, they can sometimes create even more resentment from people both above and below one on the social hierarchy, who may believe that new immigrants should not so quickly be so successful.

96. Feagin and Feagin, *Racial and Ethnic Relations*, p. 333; Arab American Institute, "Arab American Demographics."

97. Arab American Institute, "Arab American Demographics."

98. Arab American Institute Foundation, "Quick Facts about Arab Americans."

99. Feagin and Feagin, *Racial and Ethnic Relations*, p. 334.

100. Arab American Institute, "Arab American Demographics."

101. U.S. Bureau of the Census, "Selected Characteristics for All Persons: 1990"; U.S. Bureau of the Census, "Selected Characteristics for Persons of Arab Ancestry: 1990."

102. For Turkish Americans, 7.9 percent of families had no workers, 32.9 percent had one worker, 46.5 percent had two workers, and 12.7 percent had three or more workers. For Iranian Americans, 7.0 percent had no workers, 33.3 had one worker, 47.8 had two workers, and 11.9 had three or more workers. See U.S. Bureau of the Census, "Selected Characteristics for Persons of Turkish Ancestry: 1990." Internet release date February 18, 1998. www.census.gov/population/socdemo/ancestry/Turkish.txt (accessed August 8, 2003); U.S. Bureau of the Census, "Selected Characteristics for Persons of Iranian Ancestry: 1990." Internet release date February 18, 1998. www.census.gov/population/socdemo/ancestry/Iranian.txt (accessed July 27, 2003).

103. U.S. Bureau of the Census, "Selected Characteristics for All Persons: 1990."

104. U.S. Bureau of the Census, "Selected Characteristics for Persons of Turkish

Ancestry: 1990"; U.S. Bureau of the Census, "Selected Characteristics for Persons of Iranian Ancestry: 1990"; U.S. Bureau of the Census, "Selected Characteristics for Persons of Arab Ancestry: 1990."

105. "Arab Americans," p. 145.

106. Arab American Institute, "Arab American Demographics."

107. "Arab Americans," p. 145.

108. Howell, "Politics, Pragmatism, and the 'Arab Vote,'" p. 369.

109. Samhan, "Who Are Arab Americans?"

110. "Arab Americans," p. 146.

111. "Arab Americans," p. 146. Percentages for other groups were as follows: Asian Americans, 12.6 percent; Hispanic Americans, 12.5 percent; Jewish Americans, 8.1 percent; African Americans, 7.7 percent; and Italian Americans, 7.2 percent.

112. "Arab Americans," p. 146. Percentages for other groups were as follows: African Americans, 78.6 percent; Italian Americans, 76.5 percent; Asian Americans, 77.2 percent; Hispanic Americans 73.2 percent; and Jewish Americans, 70.0 percent.

113. "Arab Americans," p. 146.

114. Samhan, "Who Are Arab Americans?"; "Arab Americans," p. 148.

115. Feagin and Feagin, *Racial and Ethnic Relations*, p. 331.

116. Samhan, "Who Are Arab Americans?"

117. Feagin and Feagin, *Racial and Ethnic Relations*, p. 332.

118. Feagin and Feagin, *Racial and Ethnic Relations*, p. 331.

119. Samhan, "Who Are Arab Americans?"

120. Arab American Institute, "Roster of Arab Americans in Public Service and Political Life 2003." Last updated Monday, May 5, 2003. www.aaiusa.org (accessed July 30, 2003).

121. Samhan, "Who Are Arab Americans?"

122. Arab American Institute, "Roster of Arab Americans in Public Service and Political Life 2003."

123. Samhan, "Who Are Arab Americans?"

124. Arab American Institute, "Roster of Arab Americans in Public Service and Political Life 2003."

125. Feagin and Feagin, *Racial and Ethnic Relations*, p. 331; Kasem, "Arab Americans"; Samhan, "Who Are Arab Americans?"

126. Kasem, "Arab Americans."

127. Arab American Institute, "Roster of Arab Americans in Public Service and Political Life 2003."

128. "BBC News Online Profiles the New Head of US Central Command, Lieutenant General John Abizaid, nicknamed 'Mad Arab.'" http://news.bbc.co.uk/go/em/fr/-/1/hi/world/americas/3053242.stm (accessed August 2, 2003).

129. "BBC News Online Profiles the New Head of US Central Command."

130. Kasem, "Arab Americans."

131. For example, this was a specifically stated goal at the CAIR Leadership Conference the authors attended in spring 2003.

132. "Arab Americans," p. 146.

133. Samhan, "Who Are Arab Americans?"

134. "Arab Americans," p. 146.

135. "Arab Americans," p. 146.

136. Samhan, "Who Are Arab Americans?"

137. "Arab Americans," p. 147.

138. "Arab Americans," p. 146-147.

139. "Arab Americans," p. 147.

140. Feagin and Feagin, *Racial and Ethnic Relations*, p. 332.

141. Asian American Journalists Association, *A Journalist's Guide*, p. 21.

142. Asian American Journalists Association, *A Journalist's Guide*, p. 4; Parillo, *Strangers to These Shores*, p. 494.

143. Parillo, *Strangers to These Shores*, pp. 494–95.

144. Feagin and Feagin, *Racial and Ethnic Relations*, p. 335.

145. Parillo, *Strangers to These Shores*, p. 495.

146. Parillo, *Strangers to These Shores*, p. 495; Feagin and Feagin, *Racial and Ethnic Relations*, p. 324.

147. Arab American Institute, "Arab American Demographics."

148. Table found in Council on Islamic Education, "Teaching about Islam and Muslims in the Public School Classroom," 3d ed. www.aaiusa.org (accessed July 30, 2003).

149. Parillo, *Strangers to These Shores*, p. 495; Feagin and Feagin, *Racial and Ethnic Relations*, p. 335.

150. Parillo, *Strangers to These Shores*, p. 495.

151. Parillo, *Strangers to These Shores*, p. 354.

152. Parillo, *Strangers to These Shores*, p. 495.

153. Hasan, *American Muslims,* p. 23.

154. Asian American Journalists Association, *A Journalist's Guide*, p. 21.

155. Hasan, *American Muslims,* p. 24.

156. Karen Armstrong, *Islam: A Short History* (New York: The Modern Library, 2000), pp. 5–11; Asian American Journalists Association, *A Journalist's Guide*, p. 21.

157. Feagin and Feagin, *Racial and Ethnic Relations*, p. 336.

158. Armstrong, *Islam*, p. 5. Seyyed Hossein Nasr, *The Heart of Islam: Enduring Values for Humanity* (New York: HarperCollins, 2002), p. 8; Parillo, *Strangers to These Shores*, p. 496.

159. Parillo, *Strangers to These Shores*, p. 497.

160. Feagin and Feagin, *Racial and Ethnic Relations*, p. 336.

161. U.S. Bureau of the Census, "Selected Characteristics for Persons of Iranian Ancestry: 1990."

162. U.S. Bureau of the Census, "Selected Characteristics for Persons of Iranian Ancestry: 1990."

163. U.S. Bureau of the Census, "Selected Characteristics for Persons of Iranian Ancestry: 1990"; U.S. Bureau of the Census, "Selected Characteristics for All Persons: 1990."

164. U.S. Bureau of the Census, "Selected Characteristics for Persons of Turkish Ancestry: 1990."

165. U.S. Bureau of the Census, "Selected Characteristics for Persons of Turkish Ancestry: 1990."

166. U.S. Bureau of the Census, "Selected Characteristics for Persons of Turkish Ancestry: 1990"; U.S. Bureau of the Census, "Selected Characteristics for All Persons: 1990."

167. U.S. Bureau of the Census, "Selected Characteristics for Persons of Turkish Ancestry: 1990."

168. Even the Census does not list Pakistanis as a separate ancestry group, making it impossible to gather similar income and other demographic data for them as for Iranians and Turkish Americans. Thus, although they were another group of non-Arabs who were, for the purposes of this project Middle Eastern Americans, parallel information for them is not available.

169. U.S. Census Bureau, "Asian Alone with One Asian Category for Selected Groups . . .: Data Set: Census 2000 Summary File 1(SF 1) 100-Percent Data." http://factfinder .census.gov/servlet/DTTable?_bm = y&-geo_id = D&-ds_na   m   e = D&-_lang = en& mt_name = DEC_2000_SF1_U_PCT005 (accessed January 18, 2004).

170. Parillo, *Stranger to These Shores*, p. 365, citing U.S. Immigration and Naturalization Service, *1998 Statistical Report*, Table 3, p. 25.

171. Parillo, *Stranger to These Shores*, p. 366.

172. Parillo, *Stranger to These Shores*, p. 366, citing U.S. Immigration and Naturalization Service, *1998 Statistical Report*, Table 21, p. 81.

173. Lynette Clemetson, "Some Younger U.S. Arabs Reassert Ethnicity," *New York Times*, January 11, 2004. www.nytimes.com/2004/01/11/national/11ARAB.html?ex = 1074836131&ei = 1&en = 31e67abbd89ab068 (accessed January 11, 2004).

174. Arab American Institute, "First Census Report on Arab Ancestry Marks Rising Civic Profile of Arab Americans." www.aaiusa.org/pr/release12-03-03.htm (accessed January 18, 2004).

175. U.S. Census Bureau, "The Arab Population: 2000: Census 2000 Brief." www .census.gov/prod/2003pubs/c2kbr-23.pdf (accessed January 18, 2004), p. 2.

176. Clemetson, "Some Younger U.S. Arabs Reassert Ethnicity."

177. Arab American Institute, "First Census Report on Arab Ancestry."

178. U.S. Census Bureau, "The Arab Population," p. 2.

179. U.S. Census Bureau, "The Arab Population," pp. 4–8.

180. U.S. Census Bureau, "The Arab Population," pp. 2–3.

Chapter 2

Stereotypes of Islam and the Dubious Link with Terrorism

In this chapter we trace the development of Middle Eastern American identity in the context of two central themes: Islam and terrorism. Our goal is to high-light the forces the have forged the contemporary American view of who a Middle Eastern person is. In doing so, we discuss Islam and terrorism with the goal of addressing misconceptions and providing a general survey of the two topics for the novice reader.

ISLAM: WHAT IT MEANS TO ITS BELIEVERS AND CRITICS

The June 2003 cover photo of *Time* showed a male, white hand holding a luminescent, golden cross with the caption: "Should Christians Convert Muslims?" The article described the efforts of thousands of missionaries in Middle Eastern countries to proselytize to Muslims.[1] These missionaries are inspired by the belief that Muslims represent one of the largest and most spiritually deprived populations on the planet and are desperately in need of a spiritual rescue. They are also encouraged by the Bush administration's fairly lenient position on Christian charity organizations operating in recently "liberated" countries (i.e., Afghanistan and Iraq). For the missionaries, official statements by some members of the Bush administration further support their cause, such as the one made by Attorney General John Ashcroft in 2001. In particular, he stated that "Islam is a religion in which God requires you to send your son to die for him. Christianity is a faith in which God sends his son to die for you."[2] (Ashcroft later explained that his remarks applied to radical terrorist Islamic groups and not to average Muslims.) As a whole, this group of Christian evangelists view Islam as the main cause of global terrorism, or as one of them states, they "pray that the weapon of mass destruction, Islam, be torn down."[3]

While it is true that the evangelists do not represent a majority opinion in the United States, for many Americans the so-called war of civilizations has become a standard explanation for the political hostilities and terrorist activities that have ravaged the Middle East. Middle Eastern Americans find themselves in the midst of this purported ideological battle between the two religions. While only less than half are Muslims (the majority are Christians, as discussed in chapter 1), all Middle Eastern Americans are held accountable for the perceived threat of Islam and Islamic terrorists. Sadly, much of what is known about Islam and its differences from Christianity are based on sound bites from sensationalized news reports and talk show programs, which present out-of-context passages from the Koran (the holy text of Islam) as proof for the inherent violence and intolerance of Islam. The implied argument is that being a Muslim is a predictor of one's tendency toward violence and terrorism, a position that is officially embraced by the Justice Department and the Federal Bureau of Investigation in their law enforcement policies that have specifically targeted Middle Eastern Americans, particularly those of the Islamic faith (some of these policies are discussed later in this chapter in the section dealing with the aftermath of the September 11 terrorist attacks).

The notion that one's culture and race are impediments to becoming a "loyal American" is not new in American history and in the politics of immigration. Certainly, the same question was raised about Japanese Americans after Japan's surprise attack on Pearl Harbor on December 7, 1941, which paved the way for the United States to fully enter World War II. The fear that some Japanese Americans loyal to their ancestral home might pose a threat to U.S. security led President Franklin D. Roosevelt to sign Executive Order 9066, which provided the legal authority for placing over one hundred thousand Japanese Americans in internment or relocation camps.[4] It was not until the passage of the Civil Liberties Act of 1988 that the U.S. government officially apologized for detention of Japanese Americans and offered monetary payments to families who had lost their businesses and properties.[5]

The perceived threat of exotic cultures has not been limited to non-European immigrants. For example, a 1918 *Saturday Evening Post* article titled "Scum of the Melting Pot" offered the following warning about recent German and Russian immigrants:

We had a happy go lucky, don't care theory that nobody need worry about what the unassimilated foreigner did, as though that everything would come and transform the lazy, the weak, the vicious into hard workers, honest, desirable American citizens. We have considered the rights of every nationality in the world except our own. The immigrant who comes to America to become an American and who works at that job should be welcome; but of late years, too many of another kind have settled here. It has been the refuge of the oppressed, but it has also been the haven of a lot of rascals who have abused our hospitality.[6]

In the same way, concerns about cultural "others" have cut across many religious groups. Jewish immigrants from Eastern Europe, for example, were seen as a potential problem, as indicated in the following excerpt from an 1891 *Literary Digest* piece:

Jews expelled from Russia, whom no European country wants to receive, are assisted to immigrate to the United States in spite of protests from members of their own race residing here that they are not the kind of people to become Americanized because of their clannishness and bigotry.[7]

Similar opinions have been expressed about Middle Eastern Americans' inability to assimilate and their lack of loyalty. Particularly, following the September 11 attacks, in support of ethnic profiling, numerous editorials suggested that Muslims cannot be trusted. For example, an October 2001 editorial in the *Denver Post* reads:

What is a good Muslim? Is a good Muslim someone who will answer the call to terrorize and kill blindly? Is a good Muslim someone so fanatic about his or her cause that they cannot or should not be trusted? Or is a good Muslim a silent bystander watching his or her true faith corrupted and sabotaged by the fanatics? . . . It's hard to tell these days who or what constitutes a "good" Muslim, and even harder to sort out one from the other.[8]

Here, the character of Muslims, not unlike their Jewish counterparts a hundred years ago, is called into question. The author's point is that the distinction between "good" and "bad" Muslims is either nonexistent or impossible to detect; therefore, they should all be treated essentially the same way, with fear and suspicion.

Another editorial published in the *Chicago Sun Times* makes a more direct link between Muslim immigration and terrorism:

Ever since September 11, the immigration issue has been lurking dangerously just beneath the surface of political debate like the title character in "Jaws." As in the movie, the authorities have tried to calm public fears by denying its existence. . . . But the people see fins cutting ominously through the water. In particular, they have noticed that all 19 terrorists who carried out the September 11 attacks were legally present in the United States and that some immigrants in the growing Muslim diaspora sympathize with the denunciations of America voiced by radical Islamists. The public's fear that lax immigration policies were making life easier for terrorists has also begun to be expressed.[9]

Sadly, as some opinion polls show, this view has been shared by many Americans, both before and after the September 11 terrorist attacks. For example:

> An ABC News poll, conducted during the Persian Gulf crisis in February 1991, found 43% of Americans had a high opinion of Arabs while 41% said they had a low opinion. In that poll, majorities of Americans said the following terms applied to Arabs: "religious" (81%), "terrorists" (81%), "violent" (58%) and "religious fanatics" (56%).[10]

A *Newsweek* poll conducted shortly after the terrorist attacks on September 14–15, 2001, indicates that "32% of Americans think Arabs living in this country should be put under special surveillance as Japanese Americans were."[11] Finally, a June 2002 Gallup survey of 1,360 American adults shows that "of the five immigrant groups tested [Arabs, Hispanics, Asians, Africans, and Europeans], the public is least accepting of Arab immigrants, as 54% say there are too many entering the United States."[12] By comparison, 46 percent expressed this opinion about Hispanic immigrants, 39 percent about Asian immigrants, 29 percent about African immigrants, and 25 percent about European immigrants.[13]

Undoubtedly, these unfavorable opinions are fueled by the terrorist attacks carried out against the United States in recent decades, but the sketchy news media coverage about Islam plays no small role in exacerbating these negative attitudes. The following discussion is intended to lend some complexity to the debates about Islam and its Muslim immigrants in the United States. Our goal is not to treat Islam as a topic beyond critique; such an undertaking would move us in the direction of a fundamentalist reading of Islam, a position that we oppose. Rather, we hope to present an alternative perspective, one that calls into question the veracity of unsupported claims about differences between Islam and Christianity, or between Muslims and Christians. In doing so, we first explore the parameters of the debate (i.e., the analytic framework within which questions about Islam can be debated reasonably). We then examine three hotly debated issues in regards to Islam: (a) propensity for violence as a way of settling disputes; (b) mistreatment of women; and (c) intolerance of other faiths.

Setting the Parameters of the Debate

It is the essential nature of any religion to have followers and critics. Islam is not exempted from this rule. The fundamental principles of any religion could and should be debated, critiqued, and indeed sometimes reformed. Certainly, this has been the case with Christianity, which has undergone many reforms. For example, the differences between the doctrines of Catholicism and Protestantism sparked internal debate, and in some cases fueled brutal wars (e.g., the French Wars of Religion that lasted from 1562 to 1629).[14] External and internal debate, criticism, and reform are part of any religious doctrine. When Islam is concerned, especially in relation to the Middle East, rather than reasoned arguments and learned opinions, discussions tend to quickly degenerate into hyperbole and unfounded accusations. The problem in part is that both sides (devoted Muslims and their critics) approach the topic without contextualizing their claims. Sweeping generalizations are the norm and qualified statements are the exception. Let us consider some of the factors that could provide a context for the debate about Islam.

The Koranic Text

First, there is the matter of the Islamic text or the Koran (or the Quran or Qu'ran). According to Islamic teaching, the Koran was revealed to Muhammad at the age of forty in 610 c.e. Many Muslims consider the Koran the evidence of Muhammad's connection with the divine. Indeed, when Muhammad was asked to perform a miracle to prove that he was indeed a prophet, he referred to the Koran as his miracle and challenged his critics to imitate it. As a whole, both critics and believers concede that the Koranic text is exceptional in its poetic eloquence. The words are in fact so impressive that some have charged that Muhammad was possessed by evil forces, for only a man possessed by Satan could speak with such eloquence. As Michael Sells, the author of *Approaching the Qur'an*, notes:

> To devout Muslims, the recited Qur'an is the word of God revealed to the prophet Muhammad; its divine origin accounts for its hold over the listener. Some anti-Islamic missionaries attribute the extraordinary power and beauty of the Qur'an to a Jinni [a spirit who can assume human form] or Satan. A Marxist revolutionary from an Islamic background, who was highly critical of all religion, insisted that the genius of the Qur'an resulted from Muhammad's alleged madness and resultant close contact with the unconscious. In Middle Eastern countries, what unites these opinions and seems beyond dispute is the fact that the recited Qur'an is a distinctively compelling example of verbal expression.[15]

Despite its widely accepted eloquence, as Sells suggests, the English translations of Koran present the readers with two problems. First, there is the inherent difficulty with translating any text into another language—a problem that becomes even more noticeable when dealing with poetic texts such as

the Koran. Every word and utterance carries a certain meaning and has a special place in the rhythm of the text, which makes it impossible for a transla-
tion to be faithful to the original. Another problem for the novice English-
speaking reader is that unlike most Western texts, the Bible included, the
Koran is not a linear story. The Koran was revealed to the prophet in response
to specific events in his and his people's daily struggles. While much of the
Koran is similar to the Torah or the Old Testament in its content and instruc-
tional tone, many of the passages (*Suras*) deal with specific issues that
Muhammad and his followers faced; thus, the Koran is enigmatic and sometimes incomprehensible for a reader who is unfamiliar with its historical context and nonlinear format.

The Interpretation of the Text

In addition to the problems associated with reading the Koran, we should also
consider issues surrounding the interpretation of the text. Like the Christian
and Jewish sects (i.e., Protestant versus Catholic or Hasidic versus Kabbalis-
tic Jews), the followers of Islam also adhere to different interpretations of
their holy text and related religious rites and rituals. But this diversity in the
Islamic faith seems to be ignored by Western observers. As Seyyed Hossein
Nasr, a leading Islamic scholar, points out,

> Often in the West Islam is depicted as a monolith, and little attention is paid to the
> rich diversity within both the religion and the civilization of Islam. . . . Although the
> attempt by the media to deal more with Islam is laudable, what is presented is usu-
> ally highly selective and politically charged, dominated by the Arab-Israeli conflict
> and extremism manifesting itself in threats or acts of terror. Therefore, despite
> greater interest in covering matters pertaining to Islam, the reductionist message
> associated with extremism continues to dominate the scene, hiding from the Western
> public the great diversity of the Islamic world and the multiple interpretations of the
> Islamic religion.[16]

The main two branches of Islam are Shi'ism and Sunnism, with the majority of the world's Muslims (about 87 percent)[17] being Sunnis. The differences
between the two schools mostly have to do with disagreements about who
should have been considered the legitimate leader of the fledgling Islamic
community following the death of Muhammad in 632 c.e. For Shi'ites, the
Prophet's cousin and son-in-law, Ali, and his descendants were the legitimate
and qualified successors, whereas Sunnis embraced the tradition of the so-
called "rightly guided" caliphs (Abu Bakr, Umar, Othman, and Ali).[18]
    Within Sunnism there are a number of sects, one of which, known as Wah-
habism, is especially popular in Saudi Arabia. This branch of Sunnism was

named after its founder Muhammad ibn Abdl Wahhab (1703–1792) and is based on a very literal reading of the Koran.[19] As Nasr notes, Wahhabism rejects mainstream Sunnism and Shi'ism and their intellectual emphasis on philosophy, mysticism, and culture. Instead, Wahhabism views the fundamentalist interpretation and practice of traditional Islam as the solution to the challenges of the modern world. In recent years, the expansion and sponsorship of Wahhabist Islamic schools in Pakistan and Afghanistan have largely been supported by wealthy members of the Saudi family.[20] The notorious terrorist Osama bin Laden is a follower of Wahhabism. Also, of the nineteen terrorists who attacked the World Trade Center and the Pentagon in September 2001, at least ten were Saudi Arabian and thought to be of Wahhabi background.[21]

The Practice of Islam

Similar to its interpretation, the practice of Islam varies considerably from region to region and from person to person. On a cultural level, the religious practices typically are intermeshed with the local customs so that no two Muslim countries practice the same kind of Islam. As stated earlier, the different branches of Islam are themselves culturally and geographically marked, with most Shi'ites, a small minority in the Muslim world, being from Iran and Iraq and the followers of Sunnism being scattered throughout the Arab world and far east Asia. When considering the questions of who a Muslim is and what he or she believes, it is essential to place the answers in their appropriate cultural context. Many of the practices attributed to Islam are in fact reflections of old local customs. For example, the unequal treatment of women in some Muslim countries is more representative of centuries-old patriarchal systems than Islamic tradition per se. Thus, for example, it would be a mistake to suggest that the treatment of women under the defunct Taliban regime in Afghanistan was "true" Islam, just as it would be inaccurate to argue that Utah's polygamous Mormons are ambassadors of Christianity.

There are also vast individual differences in the practice of Islam. For example, some of the Muslim women interviewed in this book wore the veil and some did not. Similarly, some of the men grew their facial hair and some did not. On a deeper level, some Muslims in our participant observations and interviews indicated a strict following of the basic principles of Islam (i.e., daily prayer, giving alms to the poor, pilgrimage to Mecca, confession of faith, and fasting during the Islamic holy month of Ramadan) while others took a more lax attitude toward their religion. For example, while one respondent reported fasting every day during Ramadan, his close friend stated that he fasted only one day to test the strength of his will. As a whole, in judging Muslims, it is important to keep in mind these crucial regional and individual variations, which are readily afforded to the believers of other religious faiths. With this general introduction to what we have loosely referred to as the parameters of the debate, let us consider a number of controversial topics related to Islam.

Islam and Violence

An important issue for many Muslims and their critics is the extent to which Islam can be characterized as a violent religion. This question is of crucial importance for creating policies of ethnic profiling that directly target Muslims under the premise that they pose a special risk to public safety, as in the case of the FBI policy of counting mosques and Muslims throughout the country.[22] In particular, conservative Christians have been very vocal in this debate. Jerry Falwell, a leader of the Christian conservatives, for example, stated on *60 Minutes* that Muhammad was "a terrorist" who established a religion that "teaches hate."[23]

Is Islam a religion that teaches violence and hate? Many Muslims would unequivocally argue that Islam is a religion of peace that promotes acceptance of other religions. They would cite passages from the Koran that call for respect and tolerance of other faiths, or what the Koran refers to as "People of the Book." In Islamic thought, Muhammad continues the tradition of Abraham, Moses, and Jesus; he does not oppose them. This is reflected in the following passage from the Koran: "Believers, Jews, Sabaeans, and Christians—whoever believes in God and the Last Day and does what is right—shall have nothing to fear or regret."[24] In fact, in the Koran an entire chapter is named after the Virgin Mary (Maryam), and there is a detailed description of the Virgin Birth, as indicated in the following:

> The Angels said to Mary: "God bid you rejoice in a Word from Him. His name is the Messiah, Jesus son of Mary. He shall be noble in this world and in the world to come, and shall be one of those who are favored. He shall preach to men in his cradle and in the prime of manhood, and shall lead a righteous life."
>
> "Lord," she said, "how can I bear a child when no man has touched me?"
>
> He replied: "Even thus. God creates whom He will. When He decrees a thing He need only say: 'Be,' and it is."[25]

Additionally, historical records suggest that Muslim rulers were exceptionally tolerant of Christians and Jews and allowed their members to practice freely within their realms.[26] Indeed the Koran specifically instructs Muslims to:

> Be courteous when you argue with the People of the Book, except with those among them do evil. Say: "We believe in that which has been revealed to us and which has been revealed to you. Our God and your God is one. To Him we submit."[27]

There is little evidence to suggest that Islam or Muhammad called for systematic slaughter of Christians and Jews.

However, the Koranic mandate to get involved in worldly matters and to fight for social justice have thrown Muslims in the midst of militant struggles. Indeed, the Koran cites the case of David as an example of the necessity of struggle against injustice:

> David slew Goliath, and God bestowed on him sovereignty and wisdom and taught him what He pleased. Had God not defeated some by the might of others, the earth would have been utterly corrupted.[28]

Unlike the Christian notion of turning the other cheek, Muslims are instructed to "Fight in the sake of God those that fight against you, but do not attack them first, God does not love aggressors."[29] Thus it is possible to interpret the Koranic text as a call for armed struggle, or *jihad*, to change the world, as some radical groups have. However, Islamic scholars point out that jihad does not necessarily mean an armed struggle against outside forces but also refers to the personal struggle to better oneself, or to avoid sin. Furthermore, these scholars point out that jihad in the form of armed struggle should only be used for defensive purposes.[30] Thus the actions of the September 11 terrorists are not condoned under Islamic law. Regardless of how one would interpret the word jihad, it would be utterly false, or at least counter to the fundamental teachings of the Koran, to suggest that Islam is inherently aggressive toward Christians and Jews. The monotheism of Islam is inclusive and tolerant of other religions.

To the extent that Muhammad himself is accused of being a violent man, the historical record is mixed. Indeed, it is true that Muhammad was personally involved in armed struggle against the forces that opposed him at the time. However, it must also be noted that had he not defended his fledgling religion, he and his followers would have perished in the harsh environment of the Arabian Peninsula and become a footnote in world history. Rewriting the history of Islam and Muhammad to highlight their violent origins is akin to accusing Moses and his God of being violent because they drowned the Pharaoh's troops who were pursuing the fleeing Israelites to the Red Sea.

Islam and the Oppression of Women

The treatment, or mistreatment, of women in Islam has been the subject of much debate. Two prominent positions exist in this debate. On the one hand, there is the feminist critique of the gender relations in Islamic societies. Advocates of women's rights, inspired by Western feminist ideals, argue that Muslim women in societies such as Afghanistan, Iran, Pakistan, Saudi Arabia, and Sudan are treated as second-class citizens. They point out that under Islamic laws, or *shariah*, women in these countries have fewer rights than men and are essentially victims of patriarchies that sanction the mandatory covering of women's bodies, polygamy, genital circumcision, honor killings, and other abuses.

On the other hand, the defenders of the Islamic societies and Islam's position on women dismiss many of these claims as a disguised colonial attack on the native cultures of the Middle East. Furthermore, they point out that the Koran gave women the right to inheritance and divorce nearly fourteen hundred years ago, that one of the Prophet's wives, Khadija, was an independent business woman who financed the growth of Islam, and that polygamy was a historical necessity that was established to protect widows and orphaned children. Furthermore, the defenders of the Islamic perspective note that Islam elevates the role of women in society by not treating them as sexual objects, that by covering the outlines of their body and their hair, or by practicing the *hijab*, Muslim women are in fact liberated from being nothing more than objects of male desire. Indeed, the culture of the veil in many ways predates Muhammad and was not limited to Islam. Early Jewish and Christian women wore the veil long before it became associated with Islam.[31] The traditional habit of a Catholic nun is not fundamentally different from what orthodox Muslim women wear.

The reality of the role of women in Islam is most likely somewhere between the two positions of the critics and defenders of Islamic law. On the one hand, it is true that historically Western colonial powers and their intellectuals have used women's rights as a justification for colonialism. Ironically, for colonialists, while gender equality was viewed as an urgent matter abroad, it was altogether ignored at home. As Moghissi states:

> Remarkably, female domesticity and sexual purity and chastity, deemed appropriate in Europe and aggressively promoted at home, were presented for Muslim women as "evidence" of sexual slavery and signs of peculiar moral and religious deficiency of the Other.[32]

Western societies have their share of problems with abuses of women. Indeed, uncertainty regarding abortion and a woman's right to choose continues to loom in the horizon of American politics. There are also many less politically charged issues affecting women in the United States. For example, domestic abuse rates in the United States are alarmingly high. As of the early 2000s, some studies suggest that at least 28 percent and perhaps even 50 percent of women suffer some type of physical abuse from their partners, with even more suffering from emotional abuse.[33] Perhaps even more startling is the fact that almost 30 percent of men and 25 percent of *women* in the United

States believe that violence is a normal and sometimes even positive part of a marriage.[34] Twenty-six percent of all female murder victims in 1995 were in fact killed by their husbands or boyfriends.[35]

Part of the justification given for incursions into Middle Eastern countries is to rescue women from the supposed abusive men who are their husbands and fathers. Yet in our own country every day women are brutalized by their significant others and this is not treated as a similar outrage, and certainly not as an indication that our entire culture is pathological or our Judeo-Christian religious foundations are faulty. Of course, this discussion does not even begin to address the brutality committed against women in the form of rape and sexual assault by men with whom they are not involved, seemingly linked to a certain masculine ideal that relies on dominance of women. The fact that this conception of masculinity still thrives in our culture and is supportive of violence against women is at least as in need of change as the "patriarchy" of Middle Eastern societies.

Women in the United States also suffer disproportionately from eating disorders. It is estimated that one in four college women has an eating disorder; and usually, left untreated, 20 percent of those with eating disorders die.[36] Aside from eating disorders, however, there is the average American woman to consider. Every day in the United States, about 25 percent of American women are dieting, and 50 percent more are finishing or starting diets.[37] U.S. women also undergo cosmetic surgery at unusually high rates.

Perhaps some Muslim women do feel "oppressed" in some sense by the veil that they wear; and if so, this is something that Muslim feminists will need to address, in the cultural context in which they live. However, it might be argued that Western women oppress and constrain their own bodies, by succumbing to a rigorous and unobtainable standard of beauty, which requires daily starvation and hours of preparation. As mentioned previously, some Middle Eastern women we interviewed have stated that wearing the veil frees them from the concerns with which they see other women around them so obsessed. As Joan Jacobs Brumberg and Jacquelyn Jackson write:

> The female body—covered in a burka or uncovered in a bikini—is a subtle subtext in the war against terrorism. . . . Now that the Taliban's horrific treatment of women is common knowledge, dieting and working out to wear a string bikini might seem to be a patriotic act. The war on terrorism has certainly raised our awareness of the ways in which women's bodies are controlled by a repressive regime in a far away land, but what about the constraints on women's bodies right here at home, right here in America? In the name of good looks (and also corporate profits . . .) contemporary American women continue to engage in behaviors that have created major public health concerns. . . . Whether it's the dark, sad eyes of a woman in purdah or the anxious darkly circled eyes of a girl with anorexia nervosa, the woman trapped

inside needs to be liberated from cultural confines in whatever form they take. The burka and the bikini represent opposite ends of the political spectrum but each can exert a noose-like grip on the psyche and physical health of girls and women.[38]

This raises the question: Why have conservative Christians, who are vehemently opposed to women's rights at home, taken up the cause of liberating Muslim women abroad?

Having said that, there is a growing reformist/Islamic feminist movement that aims to eradicate abuses of women in the name of Islamic law. At the heart of this movement there is the recognition that Islamic texts have been interpreted in the service of patriarchal orders.[39] That Muslim women, as women in most other cultures and religions in the world, are interested in and deserve better treatment is indisputable; what remains a critical point of contention is whether the solution to gender oppression should be sought within the existing framework of indigenous Muslim cultures and practices or in reference to an outside Western ideal or standard. In our research, we did not encounter a single respondent who defended the abuses of women under the defunct Taliban rule in Afghanistan. However, most of our respondents, male and female, expressed that the model of Western feminism is not applicable in its entirety to the problems of Muslim and Middle Eastern women.

In general, the underlying theme in the debate about Islam is the capacity of the religion to adapt to modern social changes. Some critics charge that Islam is an outdated and archaic religion that is incapable of being reformed. This view reflects what Edward Said has termed Orientalism, which he suggests is based on the dogmatic notion that there is an "absolute and systematic difference between the West (which is rational, developed, humane, superior) and the Orient (which is aberrant, undeveloped, inferior)."[40] However, reason and history suggest that Muslims and Islam are adaptable and resourceful. It is likely that they will change, as they have since the inception of the religion, to cope with the challenges of their time.

Another important dimension of public perceptions of Middle Eastern Americans is the history of military conflicts and terrorism involving Middle Eastern countries. In this context, it should be noted that the history of conflict between the West and the Middle East dates back at least to the so-called Christian Crusades. During this period (1095–1291 b.c.e.), beginning under the leadership of Pope Urban II, Christians, from Western Europe and the Eastern Byzantine Empire (roughly the area of modern-day Turkey and Syria) waged several wars on Muslims and "liberated" Jerusalem. Among other things, the "holy wars" were inspired by the belief that those who fought Muslim infidels were true Christians and the punishment for their sins would be forgiven. According to a decree from Pope Urban II, referred to as "plenary indulgence": "Whosoever out of pure devotion and not for the sake of gaining honour or money, shall go to Jerusalem to liberate the Church of God, may count that journey in lieu of all penance."[41] Interestingly, the idea of a "holy war" or a "jihad" against infidels has strong roots within Christianity. The Christians who responded to this call also slaughtered Jews as part of their crusades against infidels. Indeed, after the fall of Jerusalem in the first Crusade in July 1099, all the Jewish and Muslim men, women, and children living in the city were slaughtered.[42]

We are not suggesting here that ideological distinctions between Christianity and Islam have fueled wars for centuries. On the contrary, the same economic reasons that encouraged European Christians to pursue new markets in the East centuries ago still guide Western foreign policies today. While it may be overly simplistic to argue that economic differences are solely responsible for military conflicts, it is equally naïve to deny their existence and reduce the problem to the so-called clash of civilizations.[43] As Noam Chomsky points out:

> [The clash of civilizations] is fashionable talk, but it makes little sense. Suppose we briefly review some familiar history. The most populous Islamic state is Indonesia, a favorite of the United States ever since Suharto took power in 1965, as army-led massacres slaughtered hundreds of thousands of people, mostly landless peasants, with the assistance of the U.S. . . . Suharto remained "our kind of guy," as the Clinton administration called him, as he compiled one of the most horrendous records of slaughter, torture, and other abuses of the late 20th century.[44]

Chomsky goes on to note the close association between other fundamentalist Islamic states (i.e., Pakistan and Saudi Arabia) and the United States. Thus, political and economic interests are stronger predictors of alliances and conflicts than ideological viewpoints.

It is in this broader historical context that we offer a brief review of the concept of terrorism and how it has influenced the way Arab and Iranian Americans are viewed in the United States.

TERRORISM AND ITS IMPACT ON MIDDLE EASTERN AMERICANS

A persistent assumption about Middle Eastern people is that they are "terrorists" and "violent." As stated earlier in this chapter, in a 1991 opinion poll nearly 60 percent of Americans attributed these characteristics to Arabs.[45] Clearly, these stereotypes are rooted in a list of terror attacks and hostilities that were perpetrated against U.S. citizens in the past thirty years or so both domestically and abroad (some of which will be reviewed later in this section). However, from a broader historical perspective, it would be erroneous to assume that terrorism is the specific property of Middle Easterners or Muslims.

Historians trace the origins of the word "terrorism" back to the French Revolution and the so-called Jacobin Reign of Terror. As Combs notes:

> The execution of Marie Antoinette on October 16, 1793, was one of the first incidents actually called terrorism. In this instance, the terrorists were not trying to *overthrow* the government: they *were* the government! The Committee of Public Safety, led by Robespierre, chief spokesman of the Jacobin party, governed France during the tumultuous period known as the Reign of Terror (September 1793–July 1794). It is from this period, during which an estimated 20,000 persons were killed, that the word "terrorism" has evolved.[46]

When considering the country of origin of those who have committed violence against civilian populations to advance a political goal, it is obvious that the list would include many nations outside the Middle East. For example, acts of political violence have been committed by native non-Muslim populations in Chile, Argentina, Japan, Spain, Northern Ireland, Germany, and the United States (e.g., Ted Kaczynski, the "Unabomber," and Timothy McVeigh, the Oklahoma City bomber). Some terrorism experts have pointed out that Iran in particular has a tradition of terrorism. They note that the word "assassin" could be traced back to a group of Iranian Muslims who under the influence of hashish ("assassin" is supposedly derived from "hashishan," which means hashish eaters) committed politically motivated murders.[47] However, this type of cultural analysis of terrorism is based on a very selective reading of history. As noted earlier, the responsibility for the roots of terrorism could be laid at the doorsteps of any nation such as France during the French Revolution, the United States with its history of Ku Klux Klan and other white supremacists, and Germany and Italy and their support for the atrocities committed by Nazis and Fascists. Even Jews would not be exempted from such retrospective analysis of terrorism, since the word "zealot" originally referred to a Jewish sect that committed acts of terror in the first century c.e. in opposition to the Roman rule of what is now the state of Israel.

In the most general sense, terrorism refers to clandestine, illegal violence inflicted upon civilians to influence a third party to acquiesce to certain political demands.[48] This definition encompasses two distinct aspects of terrorism: (a) its illegality (unlike conventional warfare, the violence of terrorism is not sanctioned); (b) the immorality of its methods (terrorism seeks to bring about policy change through random and secret violence inflicted on innocent targets).[49]

However, critics point out that focusing on the illegality of terrorist violence indirectly condones atrocities committed by state authorities. For example, the horrors perpetrated by the Nazi regime against the Jews were carried out under the specific legal authority of the Third Reich. At the same time, the immorality of the goals of terrorism cannot be established using objective and universal standards. For example, in the 1980s the United States supported the Contras, a paramilitary group that used highly questionable tactics to try to overthrow the Nicaraguan government led by the leftist Sandinistas. In fact, the U.S. government even provided support for Osama bin Laden "when he was part of a 'freedom fighter' group . . . [that fought] against the Soviet Union's invasion of Afghanistan in 1979."[50]

Charles Ruby notes that the most objective and widely agreed-upon feature of terrorism might be its behavior or method of operation, or the fact that terrorism inflicts deliberate harm on civilians to influence the policies of a political power. However, even at this level a certain degree of relativism enters the equation. For example, the U.S. government can be charged with employing terroristic methods when its economic embargo of Iraq, intended to overthrow Saddam Hussein's government, indirectly resulted in the deaths of thousands of children due to starvation and lack of medical supplies.

Another example of the ambiguity surrounding state-sponsored violence would be the shooting down of an Iranian airbus in the Persian Gulf on July 3, 1988. Claiming to have mistaken an Iranian passenger plane for a fighter jet, Will C. Rogers of the Navy ship *Vincennes* ordered it shot down. Two hundred and ninety passengers and flight crew were killed.[51] Though other commanders in the region had accused the captain and his crew of "aggressive 'robo-cruiser'" tactics, subsequent investigations cleared him of any wrongdoing.[52] About a year later, Will C. Rogers and his weapons officer were decorated "for exceptionally meritorious conduct in the performance of outstanding service as commanding officer."[53] The medal is considered the Armed Forces' second highest peacetime award. The accompanying citation, which did not reference the tragic incident but the skirmishes with Iranian gunboats that immediately preceded it, stated that, "Captain Rogers's dynamic leadership, logical judgment and unexcelled devotion to duty reflected great credit upon himself and were in keeping with the highest traditions of the U.S. Naval Service."[54]

Some argue that the problems associated with arriving at a precise definition of terrorism provide justification for those who oppose U.S. government policies in the Middle East through violent means directed at civilian populations. Such groups, which used to operate under the banner of Arab national-ism and have in recent decades become associated with Islam, feel that U.S. policies and military presence in the Middle East have supported dictatorships (e.g., the Saudi and Kuwaiti monarchies) at the expense of ordinary citizens.

In recent years, these terrorist organizations have been responsible for a significant number of violent acts against the United States. In this section, we review some of these tragic events and the public and official responses to them in order to better understand the forces that have shaped Middle Easterners lives in America.

The Munich Hostage Crisis of 1972

On September 5, 1972, eight Palestinian militants who called themselves the Black September group took eleven Israeli athletes hostage during the Olympic games in Munich, Germany. The hostage-takers demanded the release of over two hundred Palestinian prisoners held by Israeli authorities. Hours later, the German authorities, pretending to have conceded to the terrorists' demands for safe passage out of Germany, allowed the hostages and their captors to travel to a nearby airport. At this location, the German authorities tried to rescue the hostages, but their attempts failed. At the end all eleven hostages and five of the eight terrorists were dead.[55]

Scenes from the Olympic village, where the hostages were held, were televised worldwide. Law enforcement agencies throughout the world saw this event as a wake-up call that underscored the need for better-trained antiterrorist squads, as well as more surveillance of militant groups with ties to the conflict in the Middle East. In many ways, this tragedy brought the Arab-Israeli conflict to the West and alerted Western authorities to the threat of Middle Eastern militants sympathetic to the Palestinian cause. Some scholars have noted that the first large-scale government surveillance of Middle Eastern Americans took place immediately following this event. Specifically, in what was coded "Operation Boulder" many Arab Americans were questioned and some deported, as stated in the following excerpt from a 1973 journal article:

> Over the past four months the U.S. government has launched a campaign of harassment, intimidation and deportation against Arab-Americans and Arabs living in this country, a campaign which has precedent most recently in the suppression and intimidation of Japanese-American community in the West Coast at the beginning of World War II. The campaign was initiated in September [1972], ostensibly in response to the Palestinian commando action at the Munich Olympic games. . . . In the two months following September 30th, at least 78 Arabs were deported from the US (according to government-supplied figures). Hundreds, perhaps thousands more

have been interrogated, photographed and finger-printed by FBI and Immigration officials. Some have been jailed and forced to pay bonds for no reason, or for technical visa violations which are normally excused. They have felt the heavy hand of the state for one reason: they are "ethnic Arabs," and, presently, that's a bad thing to be in this country.[56]

This description is eerily similar to the official reaction following the September 11 attacks. Thus, the negative perceptions of Middle Eastern Americans as terrorists date back at least thirty years. Although Arab Americans have been in the United States since the early 1900s, their presence did not draw much attention from public officials, be it negative or positive, until the 1960s. The turning point was the Arab-Israeli conflict and the ensuing wars during which the United States implicitly or explicitly supported the sovereignty of the state of Israel, a stance that has remained steadfast over the decades. Since this period Middle Eastern Americans have been under pressure to prove their loyalty to their home country, and by extension, to show their support for American foreign policies in the Middle East.

The Iranian Hostage Crisis

Another key chapter in the history of Middle Eastern Americans is the Iranian hostage crisis. Shortly after the Iranian revolution that toppled the pro-American regime of the shah (Farsi word for king or monarch) of Iran, a group of radical students seized the American embassy in Tehran on November 4, 1979. Among their grievances was that the United States had given refuge to the deposed shah and supported the brutal actions of his secret police, the Savak. Fifty-three Americans were taken as hostages for 444 days. The Iranian students, backed by the fundamentalist Islamic government of Khomeini (the late spiritual and political leader of Iran) accused the American embassy personnel of being spies and threatened to try and possibly execute some of them.[57] During this period, the U.S. government explored a number of avenues for freeing the hostages, including a failed military operation. Most of this drama was played out on television with millions of Americans saddened and frustrated by their government's inability to end the crisis. The ordeal finally ended on January 20, 1981, on the day of Ronald Reagan's presidential inauguration, supposedly after the U.S. government made a number of concessions to the Iranian government (which paved the way for what later became known as the Iran-Contra scandal).

One cannot exaggerate the impact of the hostage crisis on the Americans' attitude toward Middle Easterners, and Iranians in particular. According to a 1989 Gallup poll, 89 percent of Americans had an "unfavorable" view of Iran.[58] Through the 1990s that number stayed over 75 percent and by 2002 it once again rose to 84 percent. In the months and years immediately following the hostage-taking, some Americans expressed their "unfavorable" attitude toward Iranians living in the United States in more overt ways. Consider, for example, the following excerpt about backlash against Iranians published in a December 1979 *Newsweek* article:

> James Le Fante, head of the Hudson County Bus Owner Association in New Jersey, called six drivers into his office last week and fired them—because they are Iranians. "I won't take, I can't take the way Americans are being held hostage by these degenerates," fumes Le Fante. . . . His own operation purged, Le Fante is now urging "every merchant, every restaurant owner in Jersey City to let their Iranians go and fly the American flag."[59]

The same article reports numerous other accounts of "arson, assault, and harassment."[60] These include massive dismissal of students from school simply because they were Iranian, being fired from jobs for participating in pro-Khomeini demonstrations, or receiving death threats such as a sign left at a vandalized Islamic center in New York that read "Let our people go or you will all die."[61] The words of a young Iranian in Oakland, California, in response to this violent backlash is very telling: "Now I know how the Japanese who were here in America felt during World War II."[62]

Official government policies similarly targeted Iranians living in the United States for selective enforcement of immigration laws. The same 1979 *Newsweek* article reads:

> the government has . . . a dragnet over 50,000 or so Iranian students in this country to deport those who have violated the terms of their visas. Every Iranian student is required to report to immigration officials for interviewing. . . . In the first week of the crackdown, 14,466 students were interviewed—and 11,086 were found in compliance, 1,784 were classified "deportable" and the rest are still under study. Only three students have so far been deported and seventeen have left the U.S. voluntarily.[63]

As was the case following the Munich hostage crisis, suffering from misdirected public outrage about terrorism is an all too familiar experience for Middle Eastern Americans. Sadly, the Iranian hostage crisis was not the end.

The First Gulf War

On January 16, 1991, the United States, with the aid of a massive international coalition and the backing of the United Nations, started an offensive against Iraqi forces that were occupying Kuwait at the time. Prior to this conflict Iraq was considered an ally of the United States, particularly during its war with its neighbor Iran. However, by the end of the Iran-Iraq war, faced with an economic crisis, the leader of Iraq, Saddam Hussein, attacked its other neighbor Kuwait. This act of aggression was not tolerated by the world community, and the United Nations, with strong support from the United States and President George H. W. Bush (the father of the current president), quickly moved to liberate Kuwait. Many analysts have suggested that the strong condemnation of the invasion of Kuwait was in part motivated by the terrifying prospect of Saddam controlling a significant share of the world's oil production. Regardless, faced with the massive force of over a half a million coalition troops, the Iraqi forces quickly retreated after suffering significant casualties. A cease-fire was declared by February 28, 1991. The United States and its allies imposed many restrictions on the Iraqi regime but stopped short of removing Saddam from power. This task was postponed until 2003 and carried out by the son of the former president who led the first Gulf War.

The military conflicts with Iraq have reinforced the notion that people of Middle Eastern descent are natural enemies of the United States. During the first war with Iraq, the usual rash of hate crimes against Middle Eastern Americans, and those who appeared Middle Eastern, went on. In Fairfax, Virginia, the home and car of an Afghani family was vandalized: "Their tires have been slashed. Their car windows have been shattered. Their front door splattered with spray-painted profanity."[64] In response to the hate crime, the spokesman for the county police simply stated, "Property is a silent witness. There's not a lot to go on."[65] In a school essay, the ten-year-old daughter of the family wrote, "Maybe someone can help me to understand how people can be so mean and I can help them to understand the beauty of being different."[66]

In Tulsa, Oklahoma, the house of a naturalized U.S. citizen of Iraqi descent was set on fire while the family was on vacation. According to a news report, "Family members told the police that they had received anonymous derogatory telephone calls in the last month that the Almusawi [family last name] children had been harassed at school."[67] Numerous other incidents of hate crime were reported throughout the country:

> The secretary at a Muslim-owned travel agency received a call from someone wanting to know if the business owner was Palestinian. He is Pakistani but that didn't stop the caller from threatening "to have the building blown up." The caller also threatened to rape the woman who answered the phone.
>
> A woman calling a mosque asked if people there supported Saddam Hussein and then, before anyone could answer, spewed "all the four-letter words that are not in the dictionary," as a spokesman put it.[68]

In response to the rash of violence, the senior President Bush in a meeting with Arab American leaders announced that, "There is no room for discrimination against anybody in the United States of America."[69] Meanwhile, the FBI began interviewing Arab Americans, ostensibly to warn them about a possible backlash against them, but to also assess "potential for terrorist activity."[70] In a related effort, the FBI began "seeking out Iraqi nationals who have overstayed their visas and conducting criminal investigations."[71] Interestingly, during this period, Arab and Jewish organizations formed a loose coalition to fight discrimination.[72] This was in part because anti-Jewish hate crime also increased in the aftermath of the first Gulf War, perhaps because some blamed support for the state of Israel as an unstated reason for America's involvement in the war against Iraq. In an unprecedented event, Jewish and Arab American leaders joined House Democrats on Capitol Hill to raise their objections to "the FBI investigation of prominent Arab-Americans."[73]

The first Gulf War quickly came to an end—only to be restarted twelve years later under the junior President Bush, who warned the country that Saddam Hussein was aiding terrorists and was in the process of developing nuclear and biological weapons that could be used against the United States. In this more recent conflict, thousands of American troops are stationed in Iraq indefinitely pending the establishment of a new government.

The 1993 Bombing of the World Trade Center

In what was considered the first major domestic terrorist attack against the United States, on February 26, 1993, Middle Eastern Islamic terrorists detonated a bomb in the parking garage of the One World Trade Center in Manhattan, New York. Six people were killed and hundreds of others were injured. In 1994, four of the suspects were tried and received prison sentences of 240 years each.[74] In 1996, ten other Muslim fundamentalists were convicted and sentenced in connection with this terrorist act and related plots, receiving sentences that ranged from twenty-five years to life.[75] For Middle Eastern Americans, the usual fears about a backlash were raised, but the public reaction was comparatively mild. This may be in part because the government handled this tragedy as a criminal act perpetrated by fanatics. Indeed, one of the key federal prosecutors in this case, Mary Jo White, stated that the 1993 bombing of the World Trade Center was "no reflection on the vast majority of law-abiding citizens."[76] This philosophy would be severely tested when the World Trade Center was attacked again less than ten years later.

September 11 and the War on Terror

On September 11, 2001, nineteen terrorists hijacked four planes from U.S. airports. One plane was flown into the Pentagon, killing an undisclosed number of civilians and military personnel, including the passengers on the flight. Another plane was crashed into the ground in Pennsylvania, presumably due to the heroism of the passengers and crew on board, before it reached its target in Washington, DC. The other two planes were crashed into the World Trade Center buildings, or "Twin Towers," causing them to collapse a short time after the impact. Nearly three thousand people were killed, many of them firemen and policemen who rushed to the building to rescue the inhabitants. The sights of the crash and the collapse of the buildings were captured by news reporters and amateur videographers and shown repeatedly on television. Within hours, it was clear that the attacks were committed by Islamic terrorists. The majority of the hijackers were Saudi Arabian.

Fearing additional terrorists plots, repeated official announcements urged everyone to be on the alert for suspicious activities and characters (which in this case clearly meant "Middle Eastern–looking" people). Immediately following the events, thousands of Middle Eastern people were arrested (the exact number had not been released for security reasons at the time of this writing). The usual official strategy of selective enforcement of immigration laws was put into effect, and many immigrants were held and deported for technical visa violations (the exact number is still undisclosed).

The attacks were coordinated by a Saudi millionaire, Osama bin Laden, who operated terrorist training camps in Afghanistan. The Afghan government, ruled by an Islamic fundamentalist group known as the Taliban, refused to turn over bin Laden to U.S. authorities. After an ultimatum, the Bush administration entered a war against Afghanistan and quickly overthrew the Taliban regime and established an interim government—though bin Laden evaded capture. A new doctrine was slowly emerging in the fight against terrorism. The battle against terrorism was no longer seen as a law enforcement problem but a global campaign against Islamic fundamentalism and "state-sponsored terrorism."

The domestic implication of this campaign for Middle Eastern Americans has been that they are under constant suspicion for collaborating with the enemy. The passage of numerous laws and a massive shift in public attitude have added to the decades of mistrust and fear. Our quick summary of terrorist acts and public reactions is not exhaustive. Many other incidents in recent decades have been left out of our list (e.g., the 1983 truck bombing of U.S. marines in Beirut, 1988 crash of Pan Am flight 103, and 1998 bombing of

American embassies in Kenya and Tanzania). That these acts of terrorism have shaped negative public opinions of Middle Eastern Americans should not be surprising to anyone. Televised reports of these events, often presented without contextual details, have been instrumental in constructing a stereotypical representation of Islam and the Middle East.

That these terrible tragedies have been perpetrated by Middle Easterners is undeniable. The question is: Are they representative of every man, woman, and child of that origin? Are millions of Arabs and Iranians abroad and here in America preoccupied with nothing more than committing acts of violence? The empirical data provides a resounding negative answer to these questions. For example, in the United States scores of Middle Eastern or Muslim associations have condemned the September 11 terrorist attacks. Overseas, Gallup Poll data from young Muslim men (under the age of thirty) show that 83 percent of Indonesians, 69 percent of Lebanese, 71 percent of Iranians, and 62 percent of Pakistanis stated that the September 11 attacks were not morally justified.[77] Undoubtedly, fanaticism is a problem in the Middle East, but it is neither unique to the region nor is it a universal trait of every person from that part of the world.

For example, domestic terrorists continue to pose a threat to the security of U.S. citizens. In fact, during the "orange alert" and fear of foreign terrorism in December 2003, one of the largest investigations of domestic terrorism went unnoticed. The following is one of the rare newspaper reports on the topic:

> Last month, an east Texas man pleaded guilty to possession of a weapon of mass destruction. Inside the home and storage facilities of William Krar, investigators found a sodium-cyanide bomb capable of killing thousands, more than a hundred explosives, half a million rounds of ammunition, dozens of illegal weapons, and a mound of white-supremacist and antigovernment literature.
>
> "Without question, it ranks at the very top of all domestic terrorist arrests in the past 20 years in terms of the lethality of the arsenal," says Daniel Levitas, author of *The Terrorist Next Door: The Militia Movement and the Radical Right.*
>
> But outside Tyler, Texas, the case is almost unknown. In the past nine months, there have been two government press releases and a handful of local stories, but no press conference and no coverage in the national newspapers.[78]

Ironically, while there was a less than fruitful search for weapons of mass destruction in Iraq, right here at home, in Texas, a man pleads guilty to the charge. Yet the stereotype of a "Muslim terrorist," which is broadcast relentlessly, continues to fuel hatred and disrupt the lives of Middle Eastern Americans. Consider, for example, the case of a Lebanese American from

Pittsburgh who was fired after complaining about racist remarks made by a fellow worker.

Yimin charges that he was fired by Guardian after he complained about a co-worker twice making references to getting rid of "those towel heads" in a company meeting held one week after the terrorist attacks. Guardian denies the allegation and says Yimin was dismissed for other reasons. Yimin, a third-generation American from a Lebanese family, said he was a Christian and did not wear a turban. But, he said, the comments from the co-worker seemed to be directed at him because of his appearance. "I don't look like an Irish guy," he said. "I look like a Lebanese guy." . . . In his case, Yimin alleged that the towel-head remark was made twice during the meeting. He said he let the first comment pass, hoping the topic of the meeting would turn to sales results and numbers. When the second remark came a few minutes later, Yimin said, he objected to it as offensive. After the meeting ended, Yimin said he called a supervisor on the telephone to ask that the person who made the remark be reprimanded. Yimin said he was instead asked three days later to quit and was fired when he refused to resign.[79]

Interestingly, the spokesman for the Pennsylvania Equal Employment Office Commission commenting on this case noted that:

A lot of this is perception stuff. . . . Biases are not fine-tuned. We have a number of charges from persons who are Sikhs, who for religious reasons do not cut their hair, and that leads to long beards and long hair wrapped up in a turban. People think of them as being Arabic when they are not in fact Arabic or Muslim.[80]

It is the "perception stuff," formed over decades of conflict and reinvigorated by the "War on Terror," that has cast Middle Eastern Americans as second-class citizens. As the following story suggests, the negative perceptions of "Middle-Eastern looking people" and their public scrutiny are manifest in many encounters.

Hikmat Beaini, a lawyer with the Fairfax County Human Rights Commission, recalls taking his children on a trolley tour of Washington in December [2001]. As he boarded the vehicle, he said, the driver grilled him about his origin. Beaini, who is originally from Lebanon, declared that he was a U.S. citizen—period. The other tourists stared at him nervously, and two promptly got off the bus, he said. "You have these types of things. Are they dying out? I think so. But any other attack against America, we're going to pay the price. That's what we're worried about," he said.[81]

The stereotype that all Muslim, Arab, or Iranian people support terrorism forms the basis for the way Middle Eastern Americans are treated in both informal everyday encounters and formal institutional settings such as the workplace and schools. In the next chapter, we especially focus on how some post–September 11 media reports and analyses have further ostracized Middle Easterners in the United States by drawing dogmatic distinctions between "us" (i.e., the "American self") and "them" (the Islamic others).

NOTES

1. David V. Biemma, "Missionaries under Cover," *Time,* June 30, 2003, pp. 36–44.
2. Biemma, "Missionaries," p. 38.
3. Biemma, "Missionaries," p. 38.
4. Adalberto Aguire and Jonathan Turner, *American Ethnicity: The Dynamics and Consequences of Discrimination,* 3d ed. (Boston: McGraw Hill, 2001), pp. 182–83.
5. Aguire and Turner, *American Ethnicity,* p. 184.
6. Rita J. Simon and Susan H. Alexander, *The Ambivalent Welcome: Print Media, Public Opinion and Immigration* (Westport, Conn.: Praeger 1993), p. 70.
7. Simon and Alexander, *The Ambivalent Welcome,* p. 85.
8. Ken Hamblin, "Maybe China Has the Right Idea," *The Denver Post,* October 28, 2003, p. F5.
9. John O'Sullivan, "Immigration Simmering in U.S. Pot," *Chicago Sun Times,* December 11, 2001, p. 31.
10. Jeffrey M. Jones, "Americans Felt Uneasy toward Arabs Even before September 11," *The Gallup Poll Organization* (www.gallup.com), September 28, 2001, p. 1.
11. Jones, "Americans Felt Uneasy toward Arabs," pp. 3–4.
12. Jeffrey M. Jones, "Effects of Sept. 11 on Immigration Attitudes Fading, but Still Evident," *The Gallup Poll Organization* (www.gallup.com), August 8, 2002, p. 3.
13. Jones, "Effects of Sept. 11 on Immigration," p. 3.
14. Mack Holt, *The French Wars of Religion 1562–1629* (Cambridge, U.K.: Cambridge University Press, 1995).
15. Michael Sells, *Approaching the Qur'an: The Early Revelations* (Ashland, Ore..: White Cloud Press, 1999), pp. 1–2.
16. Seyyed Hossein Nasr, *The Heart of Islam: Enduring Values for Humanity* (San Francisco: Harper, 2002), p. 57.
17. Nasr, *The Heart of Islam,* p. 65.
18. Nasr, *The Heart of Islam,* p. 66.
19. Karen Armstrong, *Islam: A Short History* (New York: Modern Library, 2000), p. 135.
20. Nasr, *The Heart of Islam,* pp. 69–70.
21. Neil McFarquhar, "Ferocious Dedication to an Unforgiving Faith," *New York Times,* October 10, 2001, A9.
22. "News Summary," *New York Times,* January 28, 2003, p. A2.
23. "In Defense of Islam: Anti-Muslim Christians Reveal a Distasteful Political Agenda," *The Ottawa Citizen,* October 15, 2002, p. A18.
24. Koran 5:69.
25. Koran 3:45–48.
26. Armstrong, *Islam,* pp. 30–31.
27. Koran 29:46.

28. Koran 2:251.

29. Koran 2:190.

30. Nasr, *The Heart of Islam*, pp. 256–66.

31. Nasr, *The Heart of Islam*, p. 195.

32. Haideh Moghissi, *Feminism and Islamic Fundamentalism* (London: Zed Books, 1999), p. 15.

33. Julia T. Wood, *Gendered Lives: Communication, Gender, and Culture*, 5th ed. (Belmont, Calif.: Thompson/Wadsworth, 2003), p. 299.

34. Wood, *Gendered Lives*, pp. 299–300.

35. Wood, *Gendered Lives*, pp. 301–02.

36. Wood, *Gendered Lives*, p. 144.

37. Wood, *Gendered Lives*, p. 144.

38. Joan Jacobs Brumberg and Jacquelyn Jackson, "The Burka and the Bikini," in *Reconstructing Gender: A Multicultural Anthology*, 3d ed., ed. Estelle Disch (Boston: McGraw-Hill, 2003), pp. 212–14.

39. Ann Sofie Roald, *Women in Islam: The Western Experience* (New York: Routledge, 2001), p. ix.

40. Edward Said, "Arabs, Islam and the Dogmas of the West," in *Orientalism: A Reader*, ed. Alexander Lyon Macfie (New York: New York University Press, 2000), p. 104.

41. "Indulgence," *Encyclopædia Britannica Online*. http://search.eb.com/eb/article ?eu = 43310 (accessed January 25, 2004).

42. "Crusade," *Encyclopædia Britannica Online*. http://search.eb.com/eb/article?eu = 118963 (accessed January 7, 2004).

43. See, for example, Samuel Huntington's *Clash of Civilizations and the Remaking of World Order* (New York: Simon and Schuster, 1998).

44. Noam Chomsky, *9-11* (New York: Seven Stories Press, 2001), pp. 78–79.

45. Jones, "Americans Felt Uneasy toward Arabs," p. 1.

46. Cindy C. Combs, *Terrorism in the Twenty-First Century* (Upper Saddle River, N.J.: Prentice Hall, 1997), p. 24.

47. Combs, *Terrorism*, pp. 20–21.

48. Jack P. Gibbs, "Conceptualization of Terrorism," *American Sociological Review* 54, no. 3 (1989): 329–40.

49. Charles L. Ruby, "The Definition of Terrorism," *Analysis of Social Issues and Public Policy* (2002): 9–14.

50. Ruby, "The Definition of Terrorism," p. 12.

51. Molly Moore, "U.S. Team Completes Iranian Airbus Inquiry; Report Due Next Week on Gulf Incident," *The Washington Post*, July 29, 1988, p. A16.

52. Simon Tisdall, "Vincennes Captain Gets a Top Medal: 'Meritorious Conduct' Citation for Gulf Skipper," *The Guardian*, April 24, 1990 (retrieved from Lexis Nexus October 15, 2003).

53. Tisdall, "Vincennes Captain."

54. Molly Moore, "2 Vincennes Officers Get Medals; Citations Do Not Mention Downing of Iranian Airliner That Killed 290," *The Washington Post*, April 23, 1990, p. A9.

55. Desson Howe, "A Moving, Tragic 'Day,'" *The Washington Post*, December 8, 2000, p. N47.

56. Joe Stork and Rene Theberge, "Any Arab or Others of a Suspicious Nature . . . ," *Middle Eastern Research and Information Project* 14 (1973): 3.

57. "Hostage Crisis; A Hot Potato for Reagan?" *U.S. News and World Report*, January 12, 1981, p. 20.

58. Lydia Saad, "Canada and Britain Top Americans' Country Ratings Once Again," *The Gallup Organization* (www.gallup.com), March 4, 2002, p. 10.

59. Dennis A. Williams, "The U.S. Backlash," *Newsweek*, December 3, 1979, p. 65.

60. Williams, "The U.S. Backlash," p. 65.

61. Williams, "The U.S. Backlash," p. 65.

62. Williams, "The U.S. Backlash," p. 65.

63. Williams, "The U.S. Backlash," p. 65.

64. Peter Baker, "Mistaken Victims of War's Fallout; Afghans Are Taken for Iraqis and Suffer Vandalism," *The Washington Post*, February 19, 1991, p. B1.

65. Baker, "Mistaken Victims," p. B1.

66. Baker, "Mistaken Victims," p. B1.

67. "Arson Fire Damages House of an Iraqi-American Family," *The New York Times*, February 22, 1991, p. 8.

68. Joni Balter and Barbara A. Serrano, "War Spawns More Hate Calls," *The Seattle Times*, January 22, 1991, p. A5.

69. "Bush Meets Arab Leaders," *St. Petersburg Times*, January 26, 1991, p. 4A.

70. Sam Vincent Meddis, "Arab Americans Assail FBI Program," *USA Today*, January 19, 1991, p. 3A.

71. David Johnson, "War in the Gulf: Security; With No Signs of Terrorism, F.B.I. Still Adds Precautions," *The New York Times*, January 20, 1991, p. 18A.

72. Adam Pertman, "War Joins US Arabs and Jews in a Common Cause," *The Boston Globe*, February 15, 1991, p. 10.

73. Pertman, "War Joins US Arabs and Jews," p. 10.

74. Richard Berstein, "Trade Center Bombers Get Prison Terms of 240 Years," *The New York Times*, May 25, 1994, p. 1.

75. Joseph Fried, "Sheik Sentenced to Life in Prison in Bombing Plot," *The New York Times*, January 18, 1996, p. 1.

76. Fried, "Sheik Sentenced," p. 1.

77. David W. Moore, "Stereotypes of Young Islamic Men Challenged," *The Gallup Organization* (www.gallup.com), March 26, 2002, p. 1.

78. Kris Axtman, "The Terror Threat At Home Often Overlooked," *Christian Science Monitor*, December 29, 2003, p. 2.

79. "Name-Calling; Salesman Charges He Was Fired for Complaining about Ethnic Taunts," *Pittsburgh Post-Gazette*, January 2002, p. E1.

80. "Name-Calling," p. E1.

81. Mary Beth Sheridan, "Backlash Changes Form," *The Washington Post*, March 4, 2002, p. B01.

Chapter 3

"Us" versus "Them"

The terrorist attacks of September 11, 2001, caused even the most politically apathetic Americans to engage in global issues and especially take an interest in the Middle East and Islam. In the weeks prior to the attacks, the most troubling media story was the sighting of unusually large numbers of sharks too close to our beaches ("The Summer of Sharks," as it was dubbed by the news media). Little did we know that the summer would end with such carnage. What happened in the aftermath of the attacks was unprecedented. The incredible suffering, heroism, and unity will continue to be a source of both pain and inspiration for all of us as ordinary citizens. Sadly, some have used this tragedy to advance a divisive political agenda that separates the Islamic other from the Western self. As Kofi Annan, the secretary general of the United Nations, notes:

> One of the most disturbing manifestations of bigotry today is Islamophobia—a new word for an old phenomenon. The Crusades and colonialism are just two examples of a poisoned past in which Muslims were first portrayed as hostile or dangerous, and then subjected to aggression and domination. In more recent decades, some have viewed Muslim countries as culturally unsuited to democracy. . . . Since the 11 September terrorist attacks on the United States, which were condemned throughout the Muslim world, many Muslims, particularly in the West, have found themselves the objects of suspicion, harassment and discrimination. And too many people see Islam as a monolith, and as intrinsically opposed to the West—when in fact Western and Islamic peoples have a long history of commerce, of inter-mingling and inter-marrying, and of influencing and enriching each other's art, literature, science and much else besides. Despite a discourse of centuries, caricature remains widespread, and the gulf of ignorance is dangerously deep.[1]

In the United States, the political ideology of "us versus them" outlined in what Annan says has dire consequences in the lives of Middle Eastern Americans. This chapter looks at how Middle Eastern Americans are socially constructed as outsiders or others. We especially look at how post–September 11 media accounts achieved this by disregarding political and socioeconomic differences in American society while at the same time exaggerating the same distinctions with the Islamic world.

To illustrate this point, we begin with a sociological explanation of what a community is and how it can be used to draw boundaries between insiders and outsiders.

Approaching the topic of "community response to terrorism" from a sociological standpoint, we ask: What is a community and how is it achieved? In this sense, rather than taking the idea of community for granted, we could study how a sense of community is created or maintained through human activities. For example, we could explore how social disturbances, such as crime or terrorism, actually serve a purpose by bringing a community together. Such an approach would pattern itself after the classic writings of Emile Durkheim, who argued that the deviant other is not "an utterly unsociable creature, a sort of parasitic element, a foreign, unassimilable body introduced into the bosom of society. He plays a normal role in social life."[2] Durkheim's controversial position is based on the view that as society punishes social outcasts, deviants, or criminals, it inadvertently defines its moral boundaries and unites the "good" against the "bad." For Durkheim, this is a "normal" and "necessary function" of crime found in all societies and all groups, even as he puts it in "a community of saints."[3] He concludes that no society can or should be free of some degree of norm violation or crime.

Following Durkheim, Kai Erikson looks at how the Puritan colonists of Massachusetts Bay went about establishing their community.[4] Separated from the influence of their homeland, the Puritans had to redefine their collective identity. They did so in part by responding to perceived threats from social outcasts (e.g., the witches of Salem). In a sense, the colonists clarified the moral boundaries of their fledgling community in response to the terrors of their time. Erikson's position, as stated in the following, echoes Durkheim's analysis of crime as a source of social solidarity:

> The deviant individual violates rules of conduct which the rest of the community holds in high respect; and when these people come together to express their outrage over the offense and to bear witness against the offender, they develop a tighter bond of solidarity than existed earlier. The excitement generated by the crime, in other words, quickens the tempo of interaction in the group and creates a climate in which the private sentiments of many separate persons are fused together into a common sense of morality.[5]

Of course, communities and nations are not distinguished simply by differences in morality. There are also economic boundaries that separate societies.

Indeed, as Joe Feagin suggests, purported cultural differences are sometimes used to justify the political oppression and economic exploitation of one group by another. Feagin states that:

> From the 1600s to the 1800s English and other European Protestants dominated the religious scene on the Atlantic coast of North America, and their religious views incorporated notions of European superiority and non-European inferiority. The early English Protestants regarded themselves as Christian and civilized, but those they conquered as unchristian and savage. Religious and cultural imperialism accompanied economic imperialism.[6]

One way in which the casting aside of minorities is achieved by a dominant group is through the process of "othering." According to sociologists, othering takes on forms such as: (a) presenting the other's differences as a shortcoming (e.g., being a minority is a deficit that has to be overcome, rather than just difference or possibly an asset); (b) objectification of the other (e.g., treating women and their bodies as sexual objects rather than treating women as persons); (c) presenting the familiar self as more superior and powerful than the other (e.g., suggesting that whites are inherently more intelligent than other groups); and (d) the assumption of the oppressive identity by the other (e.g., when Iranian Americans belittle Arab Americans for being terrorists).[7] What all these processes have in common is the creation of an inferior identity that can be used by the dominant group to economically and culturally exploit a subordinate group and deny it equal rights.

In this chapter, we examine how a sense of community was generated in response to the terrorist attacks. We are especially interested in how the reaction to the terrorist attacks gave way to a particular understanding of "community" that excluded Middle Eastern Americans and Muslims.

The sources from which we gathered our data include popular magazine articles (e.g., *Time* and *Newsweek*), editorials from local and national newspapers (e.g., the *New York Times,* paper and online versions), as well as online news reports from CNN.com and other similar outlets. These texts were published between September 2001 (immediately following the attacks) to August 2002, thus covering a time span of approximately one year. We collected over two hundred excerpts from our regular readings of these news sources. We paid particular attention to items that contained such words as "terrorism," "Arab Americans," "Islam," "patriotism," and "community." We later reduced our collection of articles using a grounded theory approach.[8] Specifically, we initially perused and coded these texts into the theme of "self versus other." We then developed two conceptual categories: minimizing differences within the Western self and magnifying differences with the Islamic other.

Approaching this data as rhetorical constructions, we were interested in how they present one version of reality by excluding other possibilities. We especially focus on how these media accounts act as interpretive frameworks or ways of making sense of the terrorist attacks and their consequences for U.S. society.[9] As we see it, asking how communities are socially constructed is to ask about their purpose and consequences. For example, in the world of politics, the notion of an "international community" encourages cooperative efforts and interdependence, whereas "national community" and "national interest" imply a more partisan stance. In this chapter, we explore how the notion of community has been defined in response to the terrorist attacks in a way that portrays Middle Easterners and Muslims as dangerous outsiders.

MINIMIZING DIFFERENCES WITHIN THE "AMERICAN" SELF

In the months following the attacks, a significant portion of the rhetorical constructions of community focused on how "*we*, as Americans, are really not all that different from each other." We label this emphasis on similarities minimizing differences within the "American" self. In the following pages, we show how this way of discounting differences was applied to the realms of race and ethnicity, politics, and economics to construct an image of Americans as a sociopolitical monolith.

Racial and Ethnic Differences

Racial differences have been at the forefront of public debate in the United States. However, many post–September 11 media reports advance the claim that the terrorist attacks in effect have eliminated a cultural preoccupation with racism and prejudice. For example, in October 2001 a *New York Times* article states the following about relations between minorities and the police:

> In Fort Greene, Brooklyn, a crew of black and Latino teenage boys say they can no longer think of the police as enemies. Since September 11, the boys say, the officers who patrol their neighborhoods, most of whom are white, no longer eye them with suspicion.
>
> Several Haitian American groups, which had angrily protested police abuse in recent years, have sent a letter to a local police chief in Crown Heights expressing admiration for the officers.[10]

This piece goes on to quote an African American teenager as saying, "[Before the attacks] I just thought of myself as black. . . . But now I feel like an American more than ever."[11] In this way, the article rhetorically discounts the problem of racial divide and emphasizes the importance of national unity (i.e., the transformation from being black to being American).

A similar piece published nine months after the attacks makes the case that the post–September 11 changes in racial attitudes are more enduring than originally expected. It states:

> Daniel Hook knows what it is like to be judged by the color of his skin. It would take no more than a ride on the subway to get the disapproving looks—the kind that screamed out: stay away. Mr. Hook is 25, black and a lifelong resident of Brooklyn. He wears baggy pants and a baseball cap and has a fondness for silver earrings. . . . But these days, Mr. Hook does not worry about the subway or the people riding them. In fact, he seeks them out. Once a week, on a day off from work, he volunteers at New York City Transit, sweeping stations and giving directions. "People are polite to me," Mr. Hook said while on duty in Jackson Heights, Queens. "My skin color doesn't seem to matter."[12]

Ironically, this piece downplays the significance of race by foregrounding the racial stereotype of a young inner-city kid with a "fondness for silver earrings." The youth in the story is textually transformed into a less threatening racial caricature (i.e., that of a docile black man who sweeps stations and gives directions). Citing the results of a recent *New York Times* and CBS News poll, the article states, "Though the widely publicized civility of New Yorkers may have lost some of its sheen, many people say the color lines remain blurred and less intimidating."[13]

This view of racial harmony is extended to Arab Americans, even as they are being subjected to ethnic profiling. For example, a CNN online article reports the community-building benefits of Justice Department interviews with thousands of Middle Eastern men. Referring to a report from the Executive Office of U.S. Attorneys [EOUSA], it states:

> few of those [Middle Eastern men who were] approached to give interviews refused. In eastern Michigan, home to a large Arab-American community, only three out 313 people refused. . . . The [EOUSA] report also concluded that a public relations campaign waged by federal authorities to go into Arab and Islamic communities and explain the program to calm their fears "has forged stronger ties between law enforcement and these communities."[14]

Other sympathetic articles about Middle Eastern communities discussed how they were facing prejudice after September 11. However, even these tended to present Middle Eastern Americans as if their lives were markedly different than those of "average" Americans, contributing to rather than decreasing the degree to which they appear "foreign" to the reader. As a whole, the post–September 11 collective identity is centered on the rejection of racial differences internally while, as we later show, simultaneously foregrounding these differences with external groups.

Political Differences

Similar rhetorical constructions (i.e., whitewashing of differences) were applied to the realms of domestic politics. For example, a September 24 article in *Newsweek* reads:

> Dividing lines of all sorts vanished in the new sense of the civilized world. . . . Gone was Washington's political sniping between Republican and Democrat; the congressional leaders of both parties held a joint meeting on the Capitol steps to pledge their support to President Bush, and then broke into a spontaneous chorus of "God Bless America."[15]

This excerpt announces the birth of a "new civilized world" that is no longer politically at odds with itself. The multiparty political system usually praised for being the hallmark of a fractious yet stable democracy is dismissed as "political sniping." In a sense, civic disagreement is made to seem "uncivilized" in the "new civilized world."

In fact, for at least a brief time, in the name of unity, the very foundational principles of laissez-faire capitalism (i.e., the unregulated pursuit of self-interest) is set aside in favor of the collective. In the following excerpt, consider how the text downgrades the desirability of economic differences:

> There are things in the world that are more important than money. Even in New York City. And even among Wall Street professionals whose business is institutionalized greed. Morality trumping Mammon is one of the few reassuring business lessons to emerge from last week's disaster. . . . Thoughts of going long were set aside in favor of getting along.[16]

Here the setting aside of greed, a staple of the capitalist economic system, becomes a symbol of the new sense of community. In the presumed struggle between money and morality, the triumph of the latter is presented as being beneficial for the community.

Discounting Domestic Terror

One potential problem with creating a sense of community as a response to outside threats and violence is the existence of domestic terror. Sometimes, the agents that threaten the community, and indeed commit acts of terror, are not outsiders. As an op-ed piece, titled "All-American Osamas," puts it:

We Americans have conjured so specific a vision of terrorists—swarthy, glowering Muslims mumbling fanatically about Allah—that we're missing the threat from home-grown nuts, people like David Burgert . . . [who] had a terror plan that made Osama bin Laden's look rinky-dink. . . .

The plan, according to Sheriff James Dupont, was for the militia to use its machine guns, pipe bombs and 30,000 rounds of ammunition to assassinate 26 officials (including Mr. Dupont), and then wipe out the National Guard when it arrived. After the panicked authorities sent in NATO troops, true American patriots would rise up, a ferocious war would ensue, and the U.S. would end up back in the hands of white Christians.[17]

While facetious in its tone, the facts of this case, as well as many others like it, do point to a serious incongruity in the rhetorical construction of community in response to outside terror. The us–them duality cannot be maintained in the face of the possibility that "All-American Osamas" could pose an even greater threat. How do media accounts deal with this challenge? Our analysis suggests that they do so by treating such cases as isolated events caused by psychologically imbalanced individuals while at the same time highlighting the endearing and familiar qualities of the American-born, white terrorist.

For example, John Walker Lindh, the so-called American Taliban, was characterized as a young man whose good intentions led him astray, as suggested in a *New York Times* op-ed about the legal case against him:

The government and John Walker Lindh, the American captured in Afghanistan last year, brought his prosecution to a reasonable conclusion yesterday when Mr. Lindh unexpectedly pleaded guilty to two felony offenses. In return the government dropped the gravest charges against him, including conspiring to kill Americans and engaging in terrorism. The plea bargain reflects the unfolding realities of the Lindh case, which had more to do with the criminal conduct of a foolish young man than the actions of a hardened terrorist.[18]

Here the distinction between a "foolish young man" and "a hardened terrorist" is key to understanding how the us–them dichotomy is maintained in light of contradictory evidence. The article, in the same passage, goes on to inform that: "The decision honors the demands of criminal justice, national security and America's commitment to constitutional rights."[19] This puts the indignant reaction to Lindh in the familiar framework of American justice: He and his treatment fall within "our" moral boundaries.

Similarly, Luke John Helder, a twenty-one-year-old who terrorized the residents of five states in spring 2002 by placing eighteen pipe bombs in rural mailboxes, was described by the authorities as "an intelligent young man with strong family ties."[20] His appearance in court was described as "clean-shaven and smiling with short-cropped hair and wearing a white shirt and tie."[21] The title of another piece about Helder reads "Pipe Bomb Suspect Known as 'Really Nice Kid.'"[22] In regards to Helder and Lindh, the violence is presented as an aberration of their *essentially* good character. Helder is described by his friends and teacher as "sweet," "very nice," "laid back," "an ordinary guy," or "just a basic guy."[23] Unlike the *terrorist other*, these "kids" are humanized (i.e., they are made to seem more like us).

Their accuracy or distortions notwithstanding, these accounts make the surprising charm of domestic perpetrators of mass violence the focal point of the news story; the agony of their victims or the amount of carnage they caused is of secondary importance. By contrast, when Islamic terrorists are concerned, occasional glimpses into their humanity are described as a facade, which itself accentuates their threat as outsiders. Accordingly, foreign terrorists only pretend to look normal or like "us," so that they could cause even greater harm. Consider, for example, this description of a suspected terrorist:

> It is not known how many of bin Laden's operatives are still on the loose. One of the most intriguing suspects may be Amer Mohammed Kamfar, 41. Last winter or fall, he showed up in Florida and took flight lessons at FlightSafety Academy. He rented a house in Vero Beach, where he had a wife, who dressed in the traditional chador, and several children. Kamfar, who called himself "John," "shopped at Wal-Mart and ate a lot of pizza," according to a neighbor.[24]

For the domestic terrorists, their normal appearance softens the gravity of their crimes. They are described as "young" and "foolish." On the other hand, the foreign terrorists' normal appearance becomes a ruse, a cause for further alarm. In this way two worlds of violence are constructed. One is the world of the unfortunate young men, like those "we know," who become tragically involved in reprehensible acts, and the other is that of the sinister men who—though they may look human—are ultimately driven to unspeakable violence that is part of their nature. Indeed, as we note in the next section, many post–September 11 media constructions create the maximum cultural and political distance between "us" and "them."

Just as media constructions render it rhetorically impossible for white Americans to be "terrorists," these same constructions make it difficult for Middle Eastern Americans to be seen as "victims." The strict us–them dichotomy sets up the Middle Eastern other as the victimizer; placing him (or her) firmly on the side of "the enemy." After September 11, this created a double burden for Middle Eastern Americans. All Americans were deeply hurt by the terrorist attacks, including Middle Eastern Americans; and all felt more vulnerable than they had prior to this outrage. Yet instead of being able to rely for support on the new sense of unity and camaraderie that developed in response to the attacks, Middle Eastern Americans became isolated in their communities. Even worse, as an additional burden, they came under suspicion and attack for supposed links with the perpetrators of the violence. After September 11, there was much talk about how all Americans were victimized by the violence to some extent; and it was in this sense of shared victimization that a sense of moral outrage and then community was created. Middle Eastern Americans, by virtue of their construction as others, were not seen as victims but only as potentially dangerous outsiders.

MAGNIFYING DIFFERENCES WITH THE ISLAMIC OTHER

As Erikson would suggest, a crucial aspect of community building is marking differences between the familiar self and the strange other, between our values and theirs. This is what Erikson calls moral boundary maintenance. He suggested that especially in times of crisis, group members find it necessary to define themselves by underscoring perceived or real differences with deviant outsiders. In Erikson's words, "The deviant is a person whose activities have moved outside the margins of the group, and when the community calls him to account for that vagrancy it is making a statement about the nature and placement of its boundaries."[25]

Similarly, the political significance of boundary maintenance as way of defining national identity is articulated by Edward Said when he states:

> The geographic boundaries accompany the social, ethnic, and cultural ones in expected ways. Yet often the sense in which someone feels himself to be not-foreign is based on a very unrigorous idea of what is "out there," beyond one's own territory. All kinds of suppositions, associations, and fictions appear to crowd the unfamiliar space outside of one's own.[26]

While Said acknowledges the presence of "real" boundaries and geographic differentiations, he argues that it is the rhetorical or "poetic" attributions that make boundaries meaningful. In his words, "space acquires emotional or even rational sense by a kind of poetic process, whereby the vacant and anonymous reaches of distance are converted into meaning for us here."[27]

In the following analysis, we particularly emphasize how such self–other distinctions rhetorically *construct* an exclusionary definition of community, one where the Middle Eastern outsiders are hateful, envious, and barbarian, whereas the Western selves are peaceful, naive, and innocent.

Differences in Socialization and Character

In much of the data we examined, there was a focus on a distinction between the "American way of life" versus depictions of "the Islamic" culture, worldview, and political system. Sometimes the contrast centers around two opposing personality types: the rational American versus the fanatic Islamic other. This is well illustrated in the writings of Dinesh D'Souza, an Indian immigrant whose astute observations have apparently led him to conclude that America is free from racism. To his list of pseudointellectual accomplishments, D'Souza has recently added Islamophobia. As quoted in an editorial, he states:

> America is a new kind of society that produces a new kind of human being. That human being—confident, self-reliant, tolerant, generous, future-oriented—is a vast improvement over the wretched, servile, fatalistic and intolerant human being that traditional societies have always produced, and that Islamic societies produce now.[28]

This quote establishes who we are as a collective by highlighting presumed psychological differences with Muslims. The praise for American society and the criticism of its Islamic counterpart offers an explanation for why they committed the acts of violence that they did on September 11. This passage also rhetorically links the essence of the American character with the attributes of being "confident, self-reliant, tolerant, generous, and future-oriented."

Many texts maximize the distinction between the American self and Islamic other by reference to the desirability of modernity over tradition. For example, another excerpt from D'Souza suggests that Islamic nations should modernize by following Western standards.[29] Accordingly, Muslims frustrated with the failures of the Islamic world, hate America; they envy American success. As one author puts it, "Hating the success of Americans is a lot easier than trying to recover their own long lost greatness."[30] Thus the Muslims are united by their hate, whereas we are united by our collective success and greatness.

Another way in which moral boundaries between the American self and the Islamic other are maintained is through social exclusion. In this way, the authenticity of who we are is presented as being under constant threat from outside influences, both physical and cultural. The assumption is that we can preserve our social solidarity only by excluding and expelling others, particularly those of the Islamic world. For example, the conservative African American analyst Thomas Sowell, in a commentary praising Pat Buchanan as a man who "understands that we are in a culture war—and [that] only one side is fighting all out,"[31] states that:

> The native-born populations in almost all Western countries are failing to have enough children. . . . These countries also have been importing large numbers of immigrants from other countries and other civilizations, people with values at cross

purposes—often dangerously so, as we learned last September 11. Because these culturally different immigrants typically have a much higher fertility rate . . . the very composition of the Western world is changing in irreversible ways that threaten the survival of the existing culture. Nor is this concern merely a matter of parochial loyalty to a familiar way of life. Despite an unceasing barrage of propaganda from many sources, proclaiming that all cultures are equal, the inescapable fact is that the actual behavior of people from virtually all the cultures in the world says the direct opposite.[32]

The immigrant other is seen as "culturally different" and possessing values that are not only at "cross-purposes" from Western values but that threaten to destroy Western civilization in its entirety. He or she is, both literally and figuratively, presented as a foreign agent that could infect and immobilize the community. Even for Middle Eastern Americans who have established themselves in the United States, these depictions drew new, and typically negative, attention to them and their communities. The increased attention created circumstances in which they were called upon to account for themselves in ways they had not been required to before.[33]

Like Sowell, other authors speak of the inability of the strange other to become part of the familiar self. For example, one editorial asserts that it is the inability of young Muslim men to adapt to Western culture that initiates them into a life of terrorism. Citing the wisdom of a "female Arab friend," the piece states:

They are mostly men who grew up in an environment where the rules were very clear. They grew up never encountering anything that shakes their core. Suddenly they are thrown into Europe, and there are a whole different set of social rules that shakes their core. They don't know how to adapt because they've never had to, so they become more insular and hold onto their [Islamic] core even more.[34]

This text goes on to explain, in relatively sympathetic terms, that it is the fact that these Muslim immigrants are unable to assimilate in European society, and thus develop a "poverty of dignity" that transforms them, almost inevitably, into terrorists.[35]

As a whole, the self–other duality as discussed in this section establishes community by pointing to irreconcilable psychological and cultural differences. That we are a community of Americans and they are backward Muslims thus becomes a cultural barrier that cannot and should not be overcome. Indeed, these texts suggest that the moral boundary between Islam and the West should become a rigid physical and legal boundary as well, one that guarantees our protection against their pathological violence. The implications of such a protective strategy for Middle Eastern Americans, taken to the extreme, could mean reactionary measures such as those taken against Japanese Americans during World War II.

Differences in Culture and Spirituality

During the year after the September 11 tragedy, another rhetorical strategy used to construct a feeling of difference from the Islamic other was to assert that the Muslim faith and religious practices are the antithesis of the American self. The following is from a story in a popular weekly news magazine:

> To the question "Why do the terrorists hate us?" Americans could be pardoned for answering "Why should we care?" The immediate reaction to the murder of 5,000 innocents is anger, not analysis. Yet anger will not be enough to get us through what is sure to be a long struggle. For that we will need answers. The ones we have heard so far have been comforting but familiar. We stand for freedom and they hate it. We are rich and they envy us. We are strong and they resent this. All of which is true.[36]

The us–them distinctions listed in this text are similar to those we have previously discussed. They are affirmed as being true and useful tools for making sense of the September 11 events. However, as the text goes on, we notice that they are only precursors to a more important dichotomy:

> But there are billions of poor and weak and oppressed people around the world. They don't turn planes into bombs. They don't blow themselves up to kill thousands of civilians. If envy were the cause of terrorism, Beverly Hills, Fifth Avenue and Mayfair would have become morgues long ago. There is something stronger at work here than deprivation and jealousy. Something that can move men to kill but also to die.
>
> Osama bin Laden has an answer—religion. For him and his followers, this is a holy war between Islam and the Western world. Most Muslims disagree. . . . But bin Laden and his followers are not an isolated cult like Aum Shinrikyo or the Branch Davidians or demented loners like Timothy McVeigh and the Unabomber. They come out of a culture that reinforces their hostility, distrust and hatred of the West—and of America in particular. This culture does not condone terrorism but fuels the fanaticism that is at its heart. To say that Al Qaeda is a fringe group may be reassuring, but it is false. Read the Arab press in the aftermath of the attacks and you will detect a not-so-hidden admiration for bin Laden. . . . This awkward reality has led some in the West to dust off old essays and older prejudices predicting a "clash of civilizations" between the West and Islam.[37]

This particular rhetorical construction involves a set of claims and counterclaims. At the end, the reader is encouraged to conclude that what "really" sets us apart is religious differences. Theirs is a religion that "reinforces . . . hostility, distrust and hatred," whereas ours, although not directly referenced, is about peace and tolerance. Unlike terrorists from other parts of the world, who supposedly are anomalies in their societies, Muslim terrorists come from a "culture" that condones their behavior.

Other media accounts continue this theme of Islam as a religion that differs from Western, Judeo-Christianity in its inherent fanaticism and violence. For example, the popular Christian evangelist Pat Robertson was called to question for stating that Islam is not a peaceful religion. In an interview with a CNN correspondent in which he was asked to clarify his comment, he not only stood behind it, but also went on to make further claims about the inherent violence of Islam:

> I'm a history major in college, and we studied about jihad, and it started right after the death of Muhammad . . . this was not a peaceful religion. They were declaring a jihad, which was war against the West, and I'm afraid they're doing it again. . . . The prime tenet of Islam is that Allah is the one true God and Muhammad is his prophet, and then Muhammad said these things. He said the second duty or the second good work a man can do is to lead a jihad against the infidels. . . . I looked it up in the Encyclopedia Britannica, and it says, "Believers are under obligation to wage war against all unbelievers." That's the Encyclopedia Britannica. I don't understand why this has suddenly become so incendiary.[38]

In order to support his construction of Islam as a religion that is radically alien to American sensibilities, Robertson relies for support on his degree in history and the *Encyclopedia Britannica*. After noting that he does have Muslim friends, but that Muhammad's teachings are incitements to violence, Robertson continues:

> And I think Osama bin Laden is probably a very dedicated follower of Muhammad. He's done exactly what Muhammad said to do, and we disagree with him obviously, and I'm sure many moderate Muslims do as well, but you can't say the religion is a religion of peace. It's not. . . . And we might as well recognize it's not just a few. It's a large number who want to hurt us.[39]

A recurring theme in the media since September 11 has been that violence is an integral part of religion for the Islamic other. This idea is then put in stark contrast with the Western view of spirituality as based on love and a sense of shared humanity.

Of course, many have gone further. Consider the words of Jerry Vines, a Southern Baptist minister:

> Islam was founded by Muhammad, a demon-possessed pedophile who had 12 wives—and his last one was a 9-year-old girl. And I will tell you Allah is not Jehovah either. Jehovah's not going to turn you into a terrorist that'll try to bomb people and take the lives of thousands and thousands of people.[40]

This statement discursively links the Muslim faith with not just violence but pedophilia and Satanism. The implication is that the Islamic other is different from the familiar self beyond any possibility of convergence. Community is rhetorically achieved in this and other similar passages by attesting the difference between "our God" versus the false God of Islamic others, who presumably causes them to commit violence, be sexually perverted, and generally be "demon-possessed." Such statements helped to stigmatize Muslim Americans, whose mosques became targets of violence directly after September 11, and on into 2003. Government policy, such as the FBI monitoring of mosque membership, certainly contributed to the perception that Muslim Americans themselves were somehow part of the "enemy other."

Differences in Types and Causes of Violence

Finally, much of the commentary in the media after September 11 centers around the brutality of the event. Certainly, the attacks were horrific beyond anything most had ever seen. Because of the calculated manner in which they were carried out, and perhaps also because the public became aware of the last moments of the lives of many of the victims, the attacks seemed all the more sinister and chilling.

However, much of the subsequent public discourse, in the media and elsewhere, reflects a belief that the perpetrators of the violent terrorist attacks were somehow, as members of a distinctly different cultural group, inherently or naturally more violent than "we" are. This view is evidenced in the following quote from a *Time* magazine article:

> What is so striking—and so alien to civilized sensibilities—about the terrorists of radical Islam is their cult of death. Their rhetoric is soaked in the glory of immolation: immolation of the infidel and self-immolation of the avenger. . . . What Western TV would feature, as does Palestinian TV, a children's song with the lyric "How pleasant is the smell of martyrs . . . the land enriched by the blood, the blood pouring out of a fresh body?" . . . The West has not known such widespread, murderous perversion of religion since the religious wars of the 17th century.[41]

Here similar revered Western slogans (e.g., "Give me liberty or give me death!" or "Death before dishonor!") are conveniently forgotten. The almost universal "cult of death," martyrdom in the name of a social cause, is presented as the distinct and peculiar character of Islam and Middle Eastern people. Like other passages quoted thus far, relativistic cultural interpretations are rejected in favor of a more reductionist declaration: They are unevolved and murderous and we are advanced and peace loving.

Similarly, Thomas Friedman writes that U.S. vulnerability lies in the fact that we are so different from the Islamic other that we "failed to imagine" the kind of evil of which they were capable. He writes:

> Imagining evil of this magnitude simply does not come naturally to the American character, which is why, even after we are repeatedly confronted with it, we keep reverting to our natural, naively optimistic selves. Because our open society is so much based on trust, and that trust is so hard-wired into the American character and citizenry, we can't get rid of it—even when we so obviously should.[42]

Using essentialist language, this passage implies that while it does not come "naturally" to Americans to imagine "evil of this magnitude," because our "natural" state is to be naive, optimistic, and trusting, conversely imagining and even carrying out exactly this type of evil comes quite naturally to the Islamic other. It also subtly suggests that our society is perhaps too "open"— that maybe we have let too many people of dubious background in, and trusted them too easily. Such commentary helps to cast suspicion on immigrants in the population.

As Said would suggest, these characterizations define the Western community in direct opposition to the outside threat.[43] In this way, "our" inherent good is juxtaposed against their essential evil. The moral boundary in this case is maintained by casting the undifferentiated other outside one's own "universe of obligation."[44] That is, the Islamic other is rhetorically placed outside the realm of civic entitlements that we naively and optimistically take for granted.

ALTERNATIVE VIEWS OF COMMUNITY

Admittedly, the self–other duality we have discussed so far was neither unanimously voiced by the media, nor did it progress in a clear and uninterrupted fashion always directed at unwelcome others. Indeed, there were many other reactions to the tragedies of September 11. One such reaction was general hysteria. For example, the mayor of Inglis (a small city in Florida) formally barred Satan from her town by issuing a proclamation stating that, "Satan, the ruler of darkness, giver of evil, destroyer of what is good and just, is not now, nor ever again will be a part of this town of Inglis."[45] Another report told the story of a man who opened fire on a civilian helicopter that was flying too close to his home. He feared that "the chopper was carrying terrorists."[46] There was also the story about a woman whose vibrating sex toy was confused with a bomb and she was consequently removed from a flight.[47] Another woman was forced to drink her own breast milk to convince airline security personnel that the liquid did not pose a threat to anyone.[48] These accounts were usually couched in terms of the unfortunate and unintended consequence of a community being constantly under the threat of outsiders. Thus they were in effect still not laid at the feet of hysterical community members or overzealous law enforcement, but blamed on evil outsiders.

There were also voices of dissent—though they were rare and typically given scant coverage by the media (less than 5 percent of our sample). For example, a *New York Times* editorial stated:

> How many times have we heard these new mantras: "we have seen the face of evil"; "these are irrational madmen." . . . Each is at once inaccurate and unhelpful. . . . The more we think that what is at stake is a clash of civilizations, the more like our enemies we become. By insisting that we are not at war with Islam, Mr. Bush deprives Mr. bin Laden of the religious battle he so intensely desires.[49]

In another piece, a CNN reporter stated that, "The Muslim world is a phrase that in itself is misleading. We're talking about more than 50 countries with a variety of forms of government."[50] Another example of this rare questioning of the us–them mind-set is found in an editorial by Maureen Dowd in which she hints at possible flaws of Judeo-Christian faiths:

> And some Jews are also displaying the deranging effects of extreme religion. The Israeli settlers' movement and many people on the Israeli right are prepared to go to terrible lengths in the name of God's promise of the land to the chosen people. They, too, treat scripture as a warrant for political aggression and outright militancy. . . . Closer to home and much less apocalyptically, the Catholic Church also provides evidence of damage that dogmatic faith can do. The pedophilia scandal engulfing a shameful number of parishes throughout the Roman Catholic world is sickening for anybody who believes that religion makes us better. . . . Evangelical Christians have also had a brush with the dark side of their shepherds. We know that the Rev. Billy Graham—America's pastor, the preacher whom President Bush credits with putting him on the right path—is a man of prejudice. Recently released Nixon tapes give incontrovertible evidence of Reverend Graham's anti-Semitism. . . . It is not news that religion has its ugly, tribalist and bellicose sides. What is news is that those sides are having a field day.[51]

Dowd calls into question the essential differences between Islam, Christianity, and Judaism. Dismissing the claim that any one faith has a monopoly on militancy and violence, she suggests the larger problem is the misuse and misinterpretation of religion in the service of power and vice. Thus, rather than promoting an us–them dichotomy, she points to a common global problem, that is, the corrupting effect of religious fanaticism.

More of these alternative views could have helped to moderate the us–them rhetoric that placed Middle Eastern Americans outside the newly constructed community after September 11. Nonetheless, objections to the misplaced fear have not contributed to a significant shift in the rhetoric of community building. The dominant response to terrorism has been that it is the manifestation of irreconcilable moral differences between the West and the Islamic other. Arguably, as Durkheim and Erikson have demonstrated, social solidarity and moral boundary maintenance are common, universal responses to perceived or real crises. Our aim in this chapter has been to demonstrate how this process is achieved through media rhetoric. We are not suggesting that the particular representations we listed here form collectively shared sentiments among all Americans. Our analysis simply shows that given the specific circumstances immediately following the tragic events of September 11, a certain version of community was promoted by many media outlets.

Having said that, rhetorical constructions are not without consequences. One of the more dangerous practical implications of the us–them method of community building is that it paves the way for indiscriminate violence against the demonized outsiders, and, as we have suggested, against insiders who have already occupied a tenuous position as U.S. citizens, but who become associated with those demonized others. Marimba Ani writes of European treatment of "cultural others":

> The cultural other is there for Europeans to define, to "make over." . . . People of other cultural traditions . . . are part of the world to be defined, it is a European world. And in this sense, the conception of the cultural other is that of the nonhuman. It is Europeans who define "humanness" in terms of their own self-image and with such intensity that the ethic and rules of behavior that apply to those who are like them do not apply to those who are not. The cultural other is, therefore, the person (object) who can be treated in any manner—with an unlimited degree of hostility and brutality, as is evident when one reviews the history of the European's relations to people of other cultures.[52]

When we magnify differences with Islamic or Middle Eastern others, we implicitly place them outside our "universe of obligations." That is, we deny them the rights and privileges that we think members of the ingroup are entitled to. In the following passage, William Gamson points out the horrifying result of this process:

> The ultimate form of exclusion is to be barricaded outside of this universe of rights merely by virtue of membership in a designated collectivity, regardless of one's own conduct or choice. Genocide, sanctioned massacres, indiscriminate bombings of civilian populations of the "enemy" in war all imply the existence of an "other" to whom one is not obliged to extend the most basic human rights.[53]

Even before the September 11 attacks, Middle Eastern Americans had been placed in a position as a distinct ethnic other in the United States. Yet certainly in the months and now years following the September 11 attacks, the dualistic rhetoric that sets Middle Eastern Americans apart as others has had even more traumatic consequences in their lives. Middle Eastern–looking people have been murdered by irate fellow citizens. Some have been denied equal access to services; for example, multiple cases have been reported where Middle Eastern Americans have been asked to leave planes or have been placed under undue scrutiny in airports. In public places, those of Middle Eastern ancestry have been subjected to verbal and physical abuse. In response to these atrocities, Middle Eastern Americans have had to learn how to fight everyday discrimination and come together as a panethnic community.[54]

We hope to suggest that if one sense of community can be constructed so could another. That is, community does not have to have a single definition and entail exclusionary practices. Alternative conceptions of community could in fact promote peace by being inclusive rather than exclusive. Instead of rhetorically exaggerating potential differences, exploring commonalities and taking concrete steps toward equal treatment of others might very well pave the way for long-lasting peace.

NOTES

1. Kofi Annan, "The Inaugural Robert Burns Memorial Lecture," New York, January 13, 2004. www.un.org/apps/sg/sgstats.asp?nid=736#.

2. Emile Durkheim, *The Rules of Sociological Method and Selected Texts on Sociology and Its Method*, ed. Steven Lukes (New York: Free Press, 1982), p. 102.

3. Durkheim, *The Rules of Sociological Method*, p. 100.

4. Kai Erikson, *Wayward Puritans: A Study in the Sociology of Deviance* (New York: John Wiley & Sons, 1966).

5. Erikson, *Wayward Puritans*, p. 4.

6. Joe Feagin, *Racist America: Roots, Current Realities, and Future Reparations* (New York: Routledge, 2000), p. 72.

7. Michael Schwable, Sandra Godwin, Daphne Holden, Douglas Schrock, Shealy Thompson, and Michele Wolkomir, "Generic Processes in the Reproduction of Inequality: An Interactionist Analysis," *Social Forces* 79, no. 2 (2000): 419–52.

8. Kathy Charmaz, "Qualitative Interviewing and Grounded Theory Analysis," in *Handbook of Interview Research: Context and Method*, ed. J. Gubrium and J. Holstein (Newbury Park, Calif.: Sage, 2002), pp. 675–94.

9. On horizons of meaning, see Jaber Gubrium, *Speaking of Life: Horizons of Meaning for Nursing Home Residents* (Hawthorne, N.Y.: Aldine de Gruyter, 1993).

10. Sonni Sengupta, "Sept. 11 Attack Narrows the Racial Divide," *The New York Times on the Web*, October 10, 2001. www.nytimes.com/2001/10/10/nyregion/10RACE .html?todaysheadlines=&pagewa nted; eqprint (accessed October 10, 2001), p. 1.

11. Sengupta, "Sept. 11 Attack Narrows the Racial Divide," p. 2.

12. Dean E. Murphy and David M. Halbfinger, "9/11 Bridged the Racial Divide, New Yorkers Say, Gingerly," *The New York Times on the Web*, June 16, 2002. www.nytimes.com/2002/06/16/nyregion/16POLL.html?tntem (accessed June 16, 2002), p. 1.

13. Murphy and Halbfinger, "9/11 Bridged the Racial Divide," p. 1.

14. Terry, Frieden, "U.S. to Interview 3,000 More 'Visitors' in Terror Probe." CNN.com, March 20, 2002.www.cnn.com/2002/US/03/20/ret.aschcroft.terrorism/index.html (accessed March 20, 2002), p. 2.

15. Kenneth Auchincloss, "We Shall Overcome," *Newsweek*, September 24, 2001, pp. 18–25, quote from p. 22.

16. Allan Sloan, "Wall Street Morality Play," *Newsweek*, September 24, 2001, p. 57.

17. Nicholas D. Kristof, "All-American Osamas," *The New York Times on the Web*, June 7, 2002. www.nytimes.com/2002/06/07/opinion/07KRIS.html?ex (accessed June 7, 2002), p. 1.

18. "Justice and John Walker Lindh," *The New York Times on the Web*, July 16, 2002. www.nytimes.com/2002/07/16/opinion/16TUE2.html?todays (accessed July 16, 2002), p. 1.

19. "Justice and John Walker Lindh," p. 1.

20. "College Student Charged in Pipe Bomb Cases," CNN.com, May 8, 2002. www.cnn.com/2002/US/05/07/mailbox.pipebombs/index.html (accessed May 8, 2002), p. 2.

21. "College Student Charged," p. 2.

22. "Pipe Bomb Suspect Known as 'Really Nice Kid,'" CNN.com, May 8, 2002. www.cnn.com/2002/US/05/08/helder.profile/ (accessed May 8, 2002), p. 1.

23. "Teacher: 'He Was Almost Sweet,'" CNN.com, May 8, 2002. www.cnn.com/2002/US/05/07/pipebombs.college.reut/index.htm (accessed May 8, 2002).

24. Evan Thomas and Mark Hosenball, "Bush: We're at War," *Newsweek*, September 24, 2001, pp. 26–34, quote from p. 33.

25. Erikson, *Wayward Puritans*, p. 11.

26. Edward Said, *Orientalism* (New York: Vintage Books, 1979), p. 54.

27. Said, *Orientalism*, p. 55.

28. Dinesh D'Souza, quoted in Michael Lind, "Three Patriotic Sages Respond to a Defining Moment," *The New York Times on the Web*, July 7, 2002. www.nytimes.com/2002/07/07/books/review/07LINDLT.html (accessed June 7, 2002), p. 3.

29. Dinesh D'Souza, quoted in Thomas Sowell, "Great America," townhall.com, May 30, 2002. www.townhall.com/columnists/thomassowell/printts2002053 (accessed May 30, 2002), p. 1.

30. Thomas Sowell, "Great America," p. 2.

31. Thomas Sowell, "Buchanan Sees 'Death of West,'" *The Chattanooga Times Free Press*, January 18, 2002, p. B7.

32. Sowell, "Buchanan Sees 'Death of West,'" p. B7.

33. These accounting practices are discussed in the next chapter.

34. Thomas Friedman, "The 2 Domes of Belgium," *The New York Times on the Web*, January 27, 2002. www.nytimes.com/2002/01/27/opinion/27FRIE.html?ex = 101315 1995&ei = 1&en = 1e8 b6765f35bbfb (accessed January 27, 2002), p. 2.

35. Friedman, "The 2 Domes of Belgium," p. 2.

36. Fareed Zakaria, "The Politics of Rage: Why Do They Hate Us?" *Newsweek* (Online version), October 15, 2001. www.msnbc.com/news/639057.asp (accessed October 15, 2001), pp. 1–8, quote from pp. 1 = 2.

37. Zakaria, "The Politics of Rage," p. 2.

38. "Robertson Stands behind Remarks on Islam," CNN.com, February 25, 2002. www.cnn.com/2002/US/02/25/robertson.islam.cnna/index/html (accessed February 25, 2002), p. 1.

39. "Robertson Stands behind Remarks on Islam," p. 2.

40. "Southern Baptist Leader Won't Reject Slurs on Islam," CNN.com, June 12, 2002. www.cnn.com/2002/US/06/12/southern.baptist.ap/index.html (accessed June 12, 2002), p. 1.

41. Charles Krauthammer, "The Greater the Evil, the More It Disarms," *Newsweek*, September 24, 2001, pp. 78–79, quote from p. 78.

42. Thomas Friedman, "A Failure to Imagine," *The New York Times on the Web*, May 19, 2002. www.nytimes.com/2002/05/19/opinion/19FRIE.html? (accessed May 19, 2002), p. 2.

43. Said, *Orientalism*.

44. Helen Fein, *Imperial Crime and Punishment: The Massacre at Jallianwalla Bagh and British Judgment, 1919–20* (Honolulu: University of Hawaii Press, 1977); William Gamson, "Hiroshima, the Holocaust, and the Politics of Exclusion: 1994 Presidential Address," *American Sociological Review* 60 (1995): 1–20.

45. "Florida Town Casts out Satan," CNN.com, January 29, 2002. www.cnn.com/2002/US/01/29/town.satan/index.html (accessed January 29, 2002), p. 1.

46. "Man, Fearing Terrorists, Fires at Helicopter," CNN.com, July 20, 2002. www.cnn.com/2002/US/07/20/helicopter.shooting.ap/index.html (accessed July 20, 2002).

47. "Woman Sues Delta over Sex Toy Incident," CNN.com, July 26, 2002. www.cnn.com/2002/TRAVEL/NEWS/07/26/airline.sex.toy.ap/index.html (accessed July 26, 2002).

48. "Woman Says Security Forced Her to Drink Breast Milk," CNN.com, August 12, 2002. www.cnn.com/2002/US/08/08/airport.breastmilk.ap/index.html (accessed August 12, 2002).

49. "Condemnation without Absolutes," *The New York Times on the Web*, October 15, 2001. www.nytimes.com/2001/10/15/opinion/15FISH.html? (accessed October 15, 2001), p. 1.

50. "Stephen Kinzer: Differences between Western and Islamic Cultures," CNN.com, October 9, 2001. www.cnn.com/ . . . 0/09/rec.kinzer.cnna/index.html (accessed October 9, 2001), p. 1.

51. Maureen Dowd, "Sacred Cruelties," *The New York Times on the Web*, April 7, 2002. www.nytimes.com/2002/04/07/opinion/07DOWD.html? (accessed April 7, 2002), p. 2.

52. Marimba Ani, *Yurugu: An African-Centered Critique of European Cultural Thought and Behavior* (Trenton, N.J.: Africa World Press, 1994), pp. 403–04.

53. Gamson, "Hiroshima, the Holocaust," p. 5.

54. We will discuss the discrimination Middle Eastern Americans face in chapter 6 and panethnic identity in chapter 7.

Part II

EVERYDAY EXPERIENCES
WITH DISCRIMINATION

Chapter 4

The Stigma of Brown Skin and "Foreign" Names

Much of what is known about Middle Eastern Americans is based on media stereotypes that feed public anxieties about terrorism. As discussed in chapter 2, a general preoccupation with the terrorist threat posed by Middle Eastern Americans, particularly those of Islamic faith, existed long before September 11, 2001. However, for some laymen, commentators, and policy makers, the tragic events of this date provided the rationale for scrutinizing every aspect of the lives of members of this ethnic minority. In this chapter we describe the strategies that Middle Eastern Americans use to cope with situations in which they are asked to explain themselves. We specifically look at how they use humor, education, or direct confrontation as a way of responding to those who call into question their sense of dignity or personhood.

ACCOUNTING FOR ONE'S IDENTITY

Receiving and wanting attention from others is a natural part of human existence. We interact with other people and would like to be noticed by them. We especially want to be recognized for our achievements (e.g., when we excel in academics or sports). It is not, however, natural to be the focus of others' scorn or suspicion, especially when you have not done anything to evoke the negative attention. For example, it is not natural to be repeatedly subjected to so-called random searches at airports under the eyes of menacing men with hands on their guns simply because of one's appearance, as the first author, Amir, has. That kind of attention is neither desired nor deserved.

Sadly, this is an all too common experience for Middle Eastern Americans. Frequently, they find themselves in social encounters in which they are asked to essentially explain themselves, or to produce an account of their identity. We borrow the term "account" from Stanford Lyman and Marvin Scott to refer to encounters in which a person is called to "explain unanticipated or untoward behavior—whether that behavior is his or her own or that of others, and whether the approximate cause of the statement arises from the actor himself or someone else."[1] Thus accounts are given when an unusual situation or something or someone out of the ordinary is presented.

It is important to note that accounts are conditioned by social factors. As Lyman and Scott point out, there are patterned differences between the people who request, judge, and possibly accept accounts versus those who have to account for themselves. In their words:

> The point with respect to accounts is their right to be requested, their establishment of social identity, and their efficacy to change in accordance with the changing status of the group involved. . . . Situations of account confusion are especially acute when a group is in transition from one status position to another and is undergoing a collective identity crisis. Racial groups provide numerous examples. Before the 1920's some Japanese in America insisted on their identity as "free white persons" in order to circumvent naturalization and franchise barriers, but found few others would accept this definition of their racial status.[2]

In many ways, the case of Middle Eastern Americans is similar to that of Japanese Americans in the first half of the twentieth century. Turmoil in the Middle East and acts of terrorism committed in the United States by Middle Easterners have created an identity crisis for those who were either born or have ancestry from that part of the world. The issue of accountability has become an everyday reality for Middle Eastern people in light of official policies that systematically demand that they explain their every action. This state of heightened awareness is exemplified by a public address by Attorney General John Ashcroft, in which he suggested that if suspected terrorists as much as spit on the sidewalk, they would be arrested.[3] Of course, the term "suspected terrorists" has become so broadly defined that thousands of Middle Eastern men were arrested for minor immigration violations, thousands more were systematically interviewed by FBI agents, and many were deported in the months following the terrorist attacks. It could be said that in a very concrete sense, thousands of Middle Eastern people were officially required to provide accounts.

Furthermore, the current terror warning system, which is intended to alert the public about potential terrorist attacks, acts as an accounting mechanism. As the level of terror is elevated, for example, from yellow to orange, public fears and suspicions are equally increased, and subsequently more Middle Eastern people are put in the position of account-givers. At the same time, the terror alert system calls on ordinary citizens to be "alert" and report anything "suspicious," in a sense, deputizing them as semiofficial account-takers. In a sense, the terror alert system makes the work of holding Middle Eastern–looking people accountable the patriotic duty of every American. In the continuing war on terrorism, the roles of Middle Eastern Americans as account-givers and other citizens as account-takers are firmly established social positions. In the following pages, using data from our interviews, we show how Middle Eastern Americans actively negotiate or account for their identities in everyday life.

For the purpose of data analysis, our interviews and Amir's personal experiences were coded broadly into styles of accounting, or ways in which the respondents and Amir accounted for being Middle Eastern when either implicitly or explicitly required to do so. This approach is similar to Joe Feagin and Karyn McKinney's "resistance strategies" in their analysis of how blacks cope with racist incidents or racist situations.[4] Feagin and McKinney found that African Americans have learned a repertoire of coping mechanisms, both through personal experience and through collective memory.[5] Despite the fact that many white Americans believe that people of color react quickly or always with anger to discrimination, Feagin and McKinney's research showed that African Americans choose carefully from this complex set of responses each time they face a discriminatory incident. The repertoire includes two main types of responses: attitudinal coping mechanisms and action-oriented resistance strategies.[6] Attitudinal coping mechanisms reported by the African American respondents included being always prepared for discrimination, avoiding internalization of the discrimination or of feelings of anger and bitterness, knowing oneself, and using spirituality and mental withdrawal. The respondents also discussed more active resistance strategies. Some of these included verbal confrontation, educating whites, protesting through formal channels, using humor, and physical withdrawal.[7]

Several of these resistance strategies described by Feagin and McKinney are similar to the accounting practices of our Middle Eastern American respondents. In the following sections, excerpts from our interviews are presented in the form of encounter stories from the respondents' and Amir's everyday experiences. Several styles of accounting emerge from the analysis: humorous accounting, educational accounting, confrontational accounting, and passing.

Humorous Accounting

When faced with questions about their ethnic identity, sometimes respondents use humor to present themselves. Consider, for example, the following cases that involve accounting for Middle Eastern–sounding names. A contractor named Ali[8] explains how he uses humor when questions about his name are raised:

> Amir: Do you get any reactions about your name? Like people asking you what kind of name is that?
> Ali: Sometimes they do; sometimes they don't. Sometimes, if they haven't met me or if they are sending me correspondence, they think it's a lady's name and a lot of correspondence comes in Ms. Ali. They think I'm either Alison or something like that. Nowadays, when my name comes up [in face-to-face contacts with clients], I use my sense of humor. For example, when they can't spell my name or ask questions about it, I say, "I'm the brother of Muhammad Ali, the boxer."

Another respondent, whose first name "Ladan" (the name of a flower in Persian) brings up unwelcome and troubling associations with the notorious terrorist Osama bin Laden, tells this story about how she used humor with an inquisitive customer:

> Amir: With the name Ladan, do you run into any problems?
> Ladan: Where I work [at a department store] we all wear nametags, with the name Ladan very clearly spelled out L A D A N. And this old couple, they approached me and I was very friendly with them—I usually chitchat with my customers. And he started asking me all these questions like, "You're so pretty, where're you from?" [I respond,] "I'm from Iran." [He says,] "What?" [I repeat,] "I'm from Iran." So he asks, "What's your name?" And I say, "Ladan." So he bent down to read my nametag and he just looked at me with a funny face and asked, "Are you related to Bin Laden?"
> Amir: Was he joking?
> Ladan: No, he was not. But I did joke back to him and I said, "Yes, he's my cousin and actually he's coming over for dinner tonight." [She chuckles.]
> Amir: So, when this sort of thing happens, you use humor to deal with it?
> Ladan: Yeah, I do, because otherwise, if I don't turn it into a joke or a laughing mood, I get upset. I get really, really offended.
> Amir: So what was this guy's reaction? Did he laugh with you?
> Ladan: When this guy realized my name is Ladan and I'm from Iran, he changed his attitude. He became reserved and he even went one step backward. When I noticed he was uncomfortable, I completed the transaction with his wife and let them leave as soon as they wanted.

Note that in this case her use of humor does not necessarily result in the proverbial "happy ending," or any kind of clearly discernible resolution. The customer turned away and ended the interaction. Clearly, an account was called for and one was given in a way that allowed Ladan to highlight the ludicrousness of the account-taker's assumptions and his right to solicit an account.

The following is the story of how Amir accounted for his name using humor. This encounter took place at a voting precinct in a small town in Pennsylvania on Election Day, November 14, 2002. He was there to vote in the midterm elections. The encounter begins with the examination of his photo identification.

> The election supervisor: Okay . . . this is a hard one! [squinting at my driver's license] You're ready? [alerting her coworker] It says "AMAR." . . . It's "A" . . . *I wait, silent and motionless, as the three old women probe my ID. I fear that any sudden movement might send people running out of the building screaming for help. "Say something!" I scream in my head. The words finally roll out of my mouth:*
> Amir: You know, my dad gave me a long name, hoping that it would guarantee my success in life. [They laugh.]
> Election Supervisor: Well, you must be a doctor because you sure sign your name like one.
> Amir: [I can't resist] Actually, I am a doctor. . . . So maybe my dad had the right idea after all.

Here humor is a method of introduction. It was not clear to Amir what the election supervisors thought about him, but he did sense that there were unanswered questions, an account had to be given for who he was. Note that the immediate substance of Amir's identity was not in question—they had his photo identification in front of them and most likely could tell from his swarthy appearance that he was not a native Pennsylvanian. Humorous accounting allowed Amir to communicate something more important about himself than simply his name, namely, that he is from a "normal" family that aspires to the universal notion of "success in life"; and that he is aware that there are concerns about his identity and is capable of responding to them in a mutually sensible way. In humorous accounting the substance of the account is incidental, as it is deliberately trivialized. Middle Eastern Americans use this way of accounting as a way of acknowledging the need to explain themselves while at the same time subtly mocking the necessity of the encounter.

Educational Accounting

Sometimes accounting takes on a deliberate pedagogical form. In such cases Middle Eastern Americans assume the role of educators, informing and instructing their fellow citizens about relevant topics. For example, in response to suspicions and antagonism from his neighbors, a Pakistani Muslim, Hassan, did a sort of door-to-door educational accounting:

> After September 11, I walked the street the whole week and talked to every single one of my neighbors for at least 3 hours. And one of my neighbors—his brother was

in Tower Two and he got out, and his mother was there and she was *furious* with
Muslims and me. And we were there for three hours, my wife, my kids, her [the
neighbor], her son and her other son that came out of the World Trade Center—he
had come down by the time the buildings came down. And I was like, "Look, that's
not Islam. That's not who Muslims are. Ask your son, what type of person am I?
What type of person is my wife? Do I oppress my wife? Do I beat my wife? Have
you ever heard me say anything extreme before?" . . . They all know I don't drink,
they all know that I pray five times a day, they all know I fast during the month of
Ramadan. At the end of Ramadan, we have a big party and invite everyone over to
help celebrate the end of fast. This year, they'll all probably fast one day with me
so they can feel what it's like.

Hassan's approach is proactive, addressing potential questions before they
are explicitly opened for accounting. In some ways, this case of educational
accounting is similar to what John P. Hewitt and Randall Stokes call "disclaimers" or a "prospective construction of meaning" in an attempt to avoid
being categorized in an undesirable way.[9] In the above excerpt, Hassan tries
to transform the relationship between him, as an account-giver, and the
account-takers who suspect him of being an "evildoer."

Middle Eastern Americans have to be selective about which inquiries are
worthy of an educational account. For example, an Iranian respondent, Mitra,
speaks of how she filters the inquiries about her culture and identity before
answering them:

If they ask about the government or the senate over there [Iran], I don't know anything about it. I know who the president is, but they ask me about the senate or the
name of the senator over there, I don't know. Since I don't know I'm not going to
get involved. I'll say I don't know or I'm not interested. If they say, "Oh, you are
from *that* country!" or "You are from the Middle East and you are a terrorist," those
kinds of comments I'm not going to get into. I'll just say, "*No*, I'm not." But if they
ask me about the culture I'll tell them, "Alright," and inform them about it—as
much as I know.

Mitra, while inclined to assume the role of an educator, is not willing or prepared to respond to every question. Part of her educational accounting strategy involves evaluating the degree of her expertise on the subject and the
tone of the questions. As she says, if the account-taker begins with accusations, such as "you are a terrorist," the only reasonable reply might be to
deny the accusation and end the interaction.

Educational accounting is a common strategy for Middle Eastern Muslim
women who wear the hijab.[10] Many of them are approached by strangers who
ask questions like: "Isn't it hot under there?" "Does that come in many col-
ors?" or simply "Why do you wear that?" or "Are you going to make *them*
[referring to the ten- and twelve-year-old girls who were standing in a grocery

store line with their mother] wear it too?" Our respondents reported that whenever time and circumstances allowed, they provide detailed accounts based on their religious teachings. Some of these answers include: "I wear it because it is my culture," "I wear it so that you won't stare at my body when you are talking to me," or "It's cooler under my scarf than you think." It should be noted that some of these women did report being verbally harassed or physically attacked (one was pelted with spitballs when she was in high school, another reported that her friend's scarf was pulled off by a teenage boy at a grocery store, and another was repeatedly yelled at "Go home!" by people in passing cars as she walked to her office on campus). However, such overt acts of discrimination were fairly isolated. The pattern for these women was that of perfect strangers literally stopping them on the street and asking questions about the hijab, sometimes so directly as to be rude.

Similarly, as a Middle Eastern sociology professor, Amir is often asked by his students to explain a wide range of topics about the region and Islam, from customs and culture to the mind-set of terrorists. Like Mitra, he evaluates each question before providing an account. For example, a student in his undergraduate criminology seminar began every session with a trivial question about Iran, such as "Do they have trees over there?" At first, Amir provided a detailed educational account whenever asked to do so, even for seemingly inane items. Given the limited time he had to cover the assigned readings, later in the semester it became necessary for Amir to remind his students that he was not paid to educate them about the Middle East; the topic of the course was crime, specifically, the criminogenic aspects of American culture. For those interested in the topic, Amir recommended a trip to the library for references on the Middle East and Iran. In this case, the educational accounting became unfeasible simply because it was consuming too much time and diverting attention from the subject matter at hand.

Indeed, a recurring problem with being Middle Eastern in a professional context is that the process of accounting for oneself (be it educational, humorous, or otherwise) could hinder one's job performance. With rare exceptions, when professional duties and the accounting demands coincide (such as the writing of this book, for example), the work of answering for one's ethnic background and religion could become a considerable chore. Another problem with becoming a "cultural ambassador" is that it tests the limits of the account-giver's knowledge about the topic.[11] The Middle East is a vast and diverse cultural entity representing many people and religions. Unstructured attempts at educating others in everyday encounters inevitably translate into sketchy overgeneralizations. Therefore, while educational accounting may be the most intelligible and productive accounting strategy

for one's identity, it is also the most time-consuming and potentially misleading approach.

Confrontational Accounting

When prompted to provide an account, some Middle Eastern Americans
make their anger and frustrations with the encounter explicitly known. We
refer to this as confrontational accounting. This strategy involves providing
information while at the same time directly challenging the other's right and
rationale to request it. For example, consider how a young Iranian woman
speaks of her experiences with a coworker:

> She [the coworker] would tell me, "I don't know which country you come from but
> in America we do it like this or that." I let it go because I was older than her and we
> had to work together. . . . But one day I pulled her aside and I told her, "For your
> information where I come from has a much older culture. And what I know, you
> can't even imagine. So why don't you go get some more education. And if you
> mention this thing again—'my country is this your country is that'—I'm going to
> take it to management and they're going to fire you or they're going to fire me."
> And that was it.

Here the accounting is not intended to repair the interaction or to restore it to
a state of equilibrium. On the contrary, the goal is to explicitly challenge
the conventional format of the encounter. Instead of aiming for consensus,
confrontational accounting foregrounds divergent and conflicting viewpoints
as it signals the account-giver's objection to the entire affair.

Confrontational strategies are used especially in times when the accounting, while seemingly a rational concern for everyone involved, crosses the
boundary of basic fairness in the eyes of the account-giver. Specifically, Middle Eastern Americans who are subjected to profiling may become confrontational in response to the practice. For example, when Amir learned that unlike
himself, his white colleagues were not asked to show ID cards upon entering
the campus gym, he felt justified in becoming confrontational. In one
instance, while pulling out his ID card from his wallet, he asked the woman
at the front counter why his white faculty friend, who had just walked in
ahead of him, was not asked to present an ID. She explained that she had not
noticed the other person entering or she would have asked that person to do
the same.

This encounter highlights the risky nature of confrontational accounting
for both parties involved in the interaction. At its core, this strategy counters
an account request with another: They ask for his ID and Amir asks why he
should be the only one subjected to this rule. In turn, the other side presents

their account and so on. What follows is a chain of accounts and counteraccounts possibly escalating into a formal dispute. Though it is possible that in some cases, when confronted, the account-takers simply back down and cease their efforts, it is just as likely that they intensify their demands, especially when they are backed by policies or other public mandates.

Since September 11, when flying, Amir has been very conscious of this fact. While Amir is certain that he has been singled out for security checks, he fears that objecting and confronting these practices would lead to additional hardships (i.e., a direct confrontation with law enforcement agents in which they have the greater authority and likelihood to win). Even after boarding the plane, he is often questioned by those seated next to him. Their inquiries typically begin with the ordinary (i.e., What is your name?) and proceed to the very personal and official matters (i.e., Are you a U.S. citizen? Do you have a green card?). In these encounters, Amir feels that to refuse to answer or to confront the other's right to ask about personal and private details of his life will lead to other more serious accounting demands.

So for Middle Eastern Americans confrontational accounting is a risky approach that could, on the one hand, rid them of a potentially humiliating process, or, on the other hand, generate additional requests and demands. Of course, confrontational accounting, when used by large numbers, can become a type of mass rebellion, as with African Americans and the passive resistance component of the Civil Rights Movement of the 1960s.

Passing or Avoiding Accounts

Sometimes, the best accounting strategy is to put oneself in a position not to have to give an account at all.[12] One way of conceptualizing such strategies is to think of them as attempts at "passing."[13] We view passing as a strategy for eliminating the need for accounting for one's identity. For many Middle Eastern Americans, passing is accomplished by manipulating their appearance. The stereotypical image of a Middle Eastern person roughly translates into someone with dark hair, large facial features, swarthy skin, non-European foreign accent, and beards in the case of men and veils and scarves in the case of women. Faced with these stereotypes, some respondents consciously altered their looks to avoid anything that might associate them with being Middle Eastern. Ironically the ultimate dubious achievement in this game of passing is hearing something like the following: "I know you are from Iran, but you don't *really* look or sound Middle Eastern. . . . You could be Hispanic for all I know."

In fact, some Middle Eastern Americans try to pass by trading their own ethnic identity with a less controversial one. The simplest way to do this is to move to an ethnically diverse region. Some of the respondents from South Florida stated that one reason they don't experience negative episodes of ethnic accounting is because they are thought to be Hispanic. For example, an Iranian woman was asked what kind of Spanish she was speaking when she was at a shopping mall having a conversation in Farsi with her teenage daughter. Another Iranian man tried to pass as Italian by placing an Italian flag vanity license plate on his car. As a general rule, displaying Western or patriotic symbols (e.g., an American flag) at work, in front of one's house, or on one's car are ways of avoiding ethnic accounting for Middle Eastern Americans. After September 11, Amir's neighbors gave him an American flag to place outside his apartment for his own safety. In a sense, the symbols of patriotism become accounting statements in their own right; they become declarations of loyalty to "the American culture."

Another strategy for passing is to give an ambiguous account in response to ethnic identity questions. For example, an Egyptian man in response to questions about his country of origin states that he is Coptic (the designation of people from pre-Islamic Egypt). He noted that in many cases the account-takers find it too embarrassing to ask follow-up questions and therefore pretend to know what "Coptic" means and drop the subject altogether. Iranians create this kind of ambiguity by stating that they are Persians (the designation of ancient Iranians).

Accounts are also circumvented by stating the name of the city of one's ancestral origin rather than one's country of birth. Amir once told a college classmate that he was from Tehran. To his astonishment, his classmate asked, "Is that near Paris?" Changing one's name is another way to pass. Some respondents change their Muslim names (e.g., Hossein) to typical American names (e.g., Michael). When asked why he changed his name, one person explained that he was tired of people slamming down the phone when he made inquiries about jobs. Some change from widely known ethnic-sounding names to lesser-known ones as in the change from Hossein to Sina. Finally, attention to clothes and grooming are equally important considerations for those who want to pass. For example, wearing jeans and having a clean shave draw less attention and lead to fewer occasions to have to account for oneself.

Passing strategies for Middle Eastern Americans are not without complications. To start with, for some, passing is tantamount to "selling out" (i.e., giving up one's native culture in favor of another). More important, for Middle Eastern Americans, passing has been construed by the media as an extension of an evil terrorist plot. After September 11, numerous media reports referred to how the hijackers were specifically instructed to wear jeans and shave their faces. Therefore, rather than being viewed as a sign of cultural assimilation, Middle Eastern Americans' conspicuous attempts at passing are sometimes considered part of a diabolical plan to deceive and destroy Americans.

Finally, especially where passing for Hispanic is concerned, Middle Eastern Americans face direct opposition and disavowals from some members of the Hispanic community. On the one hand, according to some of our respondents in South Florida, Middle Eastern Americans have been "outed" by Hispanics who point them out in public and announce to everyone that they are really Middle Eastern and not to be confused with Hispanics. On the other hand, Hispanics are self-consciously changing their self-presentation as to not be mistaken for Middle Eastern. For example, a Mexican man was warned by his wife not to wear a certain hat for fear that it made him look "Middle Eastern."

NOT A KNEE-JERK REACTION

Our respondents did not go off half-cocked, as it were. In dealing with the situations they faced, they tried to select the most reasonable reaction. It is important to note that these respondents are not passive. Their strategies are about fighting back, about speaking in a way that preserves their dignity in the face of intimidation, scrutiny, and insults. Having said that, for ethnic minorities there are situations when there is no opportunity for giving an account or talking back. For example, when a man driving by in his truck yelled at Amir, "Ragheads go home!" he had no opportunity to choose an accounting strategy or offer an account. In the same way, when the respondents in this study report being assaulted, the concept of accounting does not apply. Clearly, such aggressive or violent actions cannot be classified as requests for accounts. These are statements, declarations, or actions that by definition exclude any kind of dialogue.

The accounting strategies of Middle Eastern Americans discussed earlier also underline an important dimension of belonging to a stigmatized group. At its core, being an outcast is about having to explain oneself above and beyond what "normal" members of society are required to do. The relationship between an account-giver and an account-receiver is a relationship between a dominant and a subordinate. One party is entitled to ask questions like, "Where are you from and why are you here?" whereas the other party is expected to obediently provide legitimate replies.

This is not a mere exercise in social roles, but particularly in the context of the War on Terror, this relationship has very practical consequences for Middle Eastern Americans. Their lives have to be transparent. They have to be mindful of the fact that their attempts to protect their privacy could be misread as a clandestine plan. Furthermore, legislation, such as the PATRIOT Act, can reinforce the lower status of this minority group in relation to the white majority. In essence, the roles are becoming more institutionalized, slowly expanding beyond informal encounters and entering the realm of official policy.

NOTES

1. Stanford Lyman and Marvin Scott, *A Sociology of the Absurd* (Dix Hills, N.Y.: General Hall, 1989), p. 112.

2. Lyman and Scott, *A Sociology of the Absurd*, p. 151.

3. Siobhan Gorman, "National Security: The Ashcroft Doctrine," *National Journal* 34 (2002): 3712–19.

4. Joe Feagin and Karyn McKinney, *The Many Costs of Racism* (Lanham, Md.: Rowman & Littlefield, 2003): 147–79.

5. Feagin and McKinney, *The Many Costs of Racism*, p. 119.

6. Feagin and McKinney, *The Many Costs of Racism*, p. 123.

7. Feagin and McKinney, *The Many Costs of Racism*, pp. 124–67.

8. Most names have been fictionalized to protect the identity of respondents. In cases where it is necessary to use an actual first name, every effort is made to disguise other personal identifying information about a respondent.

9. John P. Hewitt and Randall Stokes. "Disclaimers," *American Sociological Review* 40 (1975) :1–11, specifically pp. 1–3.

10. Islamic word for modesty in dress that applies to both men and women. In the case of many Muslim women living in the United States, this means wearing a scarf that covers the hair and the neck, as well as wearing loose-fitting garments so that the outlines of the body are not exaggerated.

11. Bruce Jacobs, *Race Manners: Navigating the Minefield between Black and White Americans* (New York: Arcade Publishing, 1999), pp. 144–48.

12. See Lyman and Scott, *A Sociology of the Absurd*, pp. 126–27.

13. Erving Goffman, *Stigma: Notes on the Management of Spoiled Identity* (Englewood Cliffs, N.J.: Prentice Hall, 1963).

Chapter 5

The "Thin Veneer of Civility": Relearning the American Dream

The goal of this chapter is twofold. On the one hand, it lists the history of other ethnic and racial minorities in the United States (i.e., non-Protestant European immigrant, African, Native, Asian, and Latino Americans) to highlight the commonalties between Middle Eastern Americans and other groups that have come before them. The second part of this chapter shows what the "American Dream" means to Middle Eastern Americans as they redefine their understanding of this concept in light of their experiences with discrimination.

SIMILARITIES IN EXPERIENCE: MIDDLE EASTERN AMERICANS AND OTHER PEOPLE OF COLOR

The only black person in the school . . . was . . . the school science teacher. . . . Her poise radiated an inner beauty and self-confidence rarely found in any of the other teachers. She recalled vignettes from a childhood shaped by racial discrimination and poverty. . . . She was admired and loved by the children in her classes. Yet once in a while I would hear that some kid, usually a boy, rejected her kindness and unexpectedly hurled the word "nigger" at her in the middle of class. . . . As far as I could tell, such outbursts didn't happen often, but they always left me wondering about my own place in the neighborhood and in America as a whole.[1]

Middle Eastern Americans' experiences in the United States, while in some ways distinct, are part of a historical pattern of discrimination against people of color. Joe Feagin points out in *Racist America* that whites in the United States have most often judged newcomers along a "white-to-black status continuum," assuming those closest to white are more civilized and those who are darker are less civilized.[2] To this white–black continuum, sometimes another dimension is added, that of "foreignness."[3] Thus, some groups are judged not only on how "white" or "black" they appear, but also on how "foreign" they seem—which could be signaled by accent, clothing, food, and various home country traditions. It is likely Middle Eastern Americans are subject to being judged not only in terms of their fit along the white–black continuum but also for their degree of "foreignness," particularly in the post–September 11 United States.

Non-Protestant European Immigrants

The Anglo-Saxon Protestant settlers of the United States in some way excluded or discriminated against every group who was different from them, racially, ethnically, or religiously. Some groups, of course, have been more easily able to overcome this discrimination and assimilate into society. For example, Irish Americans faced prejudice and discrimination based on their Catholicism as well as their ethnicity when they first arrived in the United States. Interestingly, they were considered a separate "race," and were stereotyped as lazy, promiscuous, hostile, drunkards, less-than-human, unintelligent, and immoral—many of the same stereotypes applied to people of color and new immigrants today.[4] Irish were denied jobs based on these stereotypes. Later Southern European and non-Protestant European immigrants also faced similar discrimination, particularly the Italians. However, within a few generations, European immigrants were able to "become" white through a process of relinquishing some of their more visible ethnic traits, as well as through identifying with elite whites rather than with people of color along class lines. White immigrants have, since this time, always had an easier assimilation experience than have immigrants of color, because of their placement on the white–black continuum in our racist society. Still, the fact that even white immigrants faced difficulties shows that ours is a society that has historically subjected all newcomers and "others" to racism and discrimination.

African Americans

Some have placed the African American experience as the paradigmatic experience of discrimination in the United States.[5] Racism is an ideological system that was developed to justify the enslavement of African Americans and their use for free labor. To some degree it also justified the killing of Native Americans and taking of their land. Feagin writes that this system has "been extended and tailored for each new non-European group brought into the sphere of white domination. Thus, U.S. society is not a multiplicity of disconnected racisms directed at peoples of color."[6] However, African Americans were the only group ever brought to the United States involuntarily. They are the only group ever highlighted in the Constitution for treatment as less-than-human and to have been legally enslaved in the United States. Approximately six to seven million black Americans were enslaved in North America between 1619 and 1865.[7] Even after slavery ended, African Americans lived under legal segregation for nearly another century, until the 1960s. During this time, they suffered much brutality, including thousands of lynchings, which went unpunished.

Today, the effects of 350 years of oppression remain. Compared to 12 percent of the general population, 23 percent of African Americans live in poverty. As of 1999, black families were four times as likely as white families to live in poverty. Since the 1950s, African American family income has not risen above 62 percent of white family income.[8] For African Americans, the difference in wealth between them and white Americans is even more telling than difference in income. Because of persistent discrimination, African Americans have had very little opportunity to build up intergenerational assets. Because of this, wealth does not get transferred from parents to children, and black families tend to have much lower net worth than do white families with the same income. In a *New York Times* editorial, sociologist Dalton Conley summarized the wealth gap as of 2003:

> The typical white family enjoys a net worth that is more than eight times that of its black counterpart, according to the economist Edward Wolff. Even at equivalent income levels, gaps remain large. Among families earning less than $15,000 a year, the median African-American family has a net worth of zero, while the corresponding white family has $10,000 in equity. The typical white family earning $40,000 annually has a nest egg of around $80,000. Its black counterpart has about half that amount.
>
> This equity inequity is partly the result of the head start whites enjoy in accumulating and passing on assets. Some economists estimate that up to 80 percent of lifetime wealth accumulation results from gifts from earlier generations, ranging from the down payment on a home to a bequest from a parent.[9]

Lack of wealth and income mean that African Americans still experience unequal access to opportunities and resources. For example, although the gap in educational achievement between whites and African Americans has closed in the last four decades, recent evidence suggests that schools are resegregating, due to de facto housing segregation.[10] Because of this, many African American children are attending underfunded schools and thus are receiving education that is not of the same quality as white middle-class sub-urban students. This leaves them unprepared for college and the job market. High infant mortality rates and low life expectancy rates compared to whites also suggest that African Americans do not have the same access to quality health care as do white Americans.[11] Even middle-class African Americans report facing discrimination in the workplace that takes a toll on their psychological and physical health as well as on their families and communities.[12] All of these factors point to not only the effects of past discrimination but also to continuing racism. It is this systematic racism, in the form of a white–black continuum, that is applied to other incoming groups. In this sense, one could say that we live in a *colorist* racist society, in which people are judged according to how much they resemble white Europeans, or conversely, how much they resemble African Americans, the group against whom the most pervasive and long-standing discrimination has been practiced.

Native Americans

Native Americans were the first non-European group to face discrimination from European Americans in the United States. Estimates of their population prior to contact with Europeans are around two to five million, but some argue it was much larger. Even working with this conservative estimate, the population decline to around 200,000 after contact can be viewed as a near genocidal decrease.[13] After this near-genocide, Native Americans' land, their most valuable resource, was taken through multiple broken treaties. To this day, Native Americans have never been repaid for the land that was taken from them. They lost not only land but also the rights to valuable resources that were on the land. Thus, vast amounts of individual and tribal wealth were stolen from Native Americans by the U.S. government. Today, Native Americans are the most impoverished ethnic group in the United States, in part due to their isolation on or near reservations.[14] They are also still occupationally segregated in low-wage labor and have some of the most poor-quality housing of any group in the United States. Native Americans are still fighting for land rights, and for respect of their ethnic and religious symbols and images. For example, some Native American activists protest the use of stereotypical images of Native Americans as team mascots.

Asian Americans

The Asian American experience has been shaped in large part by U.S. labor needs and by political interactions with Asian countries, both of which have influenced immigration policies directed toward Asian people. Although

Asian Americans have at times been viewed as "honorary whites" or a "model minority group," they have not always been treated as such.[15] Chinese Americans were the first non-European group to immigrate in large numbers, primarily to work in mining and on the transcontinental railroad. During this time, Chinese workers began to face stereotyping, and the images that were applied to them were many of the same ones that were applied to blacks and are now applied to Middle Eastern Americans. They were portrayed as savage, immoral, and childlike, and sometimes even referred to as "niggers." When the economy faltered, European immigrants began to scapegoat Chinese workers for their loss of jobs. Eventually, Chinese began to be distinguished from African Americans, as they took on the additional element of being culturally alien, and in 1882, the Chinese Exclusion Act was passed to restrict Chinese immigration.[16] Finally during World War II, when the Chinese were a wartime ally, a very small immigration quota of 105 a year was set for their immigration.

While the Chinese were excluded, at least for a time Japanese and Filipinos were allowed to immigrate to fill the labor shortage left by the Chinese. Soon the Japanese would also face insidious institutionalized discrimination. First, because of anti-Asian sentiment, the Gentleman's Agreement of 1907 was passed to restrict Japanese immigration. Other immigration acts followed that were, in part, directed against Asian immigrants. Besides having immigration legislation passed against them, the Japanese have undergone other institutionalized racism. They are the only group ever to have been placed in internment camps in the United States. Beginning in March 1942 and lasting until January 1945, because of the bombing of Pearl Harbor, anyone at least one-eighth Japanese was relocated to internment camps, approximately 110,000 people.[17] Obviously, the dimension of foreignness that had begun to be salient with the experience of Chinese Americans was at the forefront of the racism experienced by the Japanese during World War II. Although citizens of the United States, Japanese Americans were still viewed as "foreign" or "alien" based on their membership in an ethnic group other than European American. The recent experiences of Middle Eastern Americans with heightened surveillance, although not as extreme as that of Japanese Americans during World War II, demonstrate how the treatment of ethnic others in the United States is repeated.

Today, Asian Americans, like Middle Eastern American groups, are in a unique position among U.S. ethnic groups. They have an average family income that is higher than that of white Americans. However, for Asian Americans, this is because children tend to live with their parents longer, thus contributing to the family income, and families are in general larger.[18] So more people work in a home to make the same income that a white family makes. Additionally, although many of the early, more established immigrant groups have been quite economically successful, more recent Asian immigrants, such as those from Southeast Asia, tend to be more impoverished. Indeed, many of them live below the poverty line.

Thus to suggest that Asians generally are a "model minority" is misleading. Another reason this image is misleading is because although Asian Americans have been generally successful in obtaining employment, and indeed a high percentage are employed in the professions, they still face an occupational "glass ceiling." Asian Americans are able to achieve only a certain level in business and the professions and then find that they are limited in their success. Many times, this is because of the perception that Asian people are technically oriented but do not have good social or language skills.

The model-minority myth can contribute to backlash against Asian Americans. In recent years, Asian Americans have faced both physical violence and other types of discrimination based on white resentment of their status as supposed models of achievement. For example, some colleges and universities are now setting "reverse quotas" on how many Asian students they allow in because of white resentment of their educational success.[19] Despite the fact that some argue Asian Americans have attained the status of "near whites," their "foreignness" continues to set them apart as the objects of discrimination.

Latino Americans

Like Asian Americans and Middle Eastern Americans, Latino Americans are a panethnic group made up of many different national-origin groups, with different experiences in the United States. Mexican Americans and Puerto Ricans particularly have been affected by the ideology of manifest destiny, the idea that it is God's divine will that European Americans expand their territory as much as possible. The Monroe Doctrine expressed the idea that the Western Hemisphere should be one arena for manifest destiny, and it subsequently justified invasion of Central and South American countries.[20] Mexican Americans' first contact with the United States was through confrontation and conquest, after which Mexico lost much of its land and culture, despite the Treaty of Guadalupe Hidalgo signed in 1848.[21] Puerto Rico was annexed after the Spanish American War in 1898 and then became a U.S. commonwealth in 1952.[22] Puerto Ricans have thus held a distinct status as U.S. citizens.

Cuban Americans first began to immigrate after Fidel Castro came to power in the 1960s. A second group immigrated in the 1980s, as a result of Castro's emptying of prisons and mental hospitals. The two groups were received very differently in the United States. The first group had been political refugees during the height of the Cold War, economically well-off, entrepreneurs, light-skinned, and seen by some as temporary residents. They were given generous resettlement benefits, including bilingual programs. The second group, however, was poorer, darker-skinned, and stigmatized as criminals. Their reception was the opposite of the first group—in fact, in 1980 an English-only ordinance was passed in Florida to reverse the bilingual programs.[23] The experience of Cuban Americans with how ethnic identifiability as well as political climate influences the reception of immigrants in many ways parallels the Middle Eastern American experience.

Today, Latino Americans have passed African Americans as the largest minority group in the United States, and they are the fastest-growing ethnic group. Because of this, it is of grave concern that two of the largest groups, Mexicans and Puerto Ricans, have a poverty rate that is three times that of white Americans. The median household income of Latinos is 76 percent that of white Americans. Educational achievement is lower than for non-Latinos and is lowest for the largest group, Mexican Americans (51 percent graduate high school, compared to 88.4 percent of non-Latinos; 6.9 percent graduate college, compared to 28.1 percent of non-Latinos), largely because they are concentrated in rural areas and move frequently to work in agricultural jobs. Life expectancy gaps between Latinos and non-Latinos show differential access to health care.[24]

Latino Americans face discrimination based on their growing numbers. Because many choose to maintain their cultural traditions, and specifically retain the Spanish language, many other Americans view them as a cultural threat. Again, foreignness that sets a group apart also marks it for discrimination. Physical similarities between Latinos and Middle Eastern Americans may have exacerbated Latino Americans' problems with prejudice as they are further scrutinized in public places.

Although Latinos are beginning to take their place in mainstream America, they still face much discrimination. Mexican Americans, particularly, consistently contend with prejudices and stereotyping surrounding their immigration status—many people assume that most Mexicans are illegal immigrants. Many Puerto Ricans, concentrated in the cities, not only must deal with the poverty that goes along with housing segregation but also consistently face discrimination from law enforcement through racial profiling, since many are racially perceived as "black." Additionally, based in the cities, Puerto Ricans are often viewed as a drain on the welfare system.[25] Finally, although first-wave Cuban immigrants have been relatively successful, even they have not risen to the levels of success that white immigrants have. Recent Cuban immigrants face the same discrimination as other Latino immigrants. All Latino Americans are still underrepresented politically, particularly at the national level, although this is slowly changing.

Racist Images and Stereotyping

One day, when I was five, I was sitting on the front sidewalk playing with some rocks—an innocent child not knowing what kind of hatred lurked in the world. The teenage girl who lived next door approached me and started calling me a camel jockey. Not only did she call me this, she started cheering, like a cheerleader does, about my being a camel jockey. . . . I remember sitting on the sidewalk staring at her in awe, not really understanding what she was talking about, but realizing that when she said "camel jockey," she was saying it at me and that it was a very negative word. I also remember sensing her disdain when she looked at me.

I sometimes wonder about bigoted people like our neighbors who believe that they are superior to others and have the right to hate immigrants. Do they know that they live in America? Do people have to keep reminding them what that means? Are some people just so stupid that they think immigrants traveled to their exclusive homeland to live, and not to America? This country is only about two hundred years old. It is a baby. The only people who have a right to be angered at immigrants being here are Native Americans.[26]

One of the most challenging aspects of being an ethnic or racial minority in America is dealing with dehumanizing stereotypes. Fears of ethnic others are manifested in cultural notions that they possess every characteristic that we do not. These characteristics then become stereotypes, and one can trace through the history of the United States how many of the same images are applied to different groups. The images are created to apply to each new "alien" group the opposite characteristics of what white Europeans like to think that they possess. For example, based on a content analysis of several hundred cartoons with Arab characters, Ronald Stockton concludes that:

[I]mages of Arabs cannot be seen in isolation but are primarily derivative, rooted in a core of hostile archetypes that our culture applies to those with whom it clashes . . . two hostile archetypes are particularly significant. The first was traditionally targeted at Africans, who were deemed to be inherently inferior in culture and biology; the second was traditionally targeted at Jews and describe peoples or nations with historically advanced cultures but some believed to be pathologically in error because of some inherent flaw or trait. The two . . . are . . . called racism and anti-Semitism.[27]

Stockton also mentions that images of the Japanese resemble cartoon images of Arabs. Analyzing these cartoon images, he finds several themes that parallel stereotypes of other groups: sexual depravity, creature analogies, similar derogatory physiological and psychological traits, savage leaders, deceitfulness, secret power, and being enemies of God in a war of darkness against light.[28]

Middle Eastern Americans have been characterized as irrational, barbaric, cruel, and sometimes cunning—stereotypes that originate from anti-Semitic biases. Concurrently, other racist epithets are used to describe Middle Eastern Americans, such as "sand niggers," which obviously is inspired by antiblack images.[29] Consider, for example, the following passage, in which a Middle Eastern American man from Detroit reflects on the pain of being called a "sand nigger" and its commonality with the African American experience:

> The first time I heard "sand nigger" was in the hometown of the great carmaker. I cried and beat up the kid with the big mouth. On a drive to the supermarket with my father, waiting at a stop sign, a young man crossing the street noticed the color of our skin and begged us to go back home. At the factories my uncles argued that "sand nigger" was reserved for the soul brothers from the Middle East. [One uncle] explained that the black assembly line workers said they were all immigrants, that when he arrived in Detroit on a plane from Beirut, they arrived to the city on buses and trains from Alabama, and that both were "niggers." But only they could call each other that. Charlie, the factory rats would warn, never let anyone call you a camel jockey.[30]

Thus as a whole, the experiences of Middle Eastern Americans are similar to other ethnic minority groups in that they are placed somewhere in the racist continuum that supposedly marks the distinction between white Americans and people of color. Some of the same notions about exotic others are applied again and again to different minority groups. The ideas are the same and so are the tragic consequences in the everyday lives of their targets.

With this overall orientation on ethnic and racial minorities in the United States, in this chapter, using interview data, we show how discrimination impacts the everyday lives of Middle Eastern Americans.

DEFINING DISCRIMINATION

As we began our data collection, we soon noticed a surprising pattern with many of our respondents. Some of the items on our list of questions specifically dealt with the degree of discrimination experienced by our respondents. We began with the general question: "What skills do you rely on to deal with or confront discrimination?" In answer to this item, some of our respondents indicated that they had never experienced anything that could be defined as "discrimination." However, in the follow-up questions, the same respondents would go on to report specific incidents where they lost jobs, were harassed, or even physically attacked because of their ethnicity. Given that all of our respondents were fluent in English (75 percent of them were college-educated naturalized citizens), we could not explain away this discrepancy as a simple language barrier. Our respondents' unfamiliarity with the vocabulary and motives of ethnic discrimination did not reflect linguistic misunderstanding but deeper cultural conventions about what discrimination is and when or how it should be discussed.

There are several possible reasons why respondents were reluctant to admit or recognize that they had in fact experienced discrimination. One possibility is that like other people of color in the United States, in order to survive, Middle Eastern Americans must try to overlook much of the discrimination that they face.[31] Too much time and energy would be spent dealing with discrimination if one was to attend to each instance, even if the attention given were only mental. Writing about this point in regards to African Americans, Feagin and Sikes state: "Much discrimination is overlooked if possible. There is much white hostility that blacks must ignore just to reduce the pain and to survive. If one can name racial discrimination something else, it may not hurt as much."[32] To be sure, some African Americans use "blocking out" or denial as a strategy for dealing with discrimination.[33] Some of our Middle Eastern respondents may do the same.

Some other reasons that Middle Eastern Americans may deny the existence of discrimination are similar to those of Latino and Asian Americans. Nestor Rodriguez suggests that for some Latinos, particularly those of high income, the pressure of trying to assimilate as closely as possible to being white may cause them to deny any discrimination that they face.[34] This could be similar to the experience of some Middle Eastern Americans, whose belief in the American Dream (discussed later) and their desire to assimilate into mainstream culture are incongruent with the discrimination they suffer.

Finally, some suggest that recent Latinos and Asian immigrants may not recognize or discuss discrimination because they are more concerned with fundamental necessities in their lives such as finding a job, learning the language, and putting food on their family's table. They may even be aware that discrimination exists, but they may see it as one of the expected costs of being an immigrant and have other higher priorities.[35] This also seems a possibility for some of our Middle Eastern American respondents, who, working hard to make a life for their families in the United States, very likely do not pause to think about discrimination, or, if they do, believe it to be more of a matter to be dealt with silently than discussed.

Thus, the experience of discrimination is not self-evident to ethnic or racial minorities. In this section we review how we negotiated the language of discrimination with our respondents.

NEGOTIATING A WORKING
DEFINITION OF DISCRIMINATION

For our Middle Eastern American respondents, the word "discrimination" seemed to have a narrow application. The experiences they described easily fitted the sociological definition of ethnic discrimination (i.e., being treated unequally or denied access to resources or opportunities simply because of one's ethnic background); however, these same respondents explicitly stated that they had not experienced discrimination personally. The analysis of our interviews showed three ways in which our respondents actively limited the scope of their experiences with discrimination.

First, it seems that for some of our respondents, to be discriminated against, one has to be subjected to unequal treatment persistently and globally (i.e., the discriminatory acts must occur many times and across many situations). In this context, isolated acts of hostility and aggression are not considered discrimination. For example, when asked about her experiences with discrimination, Khadija, an Egyptian woman, responded with: "Do you mean all over the United States?" When we clarified that we meant anytime and anywhere, she responded with "Maybe once, but not much." Later in the interview, the same respondent recounted numerous instances of being personally discriminated against in high school and college.

Second, discrimination has to be very explicit to be recognized and labeled as such. Consider for example, how an Iranian man speaks of his standing at work:

Interviewer: Have you ever experienced discrimination in the United States?
Respondent: Not personally, but I've seen it . . . when I was working for a big company and I felt that I had to do four times better than the other person to be promoted. Yes I felt that.

For this respondent what he "felt" did not directly translate into discrimination; for him, only overt actions fall in that category. Similarly, a Pakistani man speaks of how he was mistreated at work without considering it discriminatory.

Interviewer: Did you personally experience discrimination?
Respondent: No, not direct discrimination immediately after September 11.
[A short time later in the interview]
Respondent: My coworkers . . . I'm not sure if they feel comfortable saying these things to me or there are other motives but they said you Muslims do this you Muslims do that and then they would say, "Oh, I'm just joking."
Interviewer: So your fellow employees make references to you being a Muslim?

Respondent: Yes, in fact, there are times when they don't want me to be by myself
at work. So they always make sure somebody is there.
Interviewer: In the office?
Respondent: In the office. There is always someone else there. That happened immediately after September 11 but since then they have become relaxed with it. But
for a few weeks I noticed I was never allowed to be by myself.

Again, for this Pakistani Muslim, being watched at work did not raise to the
level of discrimination. Interestingly, the only incident that he labeled as an
act of discrimination was when he was physically attacked for his Middle
Eastern appearance.

The problem of establishing a working definition of discrimination with
our respondents reflects the fact that being treated unequally is interpreted
within a particular cultural context that may or may not favor labeling the
experience as discrimination. Indeed, Amir's familiarity with the culture suggests that for some Middle Eastern Americans, speaking of discrimination is
tantamount to speaking of personal failure. This is particularly true among
men, for whom stories of overcoming adversity are valued and respected,
whereas unresolved admissions of mistreatment show weakness of character.
At the same time, for many Middle Eastern American men, the very idea of
self-disclosure of personal suffering is looked down upon. Finally, many
Middle Eastern Americans adopt what one respondent referred to as a "don't
rock the boat mentality." That is, they fear that complaining about discrimination might be costlier than silently enduring it.

Of course, all of this makes the task of social mobilization against discrimination especially difficult. In an effort to overcome these problems, American Islamic organizations, such the Council on American-Islamic Relations
(CAIR), have begun a campaign of educating their members about the exact
definition of discrimination and the legal safeguards against it. For example,
a CAIR pamphlet informs Muslims of the following rights in the workplace
under Title VII of the 1964 Civil Rights Act:

1) Reasonable religious accommodation. The failure of an employer to reasonably
   accommodate your religious practices constitutes discrimination. "Religious practices" includes wearing a beard, hijab, prayer on the job, and going to Jumah [Fri-
   day] prayer.
2) Fairness in hiring, firing, and promotions. Your employer is prohibited from considering religion when making decisions affecting your employment status.
3) A non-hostile environment. Your employer must ensure that you are not subjected
   to anti-Muslim insults, harassment or unwelcome, excessive proselytizing.
4) Complain about discrimination without fear of retaliation. Federal law guarantees
   your right to report an act of alleged discrimination. It is illegal for your employer
   to retaliate against you for your complaint.[36]

Such measures are not unlike the consciousness-raising efforts of feminists during the 1960s. The goal is to enable the members of a minority group to mobilize against violations of their rights by first recognizing their rights have been violated and then enabling them to describe the violations in detailed terms.

In the course of our research, we too participated in consciousness raising of a sort. Specifically, we employed a number of techniques to encourage our respondents to become aware of and speak about instances of discrimination. First, by rewording the questions, we were able to facilitate discussions about unequal treatment. For example, in addition to asking if they had ever experienced discrimination, we also asked our respondents if they ever felt they were stereotyped or experienced prejudice. These rewordings generated more elaborate accounts and sometimes jolted respondents' memories of events that involved overt discrimination.

Another strategy we employed to encourage more candid discussions about discrimination was to provide specific examples of what would be considered an act of discrimination. For example, we would ask them if they had been attacked or fired from a job because of their ethnicity. In many cases, while a respondent would initially report that he or she had never experienced discrimination, after being given specific examples, she or he would reply, "Oh, yeah, that did happen to me. . . ." Finally, in some cases, we simply told our respondents that what they had experienced clearly qualified as an act of discrimination. For example, a respondent reported he had been thrown out of an elevator on a college campus by a white student who had told him he did not want to ride an elevator with people like him. However, he was not sure if the incident was considered discrimination. In this case, Amir interjected, "I think we can count that as discrimination."

In some cases, respondents answered that they had faced discrimination, but did not provide a detailed description of the experience. One way we found to get respondents to describe the situation in more detail in these instances was to encourage them to address an imaginary audience of outsiders. For example, in this passage, the second author explains to a woman how many white Americans do not understand discrimination:

Interviewer: Typically, my students don't understand what it feels like to have prejudice or discrimination directed at them. And you said when you are in a line at a store and how you can tell a different reaction to you—
Respondent: Definitely.
Interviewer: Could you just tell that—what you said?

This exchange continues (and is quoted later in the chapter). Here the second author solicits a more elaborate description, by encouraging the respondent to address her comments to a hypothetical group of skeptical white students who have no direct experience with ethnic discrimination and may doubt its very existence.

Some might criticize us for losing our objectivity. They might argue that researchers should not become directly involved in how respondents tell their stories and instead allow the "true" experiences of the research participants to emerge independently. We do not subscribe to this view. We take the view that it is impossible and immoral to distance oneself from the suffering of others: We were there, we heard their stories, and we reacted based on the belief that ethnic and racial discrimination are wrong and should be fought and eliminated.

DISCRIMINATION AND THE
AMERICAN DREAM

Our respondents' understanding of discrimination was manifested in relation to how they experienced America and its promises of equal opportunity and prosperity (i.e., the American Dream). The American Dream assumes that certain values, like equality, freedom, and justice are available to any person in the United States. However, some have pointed out the hypocrisy of the American Dream. In his research conducted in the late 1930s and early 1940s, Swedish social scientist Gunnar Myrdal and his colleagues wrote about an "American dilemma," in a work by that title.[37] This "dilemma" was the failure of U.S. society to live up to its stated values of equality and justice for everyone regardless of race. These researchers saw a great deal of conflict in the fact that although Americans held lofty ideals about fairness and equal opportunity, racism and segregation characterized the social structure of the country. The researchers also saw great potential for change in pointing out this hypocrisy, failing to consider that perhaps it is possible for people to be so invested in an economic system that they can hold values for themselves that they withhold from others.[38]

In this section, we examine three dimensions of how our respondents see the American Dream. First, we examine the respondent's view on positive potentials of the American Dream. Second, we offer accounts of the personal sacrifices our respondents endure in their attempts to fulfill the promise of the American Dream. Finally, we explore the contradictions in the American Dream, as our respondents experienced them. It is our contention that it is these contradictions, particularly in the wake of September 11, that translate into experiential knowledge of discrimination.

EMBRACING THE AMERICAN DREAM

When asked what they considered to be a positive aspect of life in the United States, almost all our respondents referred to the abundance of financial and educational opportunities and the freedom to pursue them, particularly in comparison to what was available in their home countries. A Pakistani man whose parents immigrated to the United States when he was ten states the following about the positive aspects of his immigration experience:

> The amount of opportunities that are available here, that's the whole reason our parents came here. To provide for us and to give us opportunities they never had. It's definitely a blessing coming here. You really don't notice it until you go back home.

Similarly, a Pakistani American lawyer notes this about her experiences: "I think I have a lot of opportunities here that I wouldn't have other places. . . . I mean educational opportunities, social mobility, economic mobility." For some, the notion of opportunities translates into much broader sense of freedom in general. For example, an Iranian woman, when asked what she likes about her life in America, stated:

> Respondent: Being free. Whatever I want to do I can. If I want to, have the opportunity to go to college and study. I have choice of clothing. . . . I have power in my life. . . . Back home I feel that the women are more indoor. . . . I'm not saying it's bad, but it's not much unfortunately. Even if women want to get into higher education, they give preference to people who have lost their father or brother in the war [the Iran-Iraq War of the 1980s].
> Interviewer: So having someone that died in the war helps you get an education?
> Respondent: Yeah, they have reserved admissions in a university or college that first go to those who lost their family in the war. Then the other people with the good grades, they can go. But it's not like here where they open the door for everybody.

For this respondent, who achieved a four-year degree in computer science, America was indeed the land of opportunities. In her home country of Iran, aside from the cultural barriers against the education of women, she had to contend with college admission policies that are extremely competitive and at the same time give preference to those who are ideologically and materially supportive of the government. The vast number of schools in the United States offered her the possibility of a better life.

An Iranian man also praises the educational opportunities in the United States and notes how he made the decision to become a naturalized citizen:

> When I came to the United States, I actually was never thinking about staying here. . . . I had my Bachelors of Science before I came to the States. I thought I come here and go through my masters and Ph.D. and then one day I would go back home. But

after many years, knowing what the situation is like back home [Iran], . . . I really thought that this is a better place to stay and this is a better place to live and this is a better place to establish my life. And that's why I made the decision to become a citizen and stay in this country.

Aside from the educational opportunities, some cited personal freedoms, such as the freedom of speech. For example, consider the following exchange with an Iranian American man:

Interviewer: What has been the most positive aspect of living in the United States?
Respondent: Freedom of speech . . . that you can say what comes to your mind without being punished.

Other respondents had a very positive view of the material comforts of life in the United States. For example, a Pakistani man notes, "Most positive aspect is that I have all the material benefits that I ever imagined. Most of them are within my reach." For this man, the American Dream is as much about the potential for material success (things that are within one's reach) as it is about its actual achievement. This, certainly, is the definition of the American Dream and is what many believe to be the most beneficial part of being in this country.

Finally, for some, the most important part of the American Dream is the assurance of physical safety from war and political persecution. For example, a Lebanese American respondent who had lived through the wars that devastated his country in the 1980s had this to say about his immigration experience:

There is intensity to war, which you survive. It is unparalleled to anything else in life. It [Beirut] was insanely intense. I mean you would be teaching your classes, and there was bombing and you would run to the shelter and come back and finish your lecture. It's a dangerous city, it's a wild city and you live or you don't. I didn't want to leave, I left because I had to. So immigration was really salvation. I had no alternative. And I would say for a lot of immigrants, immigration is not easy because you come into a different environment. . . . I would say, from the people that I know, that immigration is a way of hope. Because, as I said, it's not easy . . . it's not easy because it's different. . . . People have to do it because it is salvation, it's hope. It always saddens me in that the host countries don't realize that it's not easy for the immigrants. They are desperate and they're looking for a way out. . . . There's despair, there's hopelessness.

For this respondent the promise of the American Dream is not the material or educational opportunities per se, but the simple possibility of leading an ordinary life. However, this respondent acknowledges the pursuit of the American Dream involves being misunderstood by natives in the host country. Note that for this respondent the real cultural misunderstanding between the immigrants and natives is not about language or customs but the desperation and hopelessness that bring millions to the United States in search of a better life. Indeed, in one of the most blatant encounters regarding the issue of ethnicity, Amir was asked by a white male student, "Why do you people come here?" He replied, "For the same reason everyone else has come here before us, to live a better life."

Ambivalence about the American Dream

The second part of our discussion about the relationship between perceptions of the American Dream and discrimination involves the personal sacrifices that Middle Eastern Americans have to make to participate in the dream. In particular, we look at how for many Middle Eastern Americans the American Dream is a bittersweet experience. We speculate that one of the difficulties in discussing discrimination, for our respondents, lies in their reluctance to critique and thus verbally "give up on" the American Dream. All our respondents spoke of ambivalence about having to give up parts of their heritage and adopting new customs. Despair about loss of cultural heritage is particularly evident when raising children in a new environment is concerned. For example, the following excerpt from a focus group with three Pakistani American Muslim men shows their deliberations about introducing their children to Western holidays.

Respondent One: Then there's the whole thing about should you celebrate Halloween or not? Think about what Halloween celebrates, it's the sacrifice of children to Pagan gods. That's what Halloween is celebrating. It's not really a very Islamic holiday nor is it a Christian holiday for that matter. Eventually how do you tell you daughter, we can't go out trick-or-treating that's celebrating—
Respondent Two: You don't let your daughter go trick-or-treating?
Respondent One: Of course I do. I will because I did when I was a child and I don't have any problems with that. But we won't celebrate Christmas in the house. How do I explain that to my daughter three, four, five years from now when all of her friends are getting Christmas presents and putting up trees and put wreaths on the doors and decorating the house with lights? How do I explain to her why we're not doing that?
Interviewer: How will you explain that?
Respondent One: I don't know. I'll have to cross that bridge when we get to it. But she's too young to understand why we're not doing it.
Interviewer: Did your parents celebrate that sort of thing? How did they explain it?
Respondent One, Two, and Three: They didn't. [Everyone laughs.]
Respondent One: They said we're not doing it. That's the end of the story.

Ambivalence about becoming American also manifests itself in the way the respondents' day-to-day lives are affected. As seen in the following excerpt from the same focus group, a preoccupation with one's native culture and the possibility of its loss competes with the desire to fulfill the American Dream.

Interviewer: What about language?

Respondent One: We do speak two languages in the house, which is difficult for me because I don't speak the second language. I do a little bit but not enough to converse with my daughter now. So, my wife makes it a point only to speak to my daughter in Pashto.

Respondent Two: My mom speaks our native language and I speak it. When I was growing up and there was two languages being spoken, I didn't know the difference between the two, so I would have sentences with—

Respondent Three: Intermingling.

Respondent Two: Right. It didn't make sense.

Respondent Three: The funny thing with that is our kids won't have the joy of growing up with parents that speak the language. The language, the accents, that kind of stuff won't be there for them and they miss out on what we enjoy thoroughly.

We posed a similar question about the importance of language to a Lebanese American man, and his response, as shown below, reflects the importance that many Middle Eastern Americans place on transmitting their cultural heritage to their children.

Interviewer: Your children speak Arabic?

Respondent: They understand but they don't like it. The older one now is a little bit more interested. The younger one is rebellious. . . . But they understand and we're trying annually to send them to Lebanon so they keep their ears alive, as it were.

Here the use of the metaphor "keep their ears alive" is particularly enlightening. Becoming distant from one's culture is akin to having part of oneself die.

Similarly, an Iranian American man speaks of losing his cultural traditions and the problems he faces with raising his child.

Interviewer: What has been the most negative aspect of living in the United States?

Respondent: It's missing the culture. Missing the day-to-day activities that we have back home. It's difficult to try to accept a new culture, its different from what you believe and you have to go out there and face that every day. And now that I have a child, it's really about how can I raise him so that he can keep most of the traditions that I believe in and my wife believes in? And that's really the toughest question, the toughest part I have to face.

The problems of adapting to a new culture while maintaining one's own also manifest themselves in the way continuity of family experience is disrupted. In the following excerpts a Lebanese American father speaks of cultural displacement as he compares his own childhood experiences with that of his sons.

> I think it [coming to America] does change you and it does challenge you when you have a family when you have kids because then you realize the gap that is growing between you and your children. Between me and my father there wasn't much of a gap. My father could share his experiences and somehow, despite his own expulsion from Palestine, we were on his own terrain. We went to Nazareth in Palestine where he grew up, where he knew every tree and every corner. . . . And he could relate his experiences; I could relate to his experiences. I think the challenge and difficulty of immigration particularly becomes apparent, at least to me, when I have to relate to my children who are growing up as Americans. They love me and obviously understand me, but we have a lot of miscommunication because I don't relate to some of the values that they have. . . . I would also point out inability on my part to convey my own cultural experience. For example, my neighbor, he has always been fishing so he takes out his son fishing and there's a continuity of cultural experience there. This is his land; he is very familiar with it. He's grown up on hamburgers so his son will grow up on hamburgers. For us, obviously it's different. My wife always insists on cooking Arabic food and the kids are horrified and say: "What is this junk?" And from that to the rest of the social and personal goals that this society kind of encourages, which to me are devastating behaviors. So that's where it comes in. It's not typical generational gap between a father and his children. For example, yesterday I was at a parent-teacher meeting and I just cringe when I hear that the school, a Catholic school, wants the kids to go out and sell chocolate so they can raise funds. . . . I mean to me kids should be kids, they shouldn't be engaged in money. That's my view. . . . So, that's where the gap is. . . . That's where the challenge is. How do you cope with things like that?

Here the problem is not simply that one has to adapt to a new way of life, rather the cultural resources that gave meaning to one's identity and family experiences have become nothing more than fragments of a different life. At the same time, the new cultural resources, with their emphasis on material relations (e.g., kids raising money for school events), may contradict deeply held convictions.

As a whole, while the American Dream of a more successful life is something that our respondents subscribe to in one form or another, their participation in the American Dream also raises questions about navigating two cultural realms that sometimes have contradictory values. Arguably, many ethnic groups (e.g., Hispanics, African Americans, Asian Americans, or Irish Americans) have been ambivalent about assimilating into mainstream American culture. However, in the case of Middle Eastern Americans their struggle with being different has become significantly difficult in recent years, especially after the events of September 11, 2001.

Realizing the Contradictions in the American Dream in the Wake of September 11

Difficulty with cultural assimilation is a common experience for most ethnic groups; being designated public enemy number one is not. In the hours following the tragic events of September 11, 2001, being or just looking Middle Eastern became an instant offense. For members of this group this was a turning point both in terms of the way they were viewed by others and the way they defined themselves. In this section we first present several accounts of the initial shock of September 11 for our respondents. We then discuss the long-term, transformative effect of this day on the self-definition of Middle Eastern Americans, particularly in relation to perceived contradictions in the American Dream.

The Immediate Reaction to September 11

Not surprisingly, the gamut of emotions felt by our respondents was not completely different from what most other Americans experienced on September 11. Shock was a fairly common reaction. For example, in a focus group these Pakistani American men report:

> Respondent One: I was driving to work and heard it on the radio and it was that connotation that they cut the song and they said the plane hit and I figured it was a normal plane. Next thing the second one hit and I was like "Oh, crap, it's over!" I go to my work and turn on the TV and there was. . . . Yeah, it was like for real. And this was like I can't believe this is actually happening and when it collapsed I was like "oh my God." What else? I just figured the day would get worse and worse and worse. I didn't think there was any stopping. First plane hit, the second plane hit, the first collapse, the second collapse. It was like "what is next?"
>
> Respondent Two: I was on my way to the gym listening to radio when it happened. And I thought it was a hoax. And then I got to the gym and it was on TV and I was like "Oh my God, please don't let it be Muslims." That was the first thing came to my mind, "God please don't let this be one of us." Because it was a beautiful day, there was no way it was an accident. And then I went swimming, I came out and the second plane went in. I was like, "This is it!"

While the feeling of shock is similar to what everyone must have felt that day, in the case of Middle Eastern Americans, there was also a feeling of impending doom, the knowledge that their lives would never be exactly the same. Many of our respondents stated that after their sense of initial shock and sadness, the next thought they remember was that they hoped that the incident was perpetrated by domestic terrorists, as was the case with the Oklahoma City bombing. Some even mentioned their frustration that they had to be concerned with such things when they were also, like all other Americans, feeling such horror about the loss of lives that had occurred.

As the day went by, a chasm began to form between Middle Eastern Americans and their fellow citizens. The perception that Middle Easterners were the aggressors and other Americans the victims began to take hold; and out of this perception grew anger.

> Respondent: I went to class that day and came back and from then on for two days, I was glued to CNN. . . . Wherever you went you always—that day even among my friends there was talk about anger and they looked really angry. . . . There was talk about "We should bomb Palestine." And "Who cares about these people now." In a way, I understood their anger because of what had just happened. I guess it was kind of lonely that day.

In the days following the attacks, Middle Eastern Americans had to accept the fact that they were seen by many as legitimate targets of anger. The news media were full of messages about hate being an acceptable emotion under the circumstances. In that atmosphere it was indeed very "lonely" to be Middle Eastern American. What was most striking was the ordinary tone with which retaliatory violence was talked about. For example, at a school in Florida, a white woman, who served on a faculty committee with Amir, gleefully told him about a group of Middle Eastern students having "the crap beaten out of them." Supposedly, the Middle Eastern students were attacked by white students who suspected them of sympathizing with the terrorists. Anger was expressed toward any and all who resembled Middle Eastern people. For example, in an introductory race and ethnicity course taught by the second author, a young man passionately exclaimed, "I say we go bomb the Taj Mahal!" Although others in the class corrected his error in terms of his misplaced target, his general idea of bombing buildings where civilians would be the primary casualties was not disputed.

Some Middle Eastern Americans opted to show their own anger about this event and inadvertently afforded themselves protection from suspicions or attacks. For example, an Iranian American man reports:

> I was in Okeechobee Airport, working on September 11. Okeechobee is a very traditional white American city. Okay? They knew I'm not a white person, they might have had doubts about me being an Arab . . . but none of them dared to bring up the question because I was angry as those people were.

This respondent's anger toward the terrorist attack was interpreted by his colleagues as a sign of his patriotism; it transformed him from a passive target of others' emotions to the active role of one who can express his own emotions about this tragic event.

Some Middle Eastern Americans also felt a strong sense of guilt and shame about this tragedy. For example, a Pakistani man stated, "In my mind there's a kind of a debt I have to pay." The question on the minds of many Middle Eastern Americans was: "How do you explain to your fellow citizens that people who supposedly shared your faith and came from the same region as you did could be capable of committing such horrendous act of carnage?" With this lingering question came the sense of not belonging and the real possibility of being physically separated from the rest of society and placed in an internment camp.

> Respondent: Actually it was three days that felt like one day because I didn't speak much or eat much and watched CNN.
> Interviewer: You said you thought they were going to come pick you up.
> Respondent: I really thought I was going to be sent to like a camp. . . . It didn't—for those couple of days—it didn't feel like we were going to be back to normal again. Like I really didn't feel like—along with going to internment camp—I thought my life was never going to be the same. I no longer had a home here.

As indicated here, in the aftermath of September 11, perhaps the most significant realization for many Middle Eastern Americans was the awareness that their right to be part of the American Dream could be taken away for actions that they were not in any way responsible for. As this respondent puts it, realizing that one no longer has a home here was tantamount to realizing that the American Dream applied to some more than others, or that some groups were more vulnerable and more likely to be disenfranchised than others.

RETHINKING THE AMERICAN DREAM

> Arab immigrants are no longer compelled to jump into the melting pot of assimilation. Like the rest of us, they are nestled snugly in the great American "salad bowl." But beneath the leafy imagery, another message comes through: "You will not fit in here unless you behave appropriately, and this will be possible only if the differences that set you apart from us—your language, your culture, your religion, your attitude—are somehow naturalized, normalized, muted, consigned to another time, or linked to a place and a way of life you have left behind."[39]

As these authors of a study of Arab Detroit point out, despite the purported pluralism of the contemporary U.S. ethnic landscape, it becomes obvious to immigrants that in order to achieve success in the United States, they must conform to standards of Americanization. September 11 was an important turning point in the psyche of Middle Eastern Americans to the extent that it caused them to reevaluate their place in American society and its promises of freedom and equality. Consider, for example, how this Pakistani American woman (who was born in Pennsylvania) rethinks her status as an American in light of how she and her family have been treated since September 11.

> My brother was assaulted three days after September 11. It was part of the backlash. And I'm worried for my parents more than I am for myself. They've been here since 1968, longer than they ever lived in Pakistan. But they are still very much considered outsiders; and it's because of their accents largely. I feel I'm even considered an outsider a lot of the times. I sound just as American as anyone else, and I was born and raised here. . . . [After September 11] I think a lot of people thought that if you're not going to consider me American, why am I going to consider myself an American. If you're not going to protect me like other Americans, if you are going to create laws that are going to undermine me, then I shouldn't be trying so hard to fit into a culture that consistently and perpetually rejects me.

According to this respondent, after September 11, and particularly after a brutal physical attack on her younger brother, it became particularly apparent that the ideals of equality in the American Dream did not apply to her and her family. Her ethnicity transcends her identity as an American and places her in the position of a second-class citizen.

Another way in which September 11 affected Middle Eastern Americans was to make them feel uncertain about their future in this country. For example, a thirty-four-year-old Iranian American woman, who came to the United States with her parents at the age of six, told us the following:

> [Since September 11] my mind-set is a more cautious and guarded of the government. Because policies are being passed very quietly, foundation is being laid that makes it a little bit scary. I use the example of fifteen-twenty years ago my parents would say, "We'd better become citizens pretty quickly because you never know when this country is going to start looking at us and wanting to kick us out." I would get mad at them for saying that—growing up. Like, "How could you say that? They have given us a home for so many years, we have all these opportunities, that just wouldn't happen. Yeah, it happened to the Japanese, but they have learned, they're embarrassed by that. There's talk of reparations." And now all of sudden it's like, oh crap! They [my parents] knew something then. They were right! It's very possible that something like that could happen.

What at one point seemed like a tragic part of U.S. history that would never be repeated (i.e., the mass incarceration of Japanese Americans) has become a terrifying possibility for Middle Eastern Americans.

Many also worry about the future of their U.S.-born children. In the following excerpt, an Iranian American woman, whose son was born in Florida days after the terrorist attacks, expresses her worries about the boy's future:

Respondent: Sometimes I think if my son is going to school and in first grade, you know, the kids talk and they really don't know anything. . . . I don't know what is going to happen . . . how he's going to react. I know he was born here but still. I hope everything is going to be okay with him.

Interviewer: Kids can be kind of, they can say funny things to each other sometimes—

Respondent: And some kid who doesn't know anything and the first thing they notice is your parents are from Iran, or the Middle East, and they call you a terrorist. He [my son] doesn't understand that or get upset.

Interviewer: What are the best things to tell children as far as how to handle those kinds of incidents if they ever arose? How could they deal with that if a child said something to them?

Respondent: That's a good question. . . . I would tell any kid from Iran don't get into a fight. Deep down you know that you are not a terrorist, something like that. Kids tease each other and this is one thing they do. Hopefully this thing will end soon.

As was the case with the previous respondent, this woman also expresses doubt about how much protection her son's identity as a native-born American will provide against prejudice and stereotypes. Her advice for young Iranians to remember that deep down they are not terrorists shows how ethnic pride could be used as a way of coping with prejudice. Keeping in mind the authentic meaning of one's ethnic identity protects that identity from corruption by the discrimination of others. Put differently, the identity cannot become "spoiled" by the stigma[40] of a terrorist attack if it is grounded in a deeper sense of culture and tradition. This mother goes on to discuss how she plans to raise her son to know Farsi, the language of Iran, and traditions associated with his culture, to help him have a sense of being Iranian American, rather than only American.

One of the most profound effects of September 11 on the lives of Middle Eastern Americans was the realization that their daily routines (i.e., the mundane tasks of going on a trip or even to a grocery store) would be subjected to scrutiny and potentially make them vulnerable to acts of violence. As a Pakistani American respondent put it: "I always looked over my shoulder after September 11. I wasn't sure what was going to happen. . . . I was concerned and we were always cautious." Similarly, an Iranian American man describes how September 11 affected his life:

Respondent: I actually canceled a trip. We usually take a trip on Thanksgiving with about thirty to forty Iranian Americans. And that's when I realized there's a difference in this war [War on Terrorism]. There is a new order. We've been doing this [going on trips] for the past seven or eight years. Every Thanksgiving we get together with other people, mostly Iranian Americans or people who are Iranian American and have a husband or wife from a different country. We used to go to

North Carolina to South Carolina, to beautiful places and stay there for four or five days. Now that year, in November, I canceled the trip and I thought there was too much risk in taking forty people on a trip, and most of them were thinking the same way. We can't go somewhere and not play our own music. We like our own music, we like our own dance, we like our own food and tradition so we couldn't do that therefore I canceled that trip. That's when it occurred to me there's a difference.

Interviewer: Did you put any other limitations on your life because of it? Did you restrict your life in any other way?

Respondent: I'm more alert these days about how I answer people. Especially at my work, it's very important, that's the lifeline . . . losing a contract is too much for me. I can't really afford that. In the past I wouldn't mind if they asked right off the bat where I'm from. . . . But now most of the time I say "God, please don't let them ask the question."

Interviewer: The question being "Where are you from?"

Respondent: Where I'm from, yes.

Interviewer: So what do you do?

Respondent: I don't volunteer information.

Interviewer: I see. So you're more guarded?

Respondent: Yes, I'm more guarded about what I say.

For many Middle Eastern Americans, September 11 meant restricting their personal freedoms (e.g., the right to travel, go to various public places, attend mosques, or practice Islam). While many of these were self-imposed restrictions, they were nonetheless in direct response to real or perceived threats of persecution and violence. Being "more guarded" about personal speech and travel became the new way of life.

As discussed in chapter 2, Middle Eastern Americans have experienced discrimination and prejudice for at least the past two decades; however, September 11 gave new legitimacy and justification to a level of mistreatment that had never existed before. As a Pakistani American woman puts it:

[It happened before] but not with this magnitude, and not with the accusatory tone, and not with the same attitude as they did before. Before it was just out of curiosity, and it was incidental, but this is an even more demanding tone of "Who are you? And why did your people do this?" And we need to protect ourselves.

Collectively, these post–September 11 experiences have caused some Middle Eastern Americans to question the meaning of the American Dream and the extent to which its lofty promises apply to them. They have recognized that full assimilation into American culture will not provide protection against acts of ignorance and that their future in this country is uncertain. This outlook is eloquently summarized by one of our Lebanese American respondents:

I for one imagine that every immigrant coming to this country comes with at least the impression that this is a country that has laws—laws which are civil. But suddenly to realize, as I have seen it, this is a veneer, a very thin veneer of civility. At the moment that something threatening happens, that veneer is gone. For instance, the PATRIOT Act is horrific. And, of course, the bigotry and the xenophobia that flooded the media is appalling. That again was disappointing to me because, as I said, all immigrants who are coming to America are coming to an America they have seen in the movies. And, in a sense, because that's the only thing we know about America, we believe that. We come with these high values, discipline, honesty, hard work, and of course, the rule of law, justice, all these values. We have seen them in the movies, the good guys always winning at the end. . . . And suddenly when something horrific happens, that veneer is gone. . . . So my faith is shaken.

The very value of civility is that it should offer protection when things are the most tense. If it fails to do so, then it is in fact, just a "veneer." Similarly, laws, as this man suggests, are of no value unless they defend those who are least able to protect themselves (e.g., the newest immigrants) at times when they are most vulnerable. For this respondent, the fact that the immigrants' constitutional rights (i.e., due process protections) are undermined with the passage of new laws, such as the PATRIOT Act, further reveals how thin this "veneer of civility" really is.

NOTES

1. Nabeel Abraham, "To Palestine and Back: A Quest for Place," in *Arab Detroit: From Margin to Mainstream,* ed. N. Abraham and A. Shryock (Detroit: Wayne State University Press, 2000), pp. 444–45.

2. Joe R. Feagin, *Racist America: Roots, Current Realities and Future Reparations* (Lanham, Md.: Routledge, 2000), p. 210.

3. Feagin, *Racist America,* p. 211.

4. Adalberto Aguirre Jr. and Jonathan H. Turner, *American Ethnicity: The Dynamics and Consequences of Discrimination,* 4th ed. (Boston: McGraw Hill, 2004), p. 223.

5. Feagin, *Racist America,* p. 204.

6. Feagin, *Racist America,* p. 204.

7. Feagin, *Racist America,* p. 206.

8. Joe R. Feagin and Clairece B. Feagin, *Racial and Ethnic Relations,* 7th ed. (Upper Saddle River, N.J.: Prentice Hall, 2003), p. 176.

9. Dalton Conley, "The Cost of Slavery," *The New York Times.* www.nytimes.com/2003/02/15/opinion/15CONL.html?ex = 1046329331&ei = 1&en = e74182c97bad853f (accessed February 15, 2003).

10. Feagin and Feagin, *Racial and Ethnic Relations,* p. 188; G. Winter, "Schools Resegregate, Study Finds," *The New York Times,* late edition, final, section A , p. 14, column 1. www.nytimes.com/2003/01/21/education/21RACE.html? (accessed January 26, 2003).

11. Aguirre Jr. and Turner, *American Ethnicity,* p. 68.

12. Joe R. Feagin and Karyn D. McKinney, *The Many Costs of Racism* (Lanham, Md.: Rowman & Littlefield, 2003).

13. Aguirre Jr. and Turner, *American Ethnicity,* p. 106.

14. Aguirre Jr. and Turner, *American Ethnicity,* p. 118.

15. Feagin, *Racist America,* p. 210.

16. Feagin, *Racist America,* pp. 214–15.

17. Aguirre Jr. and Turner, *American Ethnicity,* pp. 195–97.

18. Aguirre Jr. and Turner, *American Ethnicity,* p. 184.

19. Aguirre Jr. and Turner, *American Ethnicity,* pp. 187–88.

20. Paul Kivel, *Uprooting Racism: How White People Can Work for Racial Justice,* rev. ed. (Gabriola Island, BC, Canada: New Society Publishers, 2002), p. 149.

21. Aguirre Jr. and Turner, *American Ethnicity,* p. 156; Kivel, *Uprooting Racism,* p. 149.

22. Aguirre Jr. and Turner, *American Ethnicity,* p. 168.

23. Aguirre Jr. and Turner, *American Ethnicity,* pp. 174–75.

24. Aguirre Jr. and Turner, *American Ethnicity,* pp. 145–52.

25. Aguirre Jr. and Turner, *American Ethnicity,* p. 180.

26. Shams Alwujude, "Daughter of America," in *Arab Detroit: From Margin to Mainstream,* ed. N. Abraham and A. Shryock (Detroit: Wayne State University Press, 2000), p. 383.

27. Ronald Stockton, "Ethnic Archetypes and the Arab Image," in *The Development of Arab-American Identity,* ed. Ernest McCarus (Ann Arbor: University of Michigan Press, 1994), p. 120.

28. Stockton, "Ethnic Archetypes," pp. 131–48.

29. Feagin and Feagin, *Racial and Ethnic Relations,* p. 326.

30. Hayan Charara, "Becoming the Center of Mystery," in *Arab Detroit: From Margin to Mainstream,* ed. N. Abraham and A. Shryock (Detroit: Wayne State University Press, 2000), p. 403.

31. See Feagin and McKinney, *The Many Costs of Racism,* p. 127.

32. Joe R. Feagin and Melvin P. Sikes, *Living with Racism: The Black Middle-Class Experience* (Boston: Beacon Press, 1994), pp. 276–77.

33. Feagin and Sikes, *Living with Racism,* p. 279.

34. Feagin, *Racist America,* p. 228.

35. Feagin, *Racist America,* p. 228.

36. *Muslim Community Safety Kit,* pamphlet from Council on American-Islamic Relations conference 2002, p. 10.

37. Gunnar Myrdal, *An American Dilemma,* vol. 1 (New York: McGraw-Hill, 1964 [1944]).

38. Feagin, *Racist America,* p. 197.

39. Andrew Shryock and Nabeel Abraham, "On Margins and Mainstreams," in *Arab Detroit: From Margin to Mainstream,* ed. N. Abraham and A. Shryock (Detroit: Wayne State University Press, 2000), p. 17.

40. Erving Goffman, *Stigma: Notes on the Management of Spoiled Identity* (New York: Simon and Schuster, 1986).

Chapter 6

Living with Discrimination

An important aspect of life in the United States for any ethnic group is coming to terms with the impact of discrimination on the workings of various social institutions such as family, workplace, housing, and education. In this chapter we examine Middle Eastern Americans' experiences with discrimination in the patterned and routinized context of social institutions. Our analysis catalogs the practical substance and consequences of the discrimination suffered by this group in various settings (workplace, schools, etc.).

TYPES OF DISCRIMINATION

In this section, we provide empirical examples of how discrimination impacts the lives of Middle Eastern Americans. After helping our respondents to articulate a definition of "discrimination" in the context of their expectations for life within the American Dream, we went on to question whether they had faced discrimination in specific types of institutional settings. Additionally, some comments regarding specific contexts in which discrimination occurred arose within our more general discussion of discrimination. Again, in nearly every instance, these stories were told as the "other side" of the positive features of life in the United States. In other words, most respondents were careful to state that generally, they are aware of the benefits of living in this country; however, they are also cognizant that their lives as Middle Eastern Americans differ from those of other citizens—particularly those of white Americans, and particularly since September 11, 2001.

The Workplace

Because most people spend a great deal of their everyday lives in the workplace, discrimination in that setting can be particularly stressful. Further, although studies show stress in the workplace is harmful to workers of any race or ethnicity, they have also found that people of color may be particularly vulnerable to certain types of occupational stress.[1] While it may seem that other kinds of stress are under one's control, stress caused by other people's reactions to one's race or ethnicity usually seem completely out of one's hands, and thus even more stressful. Further, for people of color, other stress caused by racial discrimination may be dealt with through avoidance or confrontation, yet it is often much more difficult to find a way to manage discrimination in the workplace.[2] Confrontation in the workplace can be costly, in terms of jeopardizing future raises, promotions, or even one's job itself. Many of our respondents spoke of discrimination they had faced in the workplace based on their identifiability as Middle Eastern Americans. For example, a Pakistani American told of an incident involving an e-mail that was forwarded to him:

> Respondent: It was a derogatory joke about Prophet Muhammad. Something to the effect of about some suicide bomber, he died, he went up and—[long pause]— okay so the joke said something like a suicide bomber died and he goes up to heaven, I can't remember completely but what happened was he went to the final heaven and God asked him "What would you like to have?" and the suicide bomber said "I'm looking for Muhammad." And God said "Muhammad can get you two cups of tea." I can't remember it was something like that. I did not appreciate it and I sent a reply back. It was an e-mail so I sent a reply back to my coworker. And I told him—
> Interviewer: So it wasn't an anonymous e-mail?
> Respondent: No somebody I knew.
> Interviewer: So what did you write him back?
> Respondent: I told him that I do not appreciate it. I understand that he was trying to be funny but that was something I didn't appreciate. That was the end of it.

On any given day, a person can find innumerable jokes, cartoons, and other supposed humorous short essays circulating on the Internet, both on websites and through e-mail. After September 11, the Internet was inundated with such items, as friends and coworkers forwarded them to one another—a person could expect to receive several each day. Interspersed with these, of course, were more serious "patriotic" short essays and calls to action. However, although different in tone, often the messages embedded in the two types of material was the same: that Middle Eastern Americans as a whole are somehow evil and were to blame for the attacks, or that Islam as a faith is a vicious and demented religion.

This respondent receives such an e-mail at work, distracting him from the business of the day. What is perhaps most disturbing is that the sender, first, does not have any qualms about including him on the list of recipients, and second, does not find it necessary to send the e-mail anonymously. In a post–September 11 world, such stereotypical representations of Muslim and Middle Eastern Americans not only was seen as justified by many Americans but also was sanctioned by institutional norms. This man felt that the norms of his workplace would be accepting of this behavior during work hours. He also did not take into consideration the effect that this stereotypical image of Muslims might have on his Muslim coworker.

According to our respondents, workplace discrimination occurred before the September 11 attacks. For example, many of Amir's friends changed their names from Middle Eastern–sounding ones to more American names after they were repeatedly turned down for jobs. A man named Hossein was blatantly discriminated against when potential employers hung up the phone after hearing his name. This man changed his name to Michael. Another man who worked as a real estate agent reported that customers would not shake hands with him and would ask to see another agent after they learned his name was Mohammad and he was from Iran.

Middle Eastern women, particularly those who practice Islam, have had their share of problems at work. For example, a Turkish woman tells of the following incident that happened when she was pursuing a career in teaching:

> Interviewer: And you mentioned something about a teacher, or the chair—or head of the education program—saying that he didn't want you in front of the classroom.
> Respondent: Yes.
> Interviewer: Could you describe the specifics of that encounter? You go in his office and he says?
> Respondent: Yeah, I was telling him that I would like to change the program from the regular math program to math education, and then he just simply said that he cannot put me in front of students *"like that"* [a reference to the fact that she covered her hair with a long scarf]. And then I said, "What do you mean?" And then he kind of changed and said, "Well, you don't have to be as experienced in high school."

This respondent went on to explain that it became clear to her that the head of her program meant that he could not put her in front of students wearing a hijab. When he realized that she was not going to accept his discriminatory behavior passively and without question, the administrator quickly tried to cover his initial unfair treatment.

In academic settings, one might expect that the professors and students might be more well-informed and even more accepting of difference than those in the general public. However, as indicated above, this is not always the case for Middle Eastern Americans who work in colleges and universities. The following stories show that Middle Eastern students are also subjected to unfair treatment.

Schools

For some, pursuing education full time is their primary occupation. For them, unfair treatment based on their ethnicity in an educational setting is just as serious as it would be for others in a workplace. Further, discrimination includes the denial not only of access to resources but also of access to opportunity based on race or ethnicity; so educational discrimination certainly represents one of the most egregious forms of denial of opportunity. Educational discrimination not only may deny a person the opportunity to learn in that time and place, but also may deny a person opportunities in the future, for example, to receive a well-paying job, or go on to even higher education. For this reason, some have discussed educational discrimination as being one of the key elements in structural or cyclical discrimination.[3] Several of our respondents had faced various types of discrimination in educational settings. For some, these incidents happened when they were very young. For example, a young Pakistani woman describes the difficulties of going to school:

> Interviewee: I just remember two years of my life when I did not want to take the bus to school because there was a group of boys on the bus and every day they would just harass me and my two younger brothers, *relentlessly*. [They would call us] "Mohammad, Mohammad" and swearing and asking where our turbans were, asking where our dots on our foreheads were. You know, mixing the different cultures, and just harassing us relentlessly for two years.
> Interviewer: They called you Mohammad because your brother's name is Mohammad?
> Interviewee: No! They were just saying that because we were Muslims. Or they didn't know what we were. We weren't white. . . . I would never forget that. . . . That was really, that was really really terrible because already when you're a kid, it is so hard to fit in. And already when you look different it's so much harder to fit in, and then to have people on top of it giving other kids less of a reason to be with you, or emphasizing the differences. For a kid, that's really hard. As adults we can deflect it with other things—intellect, humor, anything. But as a child, it's of paramount importance to fit in.

This woman clearly remembers how it felt to be an outsider as a young Middle Eastern American. Most children already worry about being acceptable to their peers, and no matter whether it is true, many believe that they are not. Insightfully, this young woman articulates the reality for Middle Eastern children, and probably that of children of many other groups. Not only do they have the usual adolescent angst regarding "fitting in," they have the very real worries generated by a society in which "Middle Eastern looks" subject people of all ages to stereotypes as well. Further, she notes that adults have learned coping skills, based on having dealt with these experiences many times in their lives, and likely also based on collective experience, while children have not yet incorporated such strategies into their everyday repertoires for interactions.

Common to many of the respondents' experience is the frustration of having their culture confused with others'. This Pakistani woman's memory of being asked about the dot on her head is a poignant reminder that the perpetrators of prejudice do not concern themselves with subtle cultural distinctions when evoking stereotypes. All Middle Eastern–looking people, in their minds, are essentially the same and deserving of the same unwelcoming treatment. However, as discussed in the next chapter, members of various ethnic groups use this misrecognition to their political advantage. In other words, ethnic misrecognition can become part of the basis for the creation of a panethnic identity that mobilizes diverse resources for a common cause. Thus, Arabs, Pakistanis, and Iranians—though they speak different languages and have different customs—could come together under the banner of fighting the discrimination that they all suffer.

Similar to this Pakistani woman's school bus experience, an Iranian American woman remembers being harassed in school during the Iranian hostage crisis (1979–1981):

> Interviewee: During the hostage crisis there were comments about Iranians, you know, "You terrorist." Things like that were said to me by other kids.
> Interviewer: How did you deal with that?
> Interviewee: Oh, it was hard. That was really really hard.
> Interviewer: How old were you?
> Interviewee: Eleven. Went home a couple of times crying.

After every tragic event involving the Middle East, Middle Eastern American school children become easy targets in the hands of their classmates. That children, who usually don't take an interest in politics, become so enraged as to call a classmate a terrorist based on her appearance alone shows how pervasive stereotypes of Middle Eastern Americans have become.

An Egyptian female respondent told us that other children threw spitballs in school. This behavior continued until her father finally had to go to the school to speak with the administration to get them to stop his daughter's harassment. This young woman also has recollections of how, in high school, others did not befriend her because they seemed to assume that she was strikingly "different" from them simply because she wears the hijab. Although she had many of the same interests as any other teenager, she believes that her classmates assumed she would not be interested in forming friendships with them. Instead, she told how it appeared that they only approached her in a friendly way when it seemed like they "wanted something," for example, help with difficult homework, or to study for a test. Similarly, she stated that teachers seemed to have a strange attitude toward her:

> Interviewer: Since you've come here, what has been the most negative aspect, do you think, of living in the United States?
>
> Respondent: Well, sometimes it's discrimination but it's not—well, it depends on the people you see. I had, at my first school—my first high school when I came here was in Oklahoma—I had a chemistry teacher who was racist and he was known to be racist, actually. Then I had to change this course because I couldn't get any answers in it. He doesn't pay attention to you and he doesn't care about you, so, that's one thing. But otherwise, teachers are, sometimes can be racist, but you can just feel it. Sometimes you can't—they try not to be, [not to] act toward you in a different way, but you can feel it, you can just feel it. You can feel that they are away from you or try to be cautious with you. More cautious than with other kids. In high school here, . . . some teachers . . . don't care where I'm from. I had an English teacher—I think that she was kind of cautious, more cautious with me than with any other kid. She didn't want to give me lower scores than other kids so that anything wouldn't—you know what I mean? She didn't want to get into trouble with me. She's afraid that I might do something. I might sue her or something. I wouldn't care, but, you know?

Theorists suggest that many white Americans may no longer express overt, intentional, and hostile forms of discrimination; but, instead, their racism is aversive, that is, it is experienced more as a discomfort around people of color that results in subtle and often unintentional discrimination or avoidance.[4] This type of racism is often practiced by those who otherwise believe themselves to hold egalitarian values. Sometimes fears and discomfort that adults feel toward those of another ethnic group, in this case Middle Eastern Americans, can be costly for children of that group. Although some might say that this young woman experienced "positive discrimination," in that teachers scrutinized her work less harshly, in the long run this could amount to her being less prepared, academically, for the future, if inadequate or incorrect work was allowed to slip by because teachers were trying to avoid contact with her.

These women are in their twenties now, so their experiences with discrimination as young children occurred years before September 11, 2001. However, although we did not interview children for this study, evidence suggests that the terrorist attacks likely impacted their lives as Middle Eastern Americans as well as that of adults. For example, Amir's nephew, during a soccer game, accidentally knocked the ball into another student's face. This student, responding in pain, called the Iranian American young man a "terrorist." This incident is discouraging for many reasons. First, and most obvious, is the impact it might have on the Iranian American young man, who at the time was newly arrived in the United States and not yet fully aware of either the racial and ethnic tensions that exist here or, more important, of strategies to manage them. Obviously this young man would be hurt by the other student's statement; to what degree is the only question. The incident is discouraging for another reason, however. When a person is physically hurt, the verbal response is usually spontaneous and not carefully considered. The fact that this very young, preteen boy's first reaction was to call the other boy a "terrorist" suggests just how quickly the stereotype of Middle Eastern Americans as such has become pervasive at the deepest and presumably most "innocent" levels of our society.

Shortly after September 11, Amir and Karyn were visiting a video store when suddenly, a young boy nearby began frantically tugging at his mother's shirt tail, while keeping his eyes firmly fixed on Amir. When she finally looked down at him and asked "What?" the boy said "Mommy! I thought they were all in jail!" The comments that children make may demonstrate what others in society are thinking but not verbalizing.

Other respondents spoke of discrimination in higher education. Many find their culture and traditions called into question. For example, a Pakistani woman tells the following story:

> A lot of people assume things about my family, like my mom completely dominates my father, but nobody believes that, but everybody assumes that she is really oppressed, or that she has no mind of her own. And those things bother me. . . . My best friend is Lebanese, she goes to law school with me, somebody started asking her questions about her mom, already with the underlying assumption that her mom is probably not very educated and she probably sits at home, and she is very subdued, and very subordinate. Which is not true at all, her mom is a head of the Lebanese Women's Golf Team. So my friend was trying to make a point that a lot of the women are happy, and you can't impose your values on that. This girl said to her, "I feel sorry for you, because you and those women don't even understand that they're oppressed." So I found this attitude a lot, even among the very educated class of people here.

Expecting more tolerance or even acceptance from those in academic settings, this young woman is surprised when the fundamental fairness of the gender roles in her family, and that of other Middle Eastern Americans, is called into question by her peers. Rather than having the expectation that those in academic settings will be more accepting of difference, in the case of Middle Eastern American families, academics, and particularly academic women, may be even more likely than those outside academia to be critical. Women in colleges and universities, especially those who identify as feminists, sometimes believe that all Middle Eastern women are oppressed and are in need of enlightenment to the state of their oppression. By extension, Middle Eastern men have been cast as master oppressors of women.

Although respondents were called on to speak as representatives of Middle Eastern people in educational settings before September 11, their position as spokespersons for their panethnic group was more salient after that date. Often, on university campuses, both in and out of the classroom, respondents were treated as the "token" Middle Eastern American. For example, a Pakistani law student explained:

> I ran for president of the student body, I could say before September 11 I was a shoe-in, I have a very visible presence on my campus. It was close but I think the fact that I lost was because I was Muslim, and I really got into arguments with a lot of people around that time, and I really felt like I was harassed, and I felt that accusatory "Well, you don't represent me because you're this or you're that." And I felt that hostility coming from other students, especially immediately after September 11 when emotions were really high, and people were really saying "Well, we need to protect our people from you," and things like that, and I felt like I was harassed.

This young woman has achieved success on her campus and become a leader in the student body. However, the events of September 11 changed her positive status of leader to a more negative status. Students suddenly seemed to view her suspiciously, and she now expresses feelings of being harassed. She still has a visible presence on campus, but she finds that that presence has changed in character. She continues:

> And in my classes we were studying constitutional law, and we were studying the *Koramatsu* case—it was the Japanese internment camp case—and this woman in class said, "Why don't we make this more interesting and why don't we change the hypothetical to another disputed incident of minorities, say Muslims?" And I'm like, "You are not going to put me in the situation, I'm the only Muslim in the class, and I am not going to be fielding questions from the entire class because of your ignorance." But yeah, I felt really harassed and I didn't like being in that position, and I felt like I was singled out because of my background.

In a classroom setting, when the topic turns to internment of Japanese Americans during World War II, and a fellow student suggests changing the group to Middle Eastern Americans to "make it more interesting," because she is Middle Eastern, this respondent is put under scrutiny. Although she refuses to "play along," still simply by raising the issue her ethnicity has been highlighted, and, during a time of national crisis and rising suspicion, she is stigmatized by the way in which it is invoked.

Similarly, an Egyptian respondent faces questioning from students and teachers after the terrorism. She speaks of multiple incidents in her high school. When asked generally about her experiences after September 11, she replied:

> Respondent: Some people actually get more afraid—scared of you—when they go into stores. They're thinking about all that happened and then, "Do you have a bomb?" . . . You might blow them up, you know. . . .
>
> Interviewer A: You were still going to school, I guess?
>
> Respondent: Yeah, yeah.
>
> Interviewer A: How was that?
>
> Respondent: Well, the first day was bad. The first day of school after 9/11, I had such a tough time in my English class. They were so mad. You could see it in their eyes—you could see in their eyes that they were so mad about what happened and all this. But, I didn't know what to do, you know. It's not me! So, in the beginning, people were kind of more afraid. Kind of scared. But they started to deal with—they learned so much of it from TV, the media, and all this. . . . Not all of us are that kind. We're not going to blow their buildings up.
>
> Interviewer B: So, they were angry?
>
> Respondent: I think yeah. I think they were.
>
> Interviewer B: How could you tell?
>
> Respondent: Because, they don't look at you in the same way as they were before that. They're kind of . . . they don't smile at you as much, as they were before. If someone is used to smiling at you, after this she doesn't smile at you as much. So—but they were confused.
>
> Interviewer A: Did you find yourself in any conversations with anybody about it, trying to explain to them anything?
>
> Respondent: Just this one day, that's all. In my history class, my history teacher wasn't that good. He doesn't like anyone who is different from him. That's all. He doesn't like anyone who disagrees with him. . . . And he used to have the TV on in the class, so he had to talk about us, you know about Muslims, about Arabs and all this. But you know I didn't go into a conversation with him. I know that I'm going to be losing anyways, so I'm not going to try to explain to him anything. . . .
>
> Interviewer A: So, you said that you got into some conversations with some kids. Did you bring it up or did they start asking you questions?
>
> Respondent: No, actually it started with a teacher. The teacher asked me. [Laughs]. That's why it made it public—everyone was listening.
>
> Interviewer B: What did the teacher ask you?
>
> Respondent: I think that she was asking about how I felt, or how did I react, or "What's your opinion?" That's all.
>
> Interviewer B: And then you had students start asking questions?
>
> Respondent: Mmhmm, yeah.
>
> Interviewer B: What kinds of questions?
>
> Respondent: Well, "How do you feel about this?" or "What do you think?" or "Why did they do that?" You know, "Why they did that?" "Why do they hate Americans?"

Interviewer B: And how did you answer those questions?

Respondent: Well, I said they're kind of foolish. Why would they blow up all this, all these people? Just because of what they wanted and just because of their hate for Americans? Killing, in itself, is just bad. So, why would you even kill just for hate? That's just bad. And then other people you don't know. And they killed Muslims and non-Muslims.

In what she senses is a hostile environment, and at a time when she also is likely upset about the terrorist attacks, this young woman is put in a position multiple times to speak for Muslim Americans as a whole. Not only do her peers ask her to do so, but teachers do as well. In fact, instead of protecting her from the scrutiny of her peers, some teachers actually incite that attention, being the first to ask her questions, as if she is able to give an "expert" or "representative" opinion on the issue, where in fact she too is puzzled and horrified by the actions of the terrorists.

Other respondents, as well, were held accountable on campuses for the actions of the extremist terrorists. Sometimes they were held accountable not only by being asked to answer verbally for the attacks but also by being subjected to threats and verbal abuse. For example, a Pakistani college student was yelled at by passers-by after September 11 on the campus of a small northeastern college. Ironically, this verbal assault came while he was seated at a table, collecting donations for victims of the attacks.

As in the case of the other instances of discrimination discussed in this chapter, discrimination on college campuses toward Middle Eastern Americans did not begin on September 11, 2001. A Pakistani respondent tells the following story, beginning with a brief mention of workplace discrimination:

Respondent: I think it was [discrimination]. I was passed over for a promotion and I had strong feelings it was because of my race and my ethnic origin. And then I did have a very strong discrimination once soon after the first Gulf war in my dormitory. After dinner I was going back to my floor and I was pushed out of the elevator by a white American guy saying that he doesn't want people like me riding with him.

Interviewer: And what college was this?

Respondent: University of Arkansas.

Interviewer: Arkansas. That was after the first Gulf War?

Respondent: Yes just after the first Gulf War.

Interviewer: What did you do in that case?

Respondent: I complained. I complained to the college and they never told me what they did with him. They were supposed to discipline him. But I never heard what they did to him.

Middle Eastern Americans whose countries are often engaged in political conflict with the United States have learned that discrimination against them often waxes and wanes based on political turmoil and traumas. This type of "jingoistic racism" is eloquently described by Nabeel Abraham in the following passage:

> In many ways similar to xenophobic nativism, jingoistic racism is a curious blend of knee-jerk patriotism and homegrown white racism toward non-European, non-Christian dark skinned peoples. It is a racism spawned by political ignorance, false patriotism, and hyper ethnocentrism. . . . Jingoistic violence tends to be spontaneous, reactive, and episodic. It almost always occurs during heightened international tensions (hijackings, hostage takings, and military conflict), especially if U.S. citizens are involved, and political leaders and the news media react sharply to the crisis. During such moments, the "redneck" may lash out at the "enemy" never knowing the difference between an Arab and an Iranian, a Sunni and a Shiite, a Palestinian and a Pakistani.[5]

Certainly the September 11 attacks brought on the worst episodes of jingoistic discrimination ever seen so far in the United States, yet as the Pakistani respondent's story shows, jingoistic discrimination also accompanied the first Persian Gulf War and in chapter 2 we discussed similar backlash after the Iranian hostage crisis. These events have caused Middle Eastern Americans to cautiously pay attention to the news, in order to be aware of when such discrimination is likely to occur. For example, for Amir, watching the latest news before going to work has become a vital necessity that could help explain the hateful gazes or more than usual scrutiny encountered in the course of a given day. Indeed, whenever the terror alert level is raised for the general population, say from yellow to orange, an internal terror system is raised in the psyche of Middle Eastern Americans who fear increased potential for random violence and insults.

Medical Settings

Recent reports not only by social scientists but also by organizations that oversee health care, and by doctors themselves (for example, in *The New England Journal of Medicine*), have documented racial bias in the U.S. medical care system.[6] These reports show that for centuries, medical care in the United States has been founded on and distributed according to stereotypical assumptions about people of color. Although one of the least discussed, this must be one of the most dangerous forms of discrimination. Some Middle Eastern Americans, like African Americans in previous research, report facing bias in the health care system. For example, a Pakistani respondent stated:

> I mean like last year my wife had some medical condition and we were getting several opinions, actually we got two opinions and in both cases within the first five

minutes the doctor did ask us, "So what country are you from?" And that makes us feel uncomfortable because things cross our mind that may be a factor in the treatment of us.

It is possible that doctors are just being curious when they ask those from other countries where they are from. However, in a setting in which the doctor is in a position of authority, and the patient is aware that she or he has the power to either help or neglect to help one who is in physical distress, to ask such a question either shows extremely poor judgment or that, indeed, one's country of origin will in fact make a difference in the standard of care she or he will receive. Some have suggested that doctors need better cross-cultural training, in order to understand better how to communicate with patients from other ethnic backgrounds.

For those who mean well and simply ask the wrong questions, such training would be useful. However, for others, it is likely that the place from which a patient comes may in fact play a role in the standard of care she or he receives, if not on a conscious, intentional level, in a less conscious way. For example, doctors have been found to make assumptions about how effective a particular course of treatment is likely to be given a patient's culture or background and thus preemptively deny them that treatment, under the assumption that the patient will not comply with it anyway, and thus it will be a waste of time, resources, and effort.[7] It may be the case that the doctors this man and his wife encountered were using stereotypical assumptions about "the Middle Eastern or Muslim lifestyle" to inform either their diagnosis or their course of treatment. Such action could endanger patients' health.

Amir has had similar experiences in medical settings. For example, during a dental visit shortly after September 11, his dentist, while working on his teeth, asked him in a sarcastic tone, "So do you feel persecuted?" On another occasion, when he was waiting for a medical examination, he overheard nurses whispering, "Yeah, he is an Arab." The impression he received was that the nurses were reluctant to have contact with him and were arguing over who should take his chart. It is important to place these encounters in the context of the media reports about how Middle Eastern terrorists might be plotting to infect Americans with the small pox virus, or how terrorists might be seeking medical help after inadvertently exposing themselves to anthrax or other toxins. In this context, a young Middle Eastern man's visit to a doctor's office becomes a noteworthy event for the medical staff.

Finally, bias in the health care system can sometimes keep otherwise qualified practitioners from being able to be involved in care-giving. For example, a young Arab woman spoke of her mother, a pharmacist who had immigrated to the United States and was attempting to become licensed to practice here.

She related how after many months, although all her mother needed to do was to take a board exam, she could not even get an appointment to do so. The young woman and her family believed that the interactions with the administrators and her mother had changed when they found out her mother was Arabic. Not only had she not been able to get licensed, this woman could not even get past the first level of gate-keeping—obtaining a simple appointment to take an exam.

Other Public Places

Discrimination in public places may leave a person feeling especially vulnerable, for several reasons. Because it happens in a public place, the space is more open and less protected, the person perpetrating the discrimination can do so quickly and often anonymously, and thus the action can be more severe and dangerous.[8] A Turkish respondent stated that she takes precautions in public, almost as a person would for a possible rainy day, for potential discrimination:

> Interviewer: One thing, when we asked you if you were worried at all about physical violence, or whatever, you said that you do take certain precautions.
> Respondent: Most definitely. I cannot just go around freely or comfortably. I am always cautious about what is happening around me. And, if I feel something strange or something suspicious, I always change my route a little bit.

Several respondents had encountered frightening acts of racism in public places. For example, a Pakistani woman stated:

> I can think of a million examples [of discrimination]. A couple of days after September 11, my brother, my younger brother, he is now twenty-two, he was twenty or twenty-one at the time, was jumped by a group of guys, just chanting . . . and he had his lip split open, and they bashed the windshield of his car with a beer bottle and it's crazy, and he has never even been to Pakistan.

Because of the jingoistic discrimination that arose immediately after the terrorist attacks, this woman's younger brother, who she describes elsewhere as having a beard, was brutally attacked by several assailants. As media accounts show, this kind of behavior seemed to be a way for some people to relieve their frustration, anger, and sense of helplessness after the attacks, at the expense of their fellow citizens. Council on American-Islamic Relations (CAIR) reports show that these kinds of attacks are still going on at the writing of this book, two years after the September 11 attacks.

Not only this woman's brother, but her older parents were threatened:

Respondent: I'm always worried for my dad when he goes out. I know people have threatened him. People have threatened my mom. We had guys that come to my house. Yeah, my family has had a lot of problems. . . .

Interviewer: You said they threatened your father; physically, anonymously, or someone he knows?

Respondent: Like I said, he's in real estate, and a lot of his property is in downtown [of his city], and a lot of people know him, he's been there for thirty years, and they know he's a Muslim, and people are always saying things to him, walking by his property when he's there, someone scratched his car. Things like that, nobody tried to hurt him, but after my brother was attacked, it became much more of a worry for us. So in that sense it's changed my life in that I feel more guarded and I feel more protective of my family, and of my friends that are Muslim.

This woman worries about her parents, and her father particularly. Although he has not been physically attacked, as her brother was, a sense of threat against him is a constant presence, signaled by such ominous markers as people lingering on the family's property and scratching their car. Such behavior is likely intended to intimidate the family, showing them that if a time comes when they want to, the perpetrators can escalate the behavior at will.

Some respondents, like the young Pakistani college student, have been verbally harassed by strangers in public since September 11. Having such a thing happen can suddenly change what feels like a safe street into a threatening open space. One Arabic woman, when asked about her experiences after the attacks, describes being yelled at on the street in a northeastern college town:

Respondent: Yeah, the first three months was very—

Interviewer: Difficult.

Respondent: Difficult, yes. We were scared to go to grocery stores and I was faced with several yellings at the road. I had a lot of questions from everyone, even from strangers. So many different things.

Amir himself, walking through a parking lot in Daytona Beach, Florida, where, until that point he had felt very comfortable, given its relative diversity, heard a scream directed his way shortly after September 11. At first, he was not even sure that the man, driving a pick-up truck, was yelling at him, until he realized the words that he had yelled: "Raghead, go home!" The incident was particularly terrifying for him because of the short distance between himself and the passing truck. Had the man been a little angrier or more willing to inflict physical harm, he could have easily run over him.

Such experiences can linger on in a person's consciousness and cause him or her to feel a constant sense of vulnerability. In the months following September 11, 2001, many Middle Eastern Americans scarcely had time for one such incident to fade from memory before another followed it. Further, for people of color, racism can become part of collective memory. In other words, even though a specific incident may happen to only one member of the community, it may be shared with others, in part in order to seek support for dealing with it, and in the process others also become affected by hearing about the discrimination that people like them have suffered.[9] In this way, the effects of racism may be compounded by incidents of discrimination suffered by friends and family.

Different racial and ethnic groups face heightened scrutiny in various settings. For example, Latino and African Americans often face racial profiling on the nation's highways, because of the assumption that they may be engaged in the transport of illegal drugs. Indeed, a term has been coined for the racial profiling of African Americans, particularly—"DWB," or "Driving While Black." Even before September 11, but even more so afterward, a similar type of profiling of Middle Eastern Americans, sarcastically termed "FWA," or "Flying While Arab," became an increasing problem for many, so much so that some spoke of avoiding travel altogether. Some of our respondents told of incidents of uncomfortable encounters or negative treatment they received in airports or on airplanes. In a focus group interview, three Muslim Americans discussed this problem:

> Respondent A: I always get called for the random searches.
> Respondent B: Yeah, random searches my ass! [Said sarcastically.]
> Respondent A: No. Not really. I mean now days whenever you get on a flight, people always look who's on the flight and they'll always give you—
> Respondent C: The funny thing is, you're doing the same thing.

These young men express their fears of travel—that at any time, problems could arise. They note, cynically, and yet with humor, that it is obvious to them that the "random" searches are anything but. Still, even while discussing their frustrations with what they know to be racial profiling, these young men try to see the situation from the perspective of those treating them negatively—they admit that they, too, look around on flights more nervously than they did prior to the terrorist attacks.

An Iranian woman, similarly, discusses airport scrutiny:

> Interviewer: The whole terrible things that happened on September 11, have those events changed anything about your life here in the United States? Have you noticed any difference since that?
> Respondent: Not in my life. Of course, when I'm traveling and they see my name, like even though I have an American passport but the name, they think of Iran. They look at me and they want to search me more. . . . And it's like because I'm from Iran they have to do this. That's a little bit embarrassing but I don't have

any choice and I can't do anything about it and I guess it's okay, they do their job.

Interviewer: Yeah, but you've noticed it increasing since September 11th?

Respondent: Oh yeah, in airports, oh yeah.

Although clearly aware she is being treated as she is based solely on her Iranian last name, this woman attempts to find a way to be patient with the new scrutiny in airports.

Some of the heightened awareness in airports comes not from airport personnel, but from other passengers. For example, about a year after the attacks, Amir was traveling across the country alone for the first time. Placed in first class, at one point, he heard two men behind him begin speaking to each other loudly about his presence there. Finally, one stated to the other, at a volume clearly intended for him to hear "That's okay, if he moves from that seat during this flight, he'll smell my foot." Of course, Amir's predicament was that should he have reacted to this verbal threat, he would have indeed been labeled as a terrorist. He opted to wait until the end of the flight and simply stare at the man in disgust while getting his bag from the overhead compartment.

Such reactions from fellow passengers have been so frequent that Amir has developed a routine for managing the discomfort throughout the flying process. For example, one of the worst parts of FWA is walking the "gauntlet"— boarding the plane and walking down the center aisle as every passenger already seated scrutinizes him from head to toe. In order to make this part of travel less uncomfortable for both himself and his fellow passengers, Amir travels extremely light. In fact, he tries to take absolutely nothing on the plane in his hands that might make another passenger or the crew nervous. If there are bags to be brought aboard, jackets, or books, his fellow travelers carry them. The interesting thing about discrimination, for many Middle Eastern Americans, is the lengths they must go to make sure *other* Americans are comfortable enough not to discriminate against *them.*

Finally, some discrimination in public places has of course been experienced by Middle Eastern Americans long before September 11. For example, a Turkish woman describes recurring discrimination in public places:

One example is just in grocery stores or in malls, or in anywhere you are buying something, you have something and you want to ask some questions. In front of you there are a couple of American people, obviously, and the cashier person talked to them and laughed and made jokes and stuff, even talked about the weather and stuff. And then it's your turn, my turn especially, and I ask some questions, "Do you have one more of this?" when I couldn't find it there, and the answer was very short, and very rude, sometimes even. They were just saying, "No. If it's not there, we don't have it." Or, I would say, "Could you please check this price first, because there was a sale marked, but I didn't know and I'm not sure whether this belongs to that or not." And then they just say, "Yes!" or "No!" Their answers are very short. And their face expresses a lot of stuff, a lot. The way they're looking at you is completely different than the person right in front of you that they were talking with.

This woman has repeatedly experienced incidents of being either passed over in line, as if she is invisible, or treated as if she is a problem to dispose of so that the clerk can move on to "real" customers. She believes that wearing a hijab accounts for much of this treatment. Indeed, women who are veiled experience negative reactions often in public places. This same woman stated that when she and a friend were in a grocery store on one occasion, a young man ran up and tore her friend's hijab off her head. Another woman, the American wife of one of our Iranian respondents, who wears the hijab, stated that after September 11, as she crossed a street, a car sped up as if to try to hit her. She has also, on repeated occasions, had rude comments made to her regarding her choice to wear a hijab. Finally, a young Egyptian woman spoke of being stared at in public regularly because she wears a hijab:

In the beginning, I can't remember where we were. I think in the mall. Yeah, in the mall, sometimes people would stare at you, but I don't care what they think, you know? You can do whatever you want, but I really don't care. In the beginning, I used to care. I used to care why would they look at me this way. You know? But I know why. My dad told me just not to care about it. . . . So, I just ignore them.
[Later]
Interviewer: Then, the other thing that I was wondering is that you said that it used to bother you at first, the people looking at you—
Respondent: Yeah, uh-huh.
Interviewer: How did you get past that bothering you? What did you do to make it not bother you anymore?
Respondent: Well, I used to tell my mom and dad about all of it. So, they kept . . . my mom and my dad told me that that's how people act. People are different. They don't know much about us. So, that's why they do that. And, some people are good and some are not. You have to expect that some people won't be that nice to you. . . . Just ignore them. That's all you can do, actually. Sometimes, actually, in high school, there was a kid on my school bus who used to stare at me and my brother. And another kid told me that she was staring and I said, "Yeah, I know." And, she said, "Well, stare at her back," so she wouldn't stare. I did that one time and she didn't stare again, you know what I mean? So, that's all. It gets funny. . . .
Interviewer: It's like people assume that you aren't going to do anything back—
Respondent: Uh-huh. Yeah—
Interviewer: And then you—
Respondent: Yeah. I can stare back, you know. [Laughs]

The discrimination this young woman faces is in the ability of others to make her an object of curiosity, to make her feel constantly on display. Although her parents suggest that she ignore the stares, this brings her little satisfaction. Insightfully, one of her friends suggests that she "stare back." In turning the gaze from herself and onto those who stare, she becomes, instead of an object, finally a more active subject in interracial interactions, even these non-verbal ones, on the most basic level of communication.

FIGHTING BACK

The Middle Eastern Americans we interviewed are beginning to come to terms with their status as a minority group in the United States. Although for many of them, especially the more recent immigrants, discrimination is a new experience, they are learning how to cope with it, and when possible to fight back. Sometimes fighting back means reasserting their identity as Americans. For example, during a visit to a mosque in Chicago, members of the mosque told Karyn about an incident that occurred soon after September 11, 2001. Their mosque had faced vandalism and attacks, and so members of the mosque were posted outside, around the building to guard it from would-be attackers. On the opposite side of the street, a menacing crowd had gathered. From across the street this group sang the national anthem, as loudly as possible, apparently to assert themselves as "true Americans" and bully the Middle Eastern outsiders. However, the mosque members fought back by singing the national anthem back across the street. Thus, in the midst of an autumn day in the heart of Chicago, there was a face-off between two groups that both claimed the anthem as a symbol of their identity and patriotism. One used it to intimidate outsiders and the other to announce their membership in American society. In this way, our Muslim respondents resisted being treated as unwelcome outsiders or others.

The struggle of Middle Eastern Americans against discrimination and prejudice is advancing in a number of ways. On the one hand, many are learning from the struggle of other ethnic groups with the same problem. For example, consider a young Muslim American's reflections about his future:

> I think it will get worse in the next few years. I can't really say when but it's going to come back and it's going to be—we will be accepted. Blacks have had to struggle, Jewish people have had to struggle, Cubans have had to struggle in south Florida.

The awareness that other groups have faced similar challenges both inspires this young man and provides him with a model for overcoming prejudice.

A related strategy in the struggle of Middle Eastern Americans for fair

treatment is to familiarize themselves with their legal rights and to support
advocacy organizations that represent them. As another Muslim American
puts it:

> First thing I've done and what my wife has done is we have made ourselves more
> familiar with our rights. So that if something should happen we know what our
> rights are so that we could be better prepared to respond to it. That's one of the
> biggest things that we have done. The other thing we have done, we have started
> to support Muslims' human rights organizations so that we have something to fall
> back on.

Finally, some have begun to question the cultural mandates that discourage
self-disclosure and openness to the non-Muslim world. At a national meeting
of CAIR, a Muslim American woman stated:

> With an event like this I am optimistic. I don't know if you ever listen to any of
> those sessions but there is really this grass roots lobbying movement just educating
> people, and I think that one of the biggest problems and why it is so easy to attack
> the Muslim community is because a lot of Muslims practice isolation, where they
> just keep to themselves and their only friends are each other and they don't try to
> reach out, and that's why they are easy targets. And so one thing that September 11
> did and one thing they are starting to do now with these conferences is to have a
> breakdown of that isolation and have Muslims be interacting with non-Muslims in a
> way that they never did before. And they've been forced to do that, to show people
> that we're very similar and I think that's a very positive thing, and I think that it
> could have positive consequences.

There is a realization among Muslim Americans, in particular, that to be less
vulnerable to random violence and discrimination, they must organize and
end their isolation from mainstream American society. In the next chapter we
describe how this awareness about the need for mobilization against discrimination has fostered the formation of a panethnic Middle Eastern identity.

NOTES

1. Joe R. Feagin and Karyn D. McKinney, *The Many Costs of Racism* (Lanham, Md.:
Rowman & Littlefield, 2003), p. 43.

2. Feagin and McKinney, *The Many Costs of Racism.*

3. See, for example, U.S. Commission on Civil Rights, "The Problem: Discrimination," in *Race, Class and Gender in the United States*, 6th ed., ed. Paula Rothenberg (New
York: Worth, 2004), pp. 213–23.

4. John F. Dovidio and Samuel L. Gaertner, "On the Nature of Contemporary Prejudice: The Causes, Consequences and Challenges of Aversive Racism," in *Race, Class and*

Gender in the United States, 6th ed., ed. Paula Rothenberg (New York: Worth, 2004), pp. 132–43.

5. Nabeel Abraham, "Anti-Arab Racism and Violence in the United States," in *The Development of Arab-American Identity* (Ann Arbor: University of Michigan Press, 1994), pp. 191–92.

6. For a thorough review of these studies, see Feagin and McKinney, *The Many Costs of Racism*, pp. 180–210.

7. Feagin and McKinney, *The Many Costs of Racism*, pp. 180–210.

8. These ideas draw on Joe R. Feagin and Melvin P. Sikes, *Living with Racism: The Black Middle-Class Experience* (Boston: Beacon Press, 1994), p. 56 and following.

9. Feagin and Sikes, *Living with Racism*, p. 348.

Chapter 7

"I Am a Middle Eastern American!": Ethnic Self-Identification

One way in which ethnic minorities combat discrimination is to form coalitions, or to consolidate their resources. This process, which is a type of ethnogenesis,[1] results in the creation of new ethnic forms, or in some cases panethnic identities. In this chapter we examine the rise of the Middle Eastern American identity in response to discrimination. We begin by defining the concept of ethnogenesis and underlining its historical significance in U.S. ethnic relations. Using data from news reports and our interviews, we then discuss the structural contingencies as well as individual perspectives that are beginning to shape the process of ethnogenesis among Middle Eastern Americans. We end by citing the challenges faced by Middle Eastern Americans in their efforts to form a panethnic identity.

ETHNOGENESIS AND ITS CRITICS

For our purposes, "ethnogenesis" is the process by which ethnic practices or groups are formed by combining "old" and "new" cultural elements, sometimes in response to nativistic attacks. For example, the creation of "native Anglo Saxon Americans" was the result of an ethnogenesis that combined the diverse cultural heritage of groups such as the Dutch, Swedes, Scots, and Welsh into a unified single ethnic category.[2] The same could be said about the creation of Hispanic American, Asian American, and African American groups.

Some conservative commentators have described ethnic identification as an emerging social problem, the prelude to the so-called balkanization of America. From this perspective, ethnogenesis is part of a recent multicultural movement that discourages minority members from becoming full Americans and creates social disorder. This position assumes that: (a) organized protests and demands for equal treatment under the law are inherently anti-American, and (b) American society was stable just until the arrival of ethnic malcontents. However, as Vincent Parillo[3] notes, the nostalgic view of America as a stable, culturally homogenous society is at best based on wishful revisionist history. In his words, "the fact is that multiculturalism has been an ongoing social reality in the United States, not just since its inception as a nation, but even in its primeval colonial cradle."[4] The groups that made up colonial and postcolonial America (e.g., the Irish, Germans, Scots, and Welsh) were involved in their own struggles over matters of ethnic identity. For example, at one point in the nineteenth century, the Germans in the North West Territory of the United States petitioned the Congress "to create a German state with German as the official language."[5] Similarly, early Irish immigrants struggled against oppression from the "native" Anglo Saxons, as recently depicted in Martin Scorcese's movie *The Gangs of New York*. Thus, ethnic struggle and ethnic self-identification is not an invention of liberal supporters of the 1960s Civil Rights Movement. On the contrary, ethnogenesis, the formation of new ethnic coalitions in response to political and economic oppression, is an American tradition. Indeed, one can argue that the very formation of a "native American culture" was a type of ethnogenesis in response to the British colonial rule.

Our focus in this chapter is on the contingencies that have paved the way for the formation of a Middle Eastern American identity. Of special interest to us is the notion of ethnicity as a fluid and variable phenomenon. That is to say, we don't view ethnicity as an authentic, natural feature of a group that is maintained or discovered by bona fide members. Instead, as Prema Kurien states, "ethnicity does not arise autonomously. Even, the so called 'old' ethnicity that supposedly occurs 'naturally' is shown to have been historically constituted through a complex interaction among economic, political, and social forces."[6]

In this chapter we approach ethnicity as a social construct that can be used to cope with discrimination. In particular, we are interested in the structural and individual factors that have motivated Middle Eastern Americans of various national, religious, and ethnic backgrounds to come together as a single panethnic group.

THE CREATION OF PANETHNIC GROUPS

By panethnicity, we mean the coming together of people from different linguistic, cultural, religious, or national backgrounds, or as Laurie Kay Sommers states:

Panethnic groups are a conglomerate of entities which in and of themselves each constitute a distinct "nation" defined by ethnic characteristics, but which are bound together by an even more general level of subjectively and objectively shared supraethnic traits.[7]

Panethnic groups are created by internal and external forces. Sometimes several ethnic groups are misrecognized by others and lumped together into one larger group. The dominant group may treat all these groups similarly. For example, there has been a tendency to place all Asians into one category, a placement that was resisted by first generation Asians. By the second and third generations, however, Asian Americans began to recognize that panethnic identification could be useful for resisting the discrimination that was directed at all Asians.[8] In response to being treated as foreigners or outsiders, Asians of different backgrounds and nationalities began to self-identify as Asian Americans beginning in the late 1960s and early 1970s. The same could be said for the coming together of different African tribes during slavery to form the African American panethnic group.

Panethnic identity may be developing similarly for Middle Eastern Americans, who are painted with the same wide brush by other Americans. Being singled out as foreign, and as potential enemies, despite national identity, is an experience shared by those of several different Middle Eastern ethnic backgrounds. At the same time, for some, sharing a common Muslim religion, which is connected to a common Arabic language, can also contribute to panethnicity. As one respondent pointed out, even most non-Muslim Middle Eastern Americans are familiar with the Koranic text, and this contributes to a sense of a shared history and culture.

Shared cultural symbols play a crucial role in the formation of panethnic groups. A common identity is "solidified and expressed by an overarching symbol system or 'cultural umbrella' that has the power to appeal across individual ethnic lines."[9] For example, for Latinos, the "cultural umbrella" includes the Spanish language, cultural festivals, music and dance, political movements, foreign affairs, and shared discrimination.[10] Middle Eastern Americans' "cultural umbrella" may just be beginning to take shape. As noted, for many it includes a shared language. For some, it may involve religion, which includes certain rituals and celebrations. Almost all have similar experiences with discrimination. Part of the cultural umbrella for many Middle Eastern Americans is also a common interest in foreign affairs, such as the events in Iraq as well as the ongoing Palestinian-Israeli conflict.

In what follows, we see how Middle Eastern Americans contend with the internal and external forces of panethnicity that we briefly outlined here. As our interviews show, there is a growing sentiment among Middle Eastern Americans for coming together as a united cultural group.

EXTERNAL PRESSURES

For our purposes, "external pressures" refer to experiences that make a person aware of his or her ethnic distinctiveness. For Middle Eastern Americans the main motivation for their treatment as outsiders has been the assumption that they are involved in terrorist activities. The following describes two related external sources in what has been dubbed "the War on Terrorism" that have shaped the experiences of Middle Eastern Americans as ethnic outsiders.

The Arab-Israeli Conflict, 1967–2001

While the stereotype of violent, uncivilized Arabs circulated in Western thought as early as the Christian Crusades of the eleventh century, the real possibility that Middle Eastern Americans might pose a threat to the interests of the United States became a public policy concern especially after the 1967 Arab-Israeli war. In this conflict a coalition of Arab countries (e.g., Egypt, Jordan, Syria, etc.) tried unsuccessfully to uproot the newly founded state of Israel on the ground that it was established on territories that were unlawfully taken away from Palestinians. With the United States explicitly allying itself with Israel during this conflict, the threat of possible retaliation against American interests by those sympathetic to the Palestinian cause became a practical concern, and has remained so since.

For Arabs living in the United States, many of whom were relatively unconcerned with foreign affairs, the Arab-Israeli conflict meant the transformations of their identities from ordinary American citizens to suspects in what would eventually become the war on terrorism. The words of a third-generation Arab American college student from the early 1970s are particularly instructive in this regard,

> With each event which related to the Middle East situation, the abuse and threats intensified. . . . I began to realize more and more that while I neither identify with nor understand what is happening in the Middle East, ... [I am held] accountable for the problem there. Through this rather perverted psychological process, I was forced to recognize my transformation from being an American citizen who happened to be of Arab origin, to being an Arab of American citizenship. I now need and want to know something about my cultural heritage, and the situation there. We will need to organize the community here.[11]

By all accounts, prior to the 1967 war, the existence of Arabs in this country went relatively unnoticed. Subsequently, however, a long list of tragedies, beginning with the taking of hostages and murder of Israeli athletes during the Munich Olympic games of 1972 through September 11, 2001, have made Middle Eastern Americans targets of law enforcement scrutiny and public mistrust. The persecution has been particularly intense in the aftermath of terrorist attacks—even those that had nothing to do with Middle Eastern people, such as the 1995 Oklahoma City bombing.

Beginning with Operation Boulder in 1972, the first major FBI campaign specifically targeting Arab Americans, through the PATRIOT Act of 2001, the typical law enforcement response has involved: (a) systematic interviews with members of Middle Eastern American communities in search of information about terrorism, and (b) selective enforcement of immigration laws in the form of detaining and deporting Middle Easterners on minor visa violations. At the same time, the public response has been to randomly attack people, businesses, and places of worship associated with Middle Eastern Americans. Thus, the identification and cataloging of Middle Eastern Americans as a distinct segment of the U.S. population has been a law enforcement objective and, to some degree, a public obsession for over three decades.

Ethnic Profiling: "Middle Eastern–Looking Men"

Officially, meaning under immigration laws, Middle Eastern Americans are classified as white. Indeed, most affirmative action forms specifically instruct people of Middle Eastern descent to identify themselves as "white." However, since the tragedy of September 11, a new phrase has been added to the ethnic lexicon that sets Middle Eastern Americans aside from all other ethnic groups. Specifically, the words "Middle Eastern–looking man or men," almost always used in connection with a terrorist threat, have come to connote the same meaning as the words "black suspect." Their official classification as "white" seems to have no practical relevance in everyday life as they are singled out for antiterrorism measures.

In the past few years, news report after news report has highlighted the potential gravity of a violent, or simply a suspicious, act by putting it in the context of possible involvement of Middle Eastern–looking men. Even before September 11, in the immediate aftermath of the Oklahoma City bombing (a white-supremacist-caused horror that incidentally did not pave the way for a war on white supremacy terror), news bulletins announced the search for two Middle Eastern–looking suspects.[12]

Some ordinary Americans' reaction to the presence of Middle Eastern–looking men in public places has been equally stigmatizing. After the September 11 attacks, Middle Eastern–looking people, men in particular, were verbally harassed, physically attacked, and sometimes killed, regardless of their actual nationality or association with Islam or the Middle East. In Mesa, Arizona, an Indian Sikh was shot and killed for being dark skinned, bearded, and wearing a turban.[13] The same man responsible for this crime also fired shots at a Lebanese gas station worker and an Afghan family.[14] In addition to the rash of indiscriminate violence, in several incidents across the country Middle Eastern–looking men were removed from flights after completing all security checks and being seated.[15] The reason offered in most cases was as vague as the crew not feeling safe flying with them.

In October 2001, after repairing his car at an auto mechanic shop in Nebraska, a Middle Eastern–looking man was reported to the local sheriff's office simply because he looked suspicious and had a New York license plate. The local police ran his name against an FBI watch list, which showed him to be "clean."[16] Nonetheless, the FBI was contacted and the man was followed to his destination in California where he was interviewed by the FBI. The incident is written up in the local papers as "the folks in town . . . just being cautious."[17]

In a similar incident, in May 2002, in Stoughton, Massachusetts, "three Muslims walked into BJ's Wholesale Club to use the restroom and began to say their evening prayers. The chanting caused a panic. Someone pulled the fire alarm, and State Police showed up with bomb-sniffing dogs."[18] In December 2002, in St. Louis, after a library user alerted the staff that "a Middle Eastern-looking man using the computers looked suspicious,"[19] the FBI was called. Since the man had left before the agents arrived, the records of everyone who had used the library in the past week were checked in an effort to identify the man.

In September 2002, in one of the most notable incidents of this kind, three Middle Eastern–looking men (all three U.S. citizens) were tracked across state lines from Georgia to south Florida, arrested, and held in police custody for seventeen hours while their car was being searched for bombs. The entire incident was aired live on national television. The police reaction was triggered after a woman reported that she overheard the men speak the following conversation in a restaurant, "They think they were sad on 9-11, wait until 9-13. . . . We do not have enough time to bring it down. . . . If we don't have enough to bring it down, I have contacts and we can get enough to bring it down."[20] The students denied making any statements about September 11 and claimed that the reference to "bringing it down" was about transporting a car. Law enforcement authorities found no connections between the three men and terrorism. Nonetheless, after the hospital where all three were expected to complete their medical internships received over 2,000 threatening e-mails, its administrators asked the young men to go elsewhere to complete their internship.[21] The woman who reported the incident, a white forty-four-year-old nurse from Calhoun, Georgia, was hailed by the authorities (including Florida governor Jeb Bush) as a good American who was doing her patriotic duty. Most commentators disputed the men's denials and concluded that they were guilty of playing a prank on the woman.

The prevalence and the growing use of the category Middle Eastern–looking man in everyday discourse can also be tracked in popular humor. For example, a December 2001 sports article about an upcoming game between the Detroit Lions and the Tampa Bay Buccaneers offers the following supposedly humorous advice as a sure way for Tampa Bay to score a touch-down: "Before game, make phone call to John Ashcroft and inform on Lions' 'Middle-Eastern-Looking' secondary."[22]

It is reasonable to assume that looking Middle Eastern has impacted members of this population in various institutional settings as well. For example, in New York, defense lawyers began voicing concerns that clients who look Middle Eastern might be viewed negatively by jurors. As one lawyer was quoted in the *New York Times*, "people have some sort of visceral reaction to someone who is Middle Eastern-looking."[23] Similarly, at least in the period immediately following September 11, "Middle Eastern parents removed their children from local schools to protect them from bullying and taunts of 'camel jockey,' 'terrorist' and worse."[24]

At the federal level, the Bush administration issued a directive on June 17, 2003, that declared, "Racial profiling is not merely wrong; it's ineffective . . . race-based assumptions perpetuate stereotypes that are harmful to our diverse democracy."[25] However, the same policy allows for numerous exceptions in the interest of national security. For example, the policy lists the following scenario as a possible exception: "U.S. intelligence sources report that terrorists of a particular ethnic group are planning to hijack a U.S. commercial jet in California next week. That week, authorities in California may subject members of that ethnic group to heightened security."[26] Supposedly, the directive allows for minimum use of profiling under a specific timeframe and location. However, given that by definition the threat of terrorism is indefinite and ubiquitous, the directive amounts to an official sanctioning of racial profiling at a federal level.

One can speculate that the public and governmental concerns with Middle Eastern–looking people is a passing phase that will evaporate as we move further away from the events of September 11. Sadly, Gallup opinion polls point to the contrary. Specifically, they show that while other September 11 related shifts in public opinion, such as the country becoming more religious and trusting of big government, have returned to their pre–September 11 levels, the distrust toward Middle Eastern Americans has worsened. In response to the question, "Would you say you that you now have less trust in Arabs living in this country than you did before the terrorist attacks on Sept. 11 . . . ?" an increasingly higher percentage have reported having less trust in Arab Americans.[27] Between September 2001 and September 2002, the percentage of distrust increased from 35 percent to 44 percent. If anything, these numbers suggest that the idea that Middle Eastern–looking people are not trustworthy is a growing sentiment.

For many Middle Eastern Americans, the question is no longer whether the perceptions of being mistreated are real or paranoid delusions, but how to overcome their status as second-class citizens. Based on interviews with twenty Middle Eastern Americans from Egypt, Iran, Pakistan, Lebanon, and Turkey, the next section explores some of the pathways to ethnic self-identification and ethnogenesis among Middle Eastern Americans. The construction of a panethnic identity may help to insulate Middle Eastern Americans from the damage created by this second-class citizenship status.

COMING TOGETHER: CONSTRUCTING A NEW IDENTITY

The analysis of our interview data revealed that there are four main avenues through which our respondents pursued a sense of ethnic self-identification. The following presents each of these themes.

Acknowledging a Shared Heritage and a Shared Predicament

A central theme in the creation of a sense of panethnic identity for our respondents was the acknowledgment that they have in common with other nationalities from the Middle East (a) a cultural heritage and (b) distinguishing physical characteristics that could draw uninvited attention to them. The realization of panethnic interests involves emphasizing cultural and physical similarities, while at the same time downplaying differences. For example, while our respondents were aware of national and cultural differences between Arabs and Iranians (for instance, Iranians speak Farsi, not Arabic), they also acknowledged that in the current political climate of the United States, these differences are meaningless to the average American who might suspect them of terrorism. Their indiscriminate persecution as suspected Middle Eastern–looking men has created a sense of camaraderie that transcends *old* national and ethnic differences.

The same process applies to other Middle Eastern nationals, or people who are perceived as being Middle Eastern. Consider, for example, a Pakistani man's description of how his wife was confused for a Palestinian:

> My wife, she used to work in a hospital and this lady, an American lady, she one day went to my wife and told her "I'm sorry that you guys and Jewish people have so many problems." And she said, "What are you talking about?" This lady said "Don't you have Pakistanis and Jewish people fighting in Israel?" And my wife said, "It's 'Palestine' not 'Pakistan.'" [Laughs]. She thought that was funny.

Experiences with the uniform and stereotypical ways in which they are perceived by their fellow citizens is slowly forging multiple diverse Middle Eastern ethnics into a single category for practical, everyday purposes.

Some respondents also report a more culturally derived sense of connection with others from the Middle East. For example, one respondent pointed out how the Koranic text and its calligraphic representations act as a familiar icon that unites people from the Middle East regardless of their particular language or culture. Respondents also spoke of how they had begun noticing more subtle features of a shared heritage, such as gold medallions with the word "Allah" engraved on them, which are quite common among Middle Eastern men.

The revival of religious beliefs and practices is another way a panethnic Middle Eastern American identity is achieved. For example, one respondent stated that he became a more orthodox Muslim after September 11. In his words:

> Interviewee: Prior to September 11 I was what they called—and I'm not sure if I agree with that term anymore—I was more like a non-practicing Muslim, far removed from the requirements of Islam. I did a lot of things that were not approved of in Islam. And after September 11 I had to go back and agree with it. I had to make a lot of adjustment in my value system and I'm still working.
> Interviewer: Why?
> Interviewee: Because the image of the backlash against Muslims made me think about my life and how I want to raise my kids. And I thought I had to go back and figure out what is the proper thing to do.

Other respondents similarly spoke of reestablishing their Islamic religious practices and ties to the community, or even discovering Islam for the first time, after it came under increased scrutiny. One young female lawyer, for example, who had never been particularly religious before, spoke of finding a new place for Islam in her life, based primarily on the sense of community with other Middle Eastern Americans she has found that it brings her.

Impression Management and Education

One part of the deliberate creation a new ethnic identity, especially for the consumption of the outside world, is impression management. Middle Eastern Americans, being aware that their every move is being watched, are making a conscious effort to live as model citizens and to portray a positive image of their religion and their culture. As an Iranian businessman put it, "Middle Eastern Americans . . . have to prove that they are worthy of living in the United States." In the following excerpt, a Pakistani businessman underscores this need for impression management.

> We need to act in a decent way. Even down to the most minute detail. Don't walk across a "don't walk signal." We need to be a shining example, the city upon the hill. That's the first thing. If you're not a good person yourself, then it doesn't matter what you talk to people about, it's more showing than telling.

This same man put his ideology into practice, going door to door in his neighborhood after the September 11 events to invite his neighbors first to an Independence Day celebration and later to his family's Ramadan gathering. To do so at a time when Middle Eastern–looking strangers are suspect was certainly a personal risk, but one that he stated he felt responsible for making on behalf of the larger Middle Eastern community.

A similar emphasis is placed on presenting a positive image of Islam. In particular, some respondents placed the blame for the misrepresentation of Islam on the shoulder of its practitioners and their failure to better educate the public about their religion. For example, a Turkish Muslim woman stated:

> I'm hoping that Middle Eastern people—educated Middle Eastern people—also will take the action in their hands, and they will be willing to, they will spend some time with other people to learn and to teach. One thing, people are afraid to ask questions about the religion and our culture, because they think that they will offend us. I mean, sometimes they ask me questions, but they look scared, and say, "Oh, we don't want you offended, but why is it like this?" And at that time it's the best time for me to speak up, as they say. I always say, "Please ask everything on your mind. I can answer as much as I know. If I don't know the answer, I promise you I will go, learn, come back and answer." And, this is what you are supposed to do. And a lot of Middle Eastern people, I believe, because they just hide themselves in their own group, they don't open themselves, they don't teach, they don't let the other people know about their culture and religion. I mean, we are also guilty by not letting them know what we have.

Here self-disclosure is recommended as a way of overcoming stereotypes; indeed, she stated that the best way to educate people is to "put [one's] personality up front." This is a crucial change of strategy in interpersonal relations for many Middle Eastern Americans. This *new* strategy challenges *old* cultural practices, where self-disclosure could have been construed as a psychological flaw or character weakness.

As a whole, through impression management, self-disclosure, and education, the Middle Eastern Americans we interviewed hope to create a new image of themselves and find support among their fellow citizens. In the words of an Iranian man:

> We have to start one person at a time, change them fundamentally, and that one person would be your best supporter. He goes out there and he starts defending you. It propagates from that point on.

This man believes that one way change can come for Middle Eastern Americans is through person-to-person contact. Although some question whether contact alone can end racial discrimination, it can at least begin to break down stereotypical and generalized thinking about a group that a person has not before had contact with. Personal contact may also increase the sense of empathy a person feels for another. This may be an effective "bottom-up" approach to social change.

Political Involvement

Historically, a barometer of the success of any minority group in the United States in the struggle against discrimination has been the ability of its members to form their own organizations and participate in local, state, and national politics. Middle Eastern Americans are no exception to this norm. More and more Middle Eastern Americans are beginning to realize that being organized and politically involved might help shield them from future episodes of backlash. As an Iranian American points out:

> Most Middle Eastern Americans used to be, and still are, *financial citizens* of the United States. That means they go to their work, they take their money, they go home spend it and don't want to be a part of the society. That is the worse thing that can happen [to] us. We have to become *social citizens*. By that I mean we have to participate in the board of our local hospitals, in the schools, and other associations. We didn't do that in the past. I hope the current situation is going to get us to the point that we start participating and believe in the power of voting.

This shift in attitude is similar to the need for self-disclosure discussed earlier. It is the realization that without a greater degree of public presence, Middle Eastern Americans continue to be vulnerable to stereotypes and discriminatory public policies. This respondent points out that what is needed in order to change public perceptions and gain greater political influence is a balancing of priorities between purely financial matters (i.e., success in the world of business, where historically Middle Eastern Americans have been one of the most successful groups) and social and political involvement.

The above statements also reflect the growing realization among Middle Eastern Americans that "business as usual," pun intended, will not be possible without increased political involvement. Indeed, a number of respondents reported having personally suffered or knowing people who suffered financial losses as a result of the September 11 backlash. For example, a restaurant owner in an exclusive community began losing customers after it was disclosed that he was Iranian. In a sense, the ethnogenesis of Middle Eastern Americans to some extent centers on the coupling of the *old* economic interests with *new* involvement in politics, particularly at the local level. This sentiment is echoed by another respondent:

> You have to join a community organization. The higher, the better because these are the people who are making the decisions. Ninety nine percent of people in this country don't do anything. They go to work for eight hours, they come home and watch TV for six hours; they have dinner, and go to sleep and do the exact same thing [the next day]. They go fishing on the weekend; they do whatever on the weekend. They don't make the policy of this country. But the one percent of people who do make the policies in this country, those are the people who sit on the community boards for the city, county and state. And that's what we need to do.

These astute observations about the nature of the American political system are a crucial part of how Middle Eastern Americans are going about inventing themselves. Not only are they becoming more politically involved, but they are becoming more selective about the organizations they join or support. For example, one respondent had this to say about the American Civil Liberties Union (ACLU).

> I am a card carrier of the ACLU. They are the only national organization that came to the defense of Muslims. They are the only one. Not the NAACP, nobody except for the ACLU came to the defense of Muslims after September 11 and I joined. I get their newsletter and there's not a single issue that I support in there except for the defense of Muslims. I don't support anything the ACLU is doing but they're defending me.

Here forming coalitions with other groups is understood to be a necessary part of gaining recognition and equal treatment as an ethnic group. What is particularly notable is the nuanced understanding of the American political system and its many faces. This respondent, a devout Muslim, joined an organization, which he fully understands backs other causes, such as gay rights, for example, that violate his religious principles. In addition to increased involvement in generic political groups, many other respondents mentioned joining specific Middle Eastern American organizations, indicating panethnic political affiliations. Additionally, at several Muslim and Middle Eastern American organizational gatherings, there was explicit reference made to the need to become more politically involved. Individuals were encouraged to be more personally aware and involved with issues that affect Middle Eastern Americans, and reference was made to the necessity of becoming more integrated into political life as a community, for example, by electing more Muslim and Middle Eastern Americans to public office.

CHALLENGES AND DIVISIONS

While the creation of a panethnic Middle Eastern identity might seem like an important step in overcoming the discrimination that members of this group face, it would be overly optimistic to assume that there is unanimous agreement on this course of action. There are many internal divisions among members of this group that block the aspiration of a panethnic identity. Yossi Shain[28] notes that Arab Americans, for example, are divided into "integrationists" and "isolationists." In his words, "ethnic isolationists in the United States consider their culture, religion, or tradition as alien to American culture, sometimes even superior to it."[29] On the other hand, Shain describes integrationists as Arabs who:

> identify themselves first and foremost as Americans. While protesting whatever exclusion they may feel from American society, they believe that their situation can and in time will improve and demand cultural and political recognition from mainstream institutions.[30]

The division between the isolationist and integrationist camps overlaps with other disagreements about religion and politics, and American foreign policy in particular. For example, during the first Persian Gulf War, Arab American activists found themselves torn between their loyalties to America and its foreign policies and their opposition to a war waged against other Arabs. At the same time, Christian Arab American and Muslim Arab American organizations do not always align themselves behind a united vision for political action. Similar divisions could be found in the Iranian American community, which is divided along secular and religious factions, with the latter tacitly approving of the Islamic government of Iran and the former supporting the overthrow of that regime.

Another source of division is the national differences that some Middle Eastern Americans continue to adhere to. For example, many Iranians separate themselves from Arabs and Pakistanis. An Iranian respondent stated, "most people mistake Iranian people for Arabs. We're not like them. I can tell you that Iranian people are not as religious as Arab people." Also, Turkish Americans speak a different language from both Arabs and Iranians and sometimes identify themselves with Europe more so than the Middle East.

Still, panethnicity is not necessarily an all-or-nothing prospect. In other words, groups may identify panethnically for particular purposes, but maintain their individual nationally, religiously, or politically based distinctions as well. In this sense, they may be cultures within a larger culture. Middle Eastern Americans may be learning to come together for strategic purposes panethnically, while still holding onto traditions that are linked to their specific ethnic cultures. As mentioned in chapter 1, the Census Report on Arab Americans found that some 20 percent have begun to identify panethnically.

What has eroded some of the differences between Middle Eastern Americans is the common experience with discrimination. When visiting a shopping mall in a predominantly white suburb, as an Iranian American, Amir is quick to notice other Middle Eastern Americans. Their very presence is reassuring to him. In their shared sense of vulnerability, Middle Eastern Americans might find themselves in an unspoken alliance.

NOTES

1. Andrew Greely, *Ethnicity in the United States* (New York: Wiley, 1974).

2. Eric Kaufmann, "American Exceptionalism Reconsidered: Anglo-Saxon Ethnogenesis in the 'Universal' Nation, 1776–1850," *Journal of American Studies* 33, no. 2 (1999): 437–57.

3. Vincent N. Parillo, "Diversity in America: A Sociological Analysis," *Sociological Forum* 9, no. 4 (1994): 523–45.

4. Parillo, "Diversity in America," p. 523.

5. Parillo, "Diversity in America," p. 526.

6. Prema Kurien, "Colonialism and Ethnogenesis: A Study of Kerala, India," *Theory and Society* 23 (1994): 385–417.

7. Laurie Kay Sommers, "Inventing Latinismo: The Creation of 'Hispanic' Panethnicity in the United States," *The Journal of American Folklore* 104, no. 411 (1991): 32–53, quote from p. 34.

8. Joe R. Feagin and Clairece B. Feagin, *Racial and Ethnic Relations*, 7th ed. (Upper Saddle River, N.J.: Prentice Hall, 2003), p. 302.

9. Sommers, "Inventing Latinismo," p. 35.

10. Sommers, "Inventing Latinismo."

11. Elaine Hagopian, "Minority Rights in a Nation-State: The Nixon Administration's Campaign against Arab-Americans," *Journal of Palestine Studies* 5, nos. 1 and 2 (1975–1976): 97–114.

12. "Arabs, Muslims Are Unlike the Stereotypes," *Buffalo* (N.Y.) *News*, April 29, 1995, p. 2.

13. Philip Delves, "New Prejudices Emerge in an Embittered City: New York's Arab Community Is Living in Fear of Attack," *The Daily Telegraph*, London, September 20, 2001, p. 7.

14. Delves, "New Prejudices Emerge," p. 7.

15. Anthony Brown, "Nervous Pilots Order Off 'Arab' Passengers," *The Observer*, September 23, 2001, p. 2.

16. Joe Dejka, "Middle-Eastern-Looking Driver Raises Suspicions in Ogallala," *Omaha* (Nebr.) *World Herald*, October 25, 2001, p. 1A.

17. Dejka, "Middle-Eastern-Looking Driver," p. 1A.

18. Fred Kaplan, "In Resignation or in Denial, People Live with Warnings," *The Boston Globe*, May 22, 2002, p. A28.

19. "Rights and the New Reality; Barring the Book Snoops," *Los Angeles Times*, August 8, 2003, p. 14.

20. Beverly Beckham, "Vigilant Get Profiled as Bigots," *The Boston Herald*, September 18, 2002, p. 41.

21. Beckham, "Vigilant Get Profiled," p. 41.

22. Martin Fennely, "Keyshawn Can't Go All Year without A TD—Can He?" *Tampa Tribune*, December 9, 2001, special sports section, p. 1.

23. William Glaberson, "A Nation Challenged: The Courts," *The New York Times*, October 3, 2001, p. 8.

24. Delves, "New Prejudices Emerge," p. 7.

25. "Racial Profiling; Loopholes Weaken New Policy," *Minneapolis Star Tribune*, June 20, 2003, p. 22A.

26. Jessamyn Blau, "New Rules Ban Most Racial Profiling," *St. Louis Post-Dispatch*, Missouri, June 18, 2003, p. A1.

27. Lydia Saad, "Have Americans Changed? Effects of Sept. 11 Have Largely Faded," Gallup Organization (www.gallup.com), p. 16.

28. Yossi, Shain, "Arab-Americans at a Crossroad," *Journal of Palestine Studies* 25, no. 3): 46–59.

29. Shain, "Arab-Americans," p. 49.

30. Shain, "Arab-Americans," p. 49.

Chapter 8

"Whining" for Social Justice?

In this book, we hope to have provided Middle Eastern Americans with a framework for making sense of their experiences in the broader context of the system of racial inequality in the United States. Taking their experiences out of individual context and making sense of them socially (to paraphrase the famed sociologist C. Wright Mills) could motivate Middle Eastern Americans to become better organized in their efforts against discrimination by joining organizations such as the Arab American Institute or the American-Arab Anti-Discrimination Committee. At the same time, knowing that others have had similar experiences with prejudice and discrimination should help lessen the psychological toll of prejudice that often causes the victims to wonder, "Why did this happen to me?" We have offered Middle Eastern Americans some examples of how others like themselves cope with and fight discrimination.

We also hope to dialogue with white Americans, who, as Joe Feagin[1] suggests, can be informed about their fellow citizens' struggle with discrimination. This could encourage white Americans to also protest the contradictions inherent in the American Dream[2] and the problems with its inaccessibility to all Americans, regardless of their skin color or ethnic origin. As Feagin points out, with the "browning of America," it is becoming more and more necessary for people of color and whites to form coalitions against prejudice and discrimination and change the racist value system that systematically erodes the ideals of American society and wastes valuable social resources. Racism and discrimination are costly to both whites and minorities.[3] An incredible amount of time and resources are wasted on unfounded suspicions of Middle Eastern Americans as terrorists.

Since September 11, Amir has given invited talks at college campuses about Middle Eastern Americans and the discrimination they face. Typically, such talks include a discussion of demographic information about Middle

Eastern Americans, their stereotypes, and how they cope with discrimination. Along the same lines, Amir wrote the following piece for a local paper about the daily toll of ethnic profiling:

I am an Iranian American who came to the United States twenty years ago. I was an ambitious sixteen-year-old who wanted to escape a terrible war, a senseless tragedy that consumed over a million lives (the dead I left behind were much less fortunate than me). I came for the chance to receive an education and lead a better life. Over the years there were occasional confrontations with bigots, like the man at work who, after discovering my nationality, began wearing a T-shirt that displayed a large screw with the word "Iran" wrapped around it. I viewed such encounters as comical acts of ignorance rather than a systematic assault on my humanity. "You have to have a thick skin," I reminded myself. I went on to complete my graduate work, start a family, and become a U.S. citizen. I imagine mine is a typical immigrant story. We come, we face some difficulties, and we persevere. Unfortunately, these days it seems that my immigrant story might have a different ending.

The maniacal murderers a year ago killed more than just three thousand innocent men and women; they destroyed the dreams of millions of people like myself— brown people who came here to get away from the terrible poverty and violence of their native homes. I say "brown" because no one is really interested in our particular cultural backgrounds or political views; that many of us came here precisely to escape the scourge of Islamic fundamentalism is of no consequence. Nor does it cross many minds that as citizens of this country, we too are potential targets of foreign terrorism. The incriminating evidence against us is our appearance: brown skin, black hair and large facial features. We came chasing the same promise that has brought millions of other dreamers here, but our lives changed on that horrible day. Suddenly, we became the people who resemble the mug shots of the black-hearted killers of September 11, and contempt for us became a way of soothing the national pain.

I began thinking the other day about all the things I don't do anymore because they might appear suspicious in the eyes of my fellow citizens. I compiled a long list of places and people I don't visit anymore. For example, in our family trip to Chicago last August, I had to tell my eleven-year-old daughter that we couldn't go to the Sears Tower because it was too far from our hotel. In reality, I didn't want to go because I feared being humiliated in front of her by peering eyes. My solitary camping trips in the Smokies are also out of the question. Who knows what people might think if they saw a young Middle Eastern man hiking by himself? I don't go to lunch with my Middle Eastern friends anymore either, because someone might think they heard us say something threatening or flippant and our lives will forever change. If we laugh, we might appear disrespectful. If we are too solemn, we could seem stealthy. Of course, the thought of speaking my native tongue, Farsi (not Arabic), in public would not even cross my mind. I am certain the foreign words, regardless of what they mean, will arouse suspicion. However, I didn't finish my list of self-imposed restrictions. It was too self-important. Compared to the thousands of lives that were lost last year, griping about my daily humiliation seemed petty. I don't blame my fellow citizens either. They are told that to be suspicious of people like me is to do their patriotic duty. So perhaps I should do my duty as an American and just shut up about profiling and discrimination. Others have made sacrifices for their country before, this is my turn. Maybe I should welcome the hateful glares, because somehow, in a strange way that I fail to understand, they make my neighbors feel safer. But I think logic (if not morality) dictates otherwise.

Repeated announcements about suspected terrorists among us only teach the bad guys to be on the alert. On the other hand, for honest, law-abiding Americans, who just happen to have the wrong skin color and appearance, they seem like nothing more than a campaign of intimidation. I doubt those religious fanatics who view suicidal killings as their one-way ticket to heaven will be deterred by such tactics. It is likely that these determined murderers will simply find another way to commit their crimes. It also troubles me that we would not even consider such extreme measures when other, more mainstream groups, are the potential suspects. . . . Why is it that we are willing to demand that only certain groups give up their rights in the name of national security and a greater good? It is clear that in the balance between security and justice we do have our limits. Some steps, at least insofar as the white majority is concerned, are regarded as too intrusive.

I am convinced that the seemingly indiscriminate profiling of Middle Eastern Americans does not provide anyone with a real sense of security. Fear of terrorism, it seems, is weakening our commitment to "liberty and justice for all." I tell myself and my family that this will pass, that cooler heads will prevail. Yet, deep down inside, I wonder how much longer the suspicion and contempt will grow before we all feel safe.[4]

After this piece was published, many colleagues showed their support for Amir and his family. However, a number of white students in response to this op-ed and during one of his invited presentations indicated that they were tired of all the "whining."

As we further explored this opinion, it appeared that the notion that minorities should stop "whining" is based on three fundamental assumptions. First, some assume that minorities, especially new immigrants, by coming to the United States have basically forfeited their right to criticize social conditions. As the saying goes, "If you don't like it here, leave!" And since they are not leaving, they must like it here, without question or criticism. This line of thinking basically denies minorities the fundamental human inclination for progress. It is based on the belief that we can make the world a safer place by discouraging critical thought. At its heart, it advocates the conservative ideology that things are as they should be and social change is unnecessary and undesirable.

However, we take the point of view that change is essential. Imagine what would happen if we did not try to eradicate diseases (there would be no medical advances). Imagine what would happen if we did not try to fight crime (there would be no safety and order). No rational person would make such proposals. Yet when it comes to certain conditions, particularly when they are imposed on a minority group and benefit a majority, they are to be taken for granted as "natural conditions" (e.g., "It is human nature to be suspicious and distrustful of outsiders.").

The second argument against "whining" is that U.S. immigrants are better off here than they were in their home countries; therefore, they should be content. This line of thinking suggests that even in the worst circumstances, Middle Eastern immigrants have more political rights and economic opportunities in America than they did in places like Saudi Arabia or Iraq. On the one hand, this argument is not empirically valid; many Middle Eastern immigrants give up considerable wealth and social status to come the United States. Some do so in order to avoid wars in the region that the United States is directly or indirectly involved in. As one of our respondents put it, "I came to America because I didn't want to be a victim of U.S. foreign policy."

However, let us assume that the assertion about pursuing a better life here in the West is true (as is certainly the case with women from the more oppressive countries). Do the relative improvements that come with immigration mean that one should tolerate all other forms of injustice in his or her new homeland? To underscore the fallacy of this argument, we ask our students to imagine a man who is being arrested for battering his wife. In his defense, he turns to the police officers and says, "I am innocent because my next door neighbor recently killed his wife." Is this a reasonable justification for oppression? The fact that there is more injustice in other parts of the world does not mean that we should tolerate seemingly less-threatening forms of oppression here. It is absurd to suggest that we should be more accepting of racism and prejudice in the United States because people are systematically slaughtered by tyrants in other parts of the world. As Martin Luther King noted, "Injustice anywhere is a threat to justice everywhere." And of course, there is a good bit of evidence that suggests racism and prejudice have led to atrocities against the innocent in the United States, as in the case of the lynching of African Americans and brutal racist killings that continue to the present day.

The third source of opposition to raising one's voice about racial and ethnic prejudice is that such talk is "hateful." Indeed, after a presentation about discrimination, a white student asked Amir if he hated America. He replied, "No, I love America. I am an American and so is my daughter who was born and raised here. Therefore, to hate America I would have to hate myself and my family. No, I do not hate America, but I do object to injustice." It is self-important on the part of whites to think that minorities who speak against racism hate Americans personally. The Middle Eastern people we interviewed, for example, simply want a chance to be fully accepted as Americans.

As a whole, labeling objections to discrimination as "whining" reveals the assumed superiority of white America in relation to minority groups. As in a parent–child relationship, whining signifies the pleas of a subordinate to someone in a higher position for better consideration or mercy. It linguistically transforms and discredits the demands for equality and justice into nothing more than bickering. At the same time, the attribution of "whining" condones the implicit and explicit violence of racism by blaming the victims, who are supposed to shut up and "take it like real men." In this context, the predicament of the victims of racism is not unlike what rape victims experience when the legal system and the public call into question their moral character instead of the rapist's motives and actions.[5]

As we have demonstrated throughout this book, discrimination is a real social problem with horrible consequences. The victims are not just psychologically damaged, they lose jobs, are physically attacked, and sometimes even killed. Consider, for example, this account of the bombing of a mosque from a 1980s congressional hearing titled "Ethnically Motivated Violence against Arab-Americans":

> On June 22, 1985, The Dar Us-Salaam Mosque in Southwest Houston was destroyed by two pipe bombs thrown through a window. The force of the blast moved the room's 15x30 foot wall nearly four inches from the foundation. The bomb went off less than one hour after the congregation of Dar Us-Salaam—which means the house of peace—had left from the evening prayer.[6]

The same report catalogs numerous other criminal offenses against Middle Eastern Americans, a situation that has no doubt worsened since September 11, 2001. Such atrocities have plagued the Middle Eastern American community for decades.

To speak against the evil of prejudice is not "whining" but part of the struggle against an inexcusable social ill. We should not wait until thousands more are mentally, economically, and physically hurt before we engage in social action against these injustices. Instead, what is needed is a doctrine of preemption against the terror of racism and prejudice. We need to stop these problems before they reach the level of crisis, before thousands of Middle Eastern Americans are placed in so-called internment camps, for example.

We believe that the struggle for social justice is ongoing and indefinite. The end is never completely in sight, no more than social progress itself has a finite end. We can, and should, continually strive to make America and the world a better place for all its citizens—social justice is a necessary condition for human survival. Furthermore, we believe that social justice is not an amorphous entity (i.e., it is not a pipedream), but a real possibility with clear objectives. As Feagin remarks:

> Social justice requires resources equity, fairness, and respect for diversity, as well as the eradication of existing forms of social oppression. Social justice entails a redistribution of resources from those who have unjustly gained them to those who justly deserve them, and it also means creating and ensuring the processes of truly democratic participation in decision-making.[7]

It is these same ideals, echoed in the U.S. Constitution and the Declaration of Independence, that provided the inspiration and the ideological framework for the creation of the United States as a democracy. The critics of cultural diversity would have us believe that the project of creating a democratic society in America is complete, that Americans, especially recent immigrants and minorities, should partake in the politics of their homeland only ceremonially, by displaying a flag and reciting the pledge of allegiance. Instead, we hope for a more active participation in American democracy. Why should the fervor and enthusiasm for creating a better world, which inspired the founding fathers, stop with the new Americans and people of color? Why should we not actively contribute to the creation of the American Dream, instead of passively consuming whatever version we are fed by the elite and the media? As we see it, far from being "whiners" or "anti-American," full participation in the creation and betterment of a democratic system is patriotic. As James Baldwin writes in *Notes of a Native Son*, "I love America more than any other country in the world, and, exactly for this reason, I insist on the right to criticize her perpetually."[8]

NOTES

1. Joe Feagin, *Racist America* (Lanham, Md.: Routledge, 2000).

2. Gunnar Myrdal, *An American Dilemma*, vol. 1 (New York: McGraw-Hill, 1964 [1944]).

3. Joe Feagin and Hernan Vera, *White Racism* (New York: Routledge, 1995).

4. Amir Marvasti, "Ethnic Profiling Takes Its Toll on the Innocent," *Altoona* (Pa.) *Mirror*, November 2, 2002, editorial page.

5. Rodney Kingsworth, Randall Macintosh, and Jennifer Wentworth, "Sexual Assault: The Role of Prior Relationship and Victim Characteristics in Case Processing," *Justice Quarterly* 16 (1999): 276–302.

6. "Ethnically Motivated Violence against Arab-Americans," Hearing before the Subcommittee on Criminal Justice of the House Judiciary Committee, House of Representa-

tives, Ninety-Ninth Congress, Second Session on Ethnically Motivated Violence against Arab-Americans, July 16, 1986 (serial no. 135) (Washington, D.C.: U.S. Government Printing Office, 1988), p. 200.

7. Joe Feagin, "Social Justice and Sociology: Agendas for the Twenty-First Century: Presidential Address," *American Sociological Review* 66, no. 1 (2001): 1–20.

8. Cited in Victoria Valentine, "Editor's Note: Remains of the Day," *The New Crisis*, November/December 2001, p. 6.

About the Authors

Amir Marvasti is an Iranian American. He was born in Tehran and moved to the United States in 1983 to escape the Iran-Iraq war. He is assistant professor of sociology at the Pennsylvania State University, Altoona. His research interests include race and ethnicity, deviance, and social theory. He is the author of *Being Homeless: Textual and Narrative Constructions* (2003) and *Qualitative Research in Sociology* (2004). His current research focuses on the immigration experiences of Middle Eastern Americans.

Karyn McKinney is a native of Chattanooga, Tennessee. She is assistant professor of sociology at the Pennsylvania State University, Altoona. She is the author of *The Many Costs of Racism* (2003, with Joe Feagin). She has a forthcoming book, *Being White: Stories of Race and Racism*. She has written numerous book chapters and articles on race and ethnicity. She is currently conducting research on the cross-section of race and gender identity.